Towards Understanding the Qur'ān

Vol. VIII

SŪRAHS 29 – 32

English version of

Tafhīm al-Qur'ān

SAYYID ABUL A'LĀ MAWDŪDĪ

Translated and edited by
Zafar Ishaq Ansari

The Islamic Foundation

Published by

THE ISLAMIC FOUNDATION,

Markfield Conference Centre,
Ratby Lane, Markfield, Leicester LE67 9SY, United Kingdom
Tel: (01530) 244944, Fax: (01530) 244946
E-mail: i.foundation@islamic-foundation.org.uk
Website: www.islamic-foundation.org.uk

Quran House, PO Box 30611, Nairobi, Kenya

PMB 3193, Kano, Nigeria

Distributed by: Kube Publishing Ltd.

Translated and edited by Zafar Ishaq Ansari

British Library Cataloguing in Publication Data

Mawdudi, Sayyid Abul A'la, 1903–1979
Towards Understanding the Qur'ān
Vol. 8, Surahs 29–32
1. Koran – Commentaries,
I. Title II. Ansari, Zafar Ishaq
III. Islamic Foundation
(Great Britain)
297.1'226

ISBN–13: 9780860374411
ISBN–13: 9780860374367 Pbk

بسم الله الرحمن الرحيم

Contents

Editor's Preface – Zafar Ishaq Ansari v

Sūrah 29: Al-ʿAnkabūt (Makkan Period)
Introduction 1
Text and Explanatory Notes 5

Sūrah 30: Al-Rūm (Makkan Period)
Introduction 65
Text and Explanatory Notes 73

Sūrah 31: Luqmān (Makkan Period)
Introduction 119
Text and Explanatory Notes 121

Sūrah 32: Al-Sajdah (Makkan Period)
Introduction 153
Text and Explanatory Notes 156

Glossary of Terms 179

Biographical Notes 187

Bibliography 203

Subject Index 209

Name Index 231

Transliteration Table

Arabic Consonants

Initial, unexpressed medial and final:

ء	ʼ	د	d	ض	ḍ	ك	k
ب	b	ذ	dh	ط	ṭ	ل	l
ت	t	ر	r	ظ	ẓ	م	m
ث	th	ز	z	ع	ʻ	ن	n
ج	j	س	s	غ	gh	هـ	h
ح	ḥ	ش	sh	ف	f	و	w
خ	kh	ص	ṣ	ق	q	ي	y

Vowels, diphthongs, etc.

Short:	ـَ a	ـِ i	ـُ u
Long:	ـَا ā	ـِي ī	ـُو ū
Diphthongs:		ـَوْ aw	
		ـَيْ ay	

Editor's Preface

The eighth volume of *Towards Understanding the Qur'ān*, comprising *Sūrahs* 29–32, is being sent to the press after an inordinate lapse of time. Readers from many parts of the world have had to wait for long to receive this volume. However, it was possible in the meanwhile to prepare an Abbreviated Version of *Towards Understanding the Qur'ān* for which all thanks be to God. The delay, however, is much regretted.

Not only has the publication of this volume been greatly delayed, but it is also the slimmest of all volumes published so far. Hopefully, however, the readers will enjoy the fact that this volume has a striking thematic unity. All the four *sūrahs* that go into this volume are Makkan, and each of them is focused on expounding and elucidating three fundamental doctrines of Islam – holding God as One and Unique and consecrating for Him worship, service and obedience, Prophethood and After-life. It would be no exaggeration to say that in the explanatory notes to these four *sūrahs* the readers will find a great deal that will be illuminating and thought-provoking.

The present volume, as volumes III, IV, V and VI before, has been prepared with the able assistance of Dr. A.R. Kidwai who translated into English the explanatory notes of *Tafhīm* relating to the above-mentioned *sūrahs*. That text served as the basis out of which the explanatory notes of the present volume were given the final shape after a long, tedious, and thoroughgoing process of editing and re-editing. While the assistance extended by Dr. Kidwai is gratefully acknowledged, the responsibility for the present text, whatever its worth, rests with the present writer. The English rendering of the text of the *sūrahs*, however, is entirely mine.

In this volume, as in the previous ones, we have attempted to provide as adequate documentation as we possibly could. In documenting the *Ḥadīth* we have followed the system of A.J.

Wensinck in his *Concordance*. However, instead of mentioning the number of the '*Bāb*' of the traditions concerned as done by him, we have preferred to mention the actual title of the *Bāb*. It may also be noted that while referring to notes in the works of *Tafsīr* that have been cited, we have referred to the relevant *sūrahs* and the verses which they seek to explain. As for the Bible, all quotations are from its *Revised Standard Edition*. Furthermore, we have retained in this volume the other features that characterize the previous volumes, namely Glossary of Terms, Biographical Notes, and Bibliography.

In preparing the text, I have greatly benefited from the excellent editorial suggestions of Mrs. Susanne Thackray. Dr. A.R. Kidwai also kindly looked at the draft and favoured me with useful critical comments. In providing documentation I received valuable assistance from my colleagues at the Islamic Research Institute – Dr. Asmatullah, Mr. Mubashshir Husain, Mr. Shahzad Qaiser, Mr. Abdurrahman Saaleh and Mr. Muhammad Zulqarnain Akhtar. They assisted me in a variety of ways but especially by providing a good deal of material on which the Biographical Notes are based. Mr. Gohar Zaman and Mr. Amjad Mahmood of the Institute's secretarial staff assiduously typed the manuscript many a time before it assumed its present form. Mr. Naiem Qaddoura of The Islamic Foundation did a fine job of setting the English and Arabic material. Dr. Kidwai, with an interest, zeal and meticulousness all his own, oversaw the final typesetting of the work. Dr. M. Manazir Ahsan of the Foundation merits the ample thanks of this writer. His frequent reminders did not permit him to remain indolent for long. Khurshid Ahmad, my life-long friend, remains a pillar of strength and an enduring source of inspiration.

Over the years my sons and sons-in-law, my daughters and daughters-in-law, and the steadily growing army of my grandchildren have been the sunshine of my life. I have no words to thank God enough for this benevolent provision to keep me happy and cheerful.

To all those mentioned above, and to many others who assisted, encouraged and inspired me in one way or the other, I record my profound sense of gratitude.

May Allah bless them all.

Islamabad
August 2007

Zafar Ishaq Ansari

Sūrah 29

Al-ʿAnkabūt

(The Spider)

(Makkan Period)

Title

The title of this *sūrah* is derived from the word *ʿankabūt* ("spider") used in the verse: "The case of those who took others than Allah as their protectors is that of a spider…." (verse 41). To put it differently, it is the *sūrah* in which the word spider occurs.

Period of Revelation

Verses 56-60 seem to indicate that the *sūrah* was revealed on the eve of some Muslims' migration to Abyssinia, which took place during the Makkan period of the Prophet's life. This is borne out by fragments of internal evidence. The state of affairs obtaining at that time quite conspicuously forms the *sūrah*'s background.

Some Qur'ānic scholars, however, are of the view that the first ten verses of the *sūrah* were revealed in Madīnah whereas the rest of the *sūrah* was a Makkan revelation. This assumption rests on the premise that there is a reference to hypocrites in the *sūrah*. Now, since hypocrites only appeared in the Madīnan period, these scholars consider the early verses to have been revealed at the same time. This opinion, however, is incorrect, because the hypocrisy mentioned in this *sūrah* is of a very different kind from that which became evident during the Madīnan period. What is referred to here as hypocrisy had its roots in the fear that severe persecution and torture would be perpetrated on the believers if they remained faithful to Islam. Quite obviously, this kind of hypocrisy could only have surfaced in the Makkan rather than the Madīnan period. For in the Madīnan period, hypocrisy arising from fear of persecution was evidently out of the question.

In like manner, other scholars of the Qur'ān, taking note of the directive to migrate in the *sūrah,* concluded that *al-ʿAnkabūt* was the last *sūrah* revealed in Makkah. Again, this conclusion is not sound. For, before migrating to Madīnah, some Muslims had sought refuge in Abyssinia. It is pertinent to note that these views about the time-frame of the *sūrah*'s revelation are of a conjectural nature. They are based on evidence provided by the *sūrah*'s contents and are not directly corroborated by authentic traditions. However, if one studies the contents of the *sūrah* as a whole, it is evident that the conditions mentioned therein are in fact those obtaining at the time of the Muslims' migration to Abyssinia rather than to Madīnah.

Subject Matter and Main Themes

It is evident from a study of the *sūrah* that, at the time of its revelation, the Muslims were exposed to severe persecution and torment in Makkah. This was when the unbelievers vigorously opposed Islam and committed untold excesses against the Muslims. It was against this backdrop that God revealed this *sūrah,* on the one hand to raise the true believers' morale and on the other to arouse a sense of shame among those believers whose faith was weak. At the same time, the Makkan unbelievers were also warned not to invite God's scourge upon themselves, the kind of scourge that enemies of the Truth have encountered throughout all ages.

In this connection, some of the questions agitating a number of Muslim youths of the time are also addressed. These youths were being compelled by their parents to dissociate themselves from the Prophet Muḥammad (peace be on him). The unbelievers on occasion even reminded them that the very Qur'ān in which they believed made it imperative that they be dutiful towards their parents. Citing this Qur'ānic instruction, they urged them to comply with their parents' command. They stressed that if the believers failed to do so, they would be guilty of violating an injunction of their own faith. A response to this is made in verse 8.

Likewise, fellow tribesmen of some new converts to Islam asked them to renounce Islam. They assured these converts that they would bear the consequences of the latters' forsaking their faith, that they would bear the brunt of Divine punishment. Furthermore, they said that they would step forward in the Hereafter and admit that they had impelled these converts to renounce Islam. The point being stressed here is that it would be those who had persuaded the believers to abjure their faith, rather than those who abjured as a result of their pleading who would be punished. A response to this is made in verses 12-13.

The stories recounted in the *sūrah* draw attention to God's Prophets of yore, stressing how they too were subjected to harrowing torture and often for long periods of time, but eventually God came to their rescue. The moral of the stories being that the Makkan Muslims need not panic for they too, like those earlier Prophets, are bound to receive God's help but first they too must go through a period of test and trial.

Apart from imparting this lesson to the Muslims, the *sūrah* also carries a note of dire warning to the Makkan unbelievers. The fact that they were not being punished instantly should not delude them into believing that they will not face such punishment. They were witnesses to the ruins of earlier nations. Was this not enough to drive home to them that doom ultimately overtakes evil-doers, whereas God comes to the aid of His Prophets?

The Muslims were also directed that if they could no longer bear the persecution perpetrated against them, they should forsake their hearths and homes and migrate to some other land rather than forsake their faith. God's earth, in any case, is immensely vast. They should migrate to any land where it would be possible for them to freely serve and worship Him.

Besides this, the unbelievers are also admonished. Their attention is drawn, on the one hand, to arguments in support of monotheism and the Hereafter. On the other hand, polytheism is refuted. Furthermore, the multitude of Signs in the Universe corroborate the truth of the Prophet Muḥammad's message.

In the name of Allah, the Most Merciful, the Most Compassionate.	بِسۡمِ ٱللَّهِ ٱلرَّحۡمَٰنِ ٱلرَّحِيمِ
(1) *Alif. Lām. Mīm.* (2) Do people think that they will be let go merely by saying: "We believe," and that they will not be tested,[1]	الٓمٓ ﴿١﴾ أَحَسِبَ ٱلنَّاسُ أَن يُتۡرَكُوٓاْ أَن يَقُولُوٓاْ ءَامَنَّا وَهُمۡ لَا يُفۡتَنُونَ ﴿٢﴾

1. To appreciate the import of this verse, the following context should be borne in mind. The state of affairs obtaining at the time this *sūrah* was revealed was such that no sooner had someone embraced Islam in Makkah than a storm of persecution and torture was let loose. If the person happened to be a slave or poor, he was mercilessly manhandled and subjected to exacting torment. If he were a shopkeeper or craftsman, he was made the victim of economic boycott, which led to straightened circumstances and even starvation. If he belonged to an influential family, his family members made life miserable for him, exerting pressure on him and subjecting him to a variety of vexing measures. As a result of this wide-scale persecution, the atmosphere in Makkah was charged with dread and fright. Fearful of facing terrible consequences, many who recognised the truth of the Prophet's message hesitated to declare their faith. Furthermore, some who had embraced Islam gave in to the unbelievers' torture and recanted their faith.

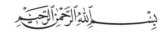

These adverse circumstances, however, did not weaken the firm resolve of true believers – the deeply-convinced Companions of the Prophet (peace be on him) – to remain faithful to Islam. Nevertheless, they too were only human, and inevitably, at times, felt upset and worried. Illustrative of this state is a report by Khabbāb ibn al-Arat, recorded in Bukhārī, Abū Dāwūd and Nasā'ī. Khabbāb narrates as follows: "At the time when we faced the polytheists' excesses, one day I saw the Prophet (peace be on him) seated in the shade of the Ka'bah's wall. I submitted to him: 'O Messenger of Allah! Do you not pray for us [that we be delivered from this miserable state]?' On hearing this, the Prophet's face turned red with emotion and he said: 'The believers before you were subjected to even greater excesses. Pits were dug for some of them and they were made to sit in them and they were sawed into two pieces from head to foot. The joints of some others were rubbed with iron combs. All this was done to make them recant their faith. By Allah, this [mission] is bound to be accomplished so that one day a person will travel from Ṣanʿā' to Ḥadramawt without having fear of anyone except God.'" (See Bukhārī, *K. al-Manāqib, Bāb: ʿAlāmāt al-Nubūwah fī al-Islām*; Abū Dāwūd, *K. al-Jihād, Bāb: Fī al-Asīr yukrahu ʿalā al-Kufr*; Nasā'ī, *K. al-Zīnah, Bāb: Libs al-Burūd* – Ed.)

In order to transform the believers' state of perturbance and anxiety into one of calm patience and endurance, God informed the believers that a person is not eligible for His promise of success and felicity in this world, as well as in the Next, merely by claiming that he is a believer. Instead, he has to establish the truthfulness of his claim by successfully going through a crucible of tests and trials. Admission to Paradise demands far more than the mere verbal profession of faith. Nor can anyone expect to be blessed with God's special bounties even in this world by merely professing to be a believer. To obtain these rewards it is essential that one be put to hard tests, even to the point of loss of life and all one's belongings. Mentally, one should be prepared for all kinds of suffering and discomfort. Further, one will also be exposed to temptation and intimidation and will have to sacrifice everything one holds dear in the cause of one's faith. It is only after one has gone through all this that the truthfulness or otherwise of one's claim to be a believer is established.

This point is stressed in all Qur'ānic passages that mention Muslims' perturbance and disconcertment in the face of the hardships and difficulties they confronted. In the early days of the Madīnan period following the *Hijrah,* the Muslims were vexed by a host of problems – financial stringency, the threat of aggression without, and the mischievous machinations of the Jews and hypocrites within. At this point in time the Qur'ān gave the Muslims the following message:

> Do you suppose that you will enter Paradise untouched by the suffering endured by the men of faith who passed away before you? They were afflicted by misery and hardship and were so convulsed that the Messenger and the believers with him cried out: 'When will Allah's help arrive?' They were assured that Allah's help was close by. (*al-Baqarah* 2:214)

Likewise, when the Muslims were confronted with a host of sufferings after the Battle of Uḥud, God addressed them in the same vein:

(3) for We indeed tested those who went before them.[2] Allah will most certainly ascertain[3] those who spoke the truth and those who lied.

وَلَقَدْ فَتَنَّا ٱلَّذِينَ مِن قَبْلِهِمْ ۖ فَلَيَعْلَمَنَّ ٱللَّهُ ٱلَّذِينَ صَدَقُوا۟ وَلَيَعْلَمَنَّ ٱلْكَـٰذِبِينَ ﴿٣﴾

> Did you think that you would enter Paradise even though Allah has not yet seen who among you strove hard in His way and remained steadfast? (*Āl 'Imrān* 3:142)

More or less the same truth features in *Āl 'Imrān* 3:79, *al-Tawbah* 9:6 and *Muḥammad* 47:31. God, thus, conveyed to the Muslims the plain truth that it is only by going through the crucible of test and trial that crowns of sterling gold can be separated from those that are fake and counterfeit. When tested, those deficient in firmness of faith will automatically abandon the path of God. This is how true men of faith are identified, how the shallow and weak are winnowed out and how it is only those who are true who receive God's rewards.

2. There was nothing new about the tests to which the Muslims were being subjected. History testifies that in the past all those who claimed to be believers were put to similar trials. Since their predecessors were not rewarded until they had been so tested, the Muslims too should not expect any reward until they have successfully gone through their tests and proven their worth. There is, after all, no good reason why any exception should be made in their case.

3. Regarding this test, the Qur'ān says: "Allah will most certainly ascertain those who spoke the truth and those who lied". When one reads this verse, a likely question that arises is: since God knows fully what everyone's conduct will be, what is the point in testing him? The answer is that as long as a person does not commit a certain action, irrespective of his ability to do so, the dictates of justice require that he should neither be rewarded or punished. One person might be potentially trustworthy and another potentially untrustworthy. However, unless they act in one manner or the other, it is discordant with God's justice to reward or

(4) Do the evil-doers[4] suppose that they will get the better of Us?[5] How evil is their judgement!

أَمْ حَسِبَ ٱلَّذِينَ يَعْمَلُونَ ٱلسَّيِّـَٔاتِ أَن يَسْبِقُونَا ۚ سَآءَ مَا يَحْكُمُونَ ﴿٤﴾

punish them only on the basis of His knowledge of those actions that will take place in the future. God, no doubt, has knowledge of both the past and the future, yet this does not have a bearing on the manner in which He will dispense justice. He does not punish anyone simply because he is inclined to steal or because he is likely to steal in the future. Rather, His punishment is contingent upon the person actually stealing. By the same token, God does not bestow His rewards on someone just because they will grow into excellent believers or as excellent fighters in God's cause. On the contrary, this person too only earns his reward by dint of his actually having sincere faith and striving in God's cause.

4. This verse has universal import and embraces all those who are disobedient of God. Nonetheless, it is especially directed at the oppressive Quraysh chiefs, Walīd ibn al-Mughīrah, Abū Jahl, 'Utbah, Shaybah, 'Uqbah ibn Abī Mu'ayṭ and Ḥanẓalah ibn Wā'il, who relentlessly opposed Islam and persecuted the Muslims. (See Ālūsī, *Rūḥ al-Ma'ānī*; Ibn al-Jawzī, *Zād al-Masīr*; al-Qurṭubī, *al-Jāmi' li Aḥkām al-Qur'ān*; Abū Ḥayyān, *al-Baḥr al-Muḥīṭ*, for comments on *al-'Ankabūt* 29:4 – Ed.) The context demanded that alongside exhorting the Muslims to show steadfastness in the face of persecution, words of reproach and censure also be directed at those guilty of perpetrating excesses on the votaries of Truth.

5. This might also be taken to mean that the unbelievers fancy that God will not be able to seize them. The Arabic expression used in the text, however, literally means: "They will get the better of Allah." This could mean either of two things. First, that the unbelievers are of the view that what God wants – the success of the Prophet's mission – will not come to pass, and what they themselves want – to reduce the Prophet's mission to ignominy – will come to pass. Secondly, that while God wants to punish the unbelievers for the excesses they committed against the believers, the unbelievers entertain the illusion that this will not happen and that they will be able to elude God's grasp.

(5) Let him who looks forward to meeting Allah know that Allah's appointed term will surely come to pass.[6] He is All-Hearing, All-Knowing.[7] (6) Whosoever strives[8] (in

مَن كَانَ يَرْجُواْ لِقَآءَ ٱللَّهِ فَإِنَّ أَجَلَ ٱللَّهِ لَأٰتٍ ۚ وَهُوَ ٱلسَّمِيعُ ٱلْعَلِيمُ ۝ وَمَن جَٰهَدَ

6. The case of the person who does not believe in the Afterlife, who does not consider himself accountable to anyone, who is convinced that there will never come a time when his deeds will be subjected to reckoning, is quite different. Such a person is free to remain engrossed in his negligence and to act as recklessly as he wants. A Day will surely come, however, when he will be confronted with reality, which will be quite contrary to his estimates. As for those who recognise that one Day they will have to appear before God and will be rewarded or punished in accordance with their deeds should not delude themselves that death is a remote possibility. Rather, they should think that death is just around the corner and that the term granted them to reveal their true natures is about to end. This should prompt them to do whatever they can for their own good in the Hereafter. There is no reason why they should defer efforts to reform themselves in the vain hope that they will live a long life.

7. They should not succumb to the delusion that they will have to deal with an ill-informed sovereign. On the contrary, the Lord before Whom they are required to appear is All-Hearing and All-Knowing. Nothing about them is hidden from Him.

8. *Mujāhadah* means to strive against a hostile force. If no enemy is specified, the word signifies a person's engagement in a pervasive, all-out struggle. A believer has to undertake this struggle throughout his life. At one level, he has to fight against Satan who constantly seeks to deter him from good deeds by frightening him with the prospect of the losses he will incur and tempting him to evil by pointing out the advantages and pleasures it will yield. Furthermore, he has to strive against his own self that is wont to prompt him to become a slave of his desires. Likewise, he has to strive against fellow-beings whose ideas, predilections, moral concepts, customs and usages, cultural patterns and socio-economic laws

the cause of Allah) does so to his own good. Surely Allah stands in no need of anyone[9] in the whole Universe. (7) Those who believe and do good deeds, We shall cleanse them of their evil deeds and reward them according to the best of their deeds.[10]	فَإِنَّمَا يُجَٰهِدُ لِنَفْسِهِۦٓۚ إِنَّ ٱللَّهَ لَغَنِىٌّ عَنِ ٱلْعَٰلَمِينَ ۝٦ وَٱلَّذِينَ ءَامَنُوا۟ وَعَمِلُوا۟ ٱلصَّٰلِحَٰتِ لَنُكَفِّرَنَّ عَنْهُمْ سَيِّـَٔاتِهِمْ وَلَنَجْزِيَنَّهُمْ أَحْسَنَ ٱلَّذِى كَانُوا۟ يَعْمَلُونَ ۝٧

are discordant with the true faith. He has also got to pit himself against that state which, claiming its right to remain free of God's obedience, exercises and enforces its authority and directs its power to promote evil rather than good. This striving is not limited to any one particular day, but extends across a believer's whole life, embracing every moment of his day and night. Furthermore, this striving is not confined to any particular domain of life; instead, it embraces each and every aspect of it. Ḥasan al-Baṣrī refers to this very *mujāhadah* when he says: "A man makes *jihād* even though he might never have struck [anyone] with his sword."

9. God does not ask the believers to engage in this striving because He stands in need of them to establish and maintain His sovereignty, or because His sovereignty would not operate unless they help Him. The truth is that God is not in need of man's help at all. Hence, if He still directs human beings to engage in this striving, it is because this is conducive to man's own growth. This striving helps human beings free themselves from the clutches of evil and waywardness and helps them proceed along the path of goodness and truth. This also infuses into them the strength that transforms them into champions of goodness and virtue and makes them worthy of Paradise. Hence, by engaging in this striving, they do God no favour; rather, they do good to themselves.

10. Belief consists of truthfully accepting all what God's Book and His Messenger ask the person to believe in. As for good deeds, they consist in carrying out the directives of God and His Messenger. A person's

(8) We have enjoined upon man kindness to his parents, but if they exert pressure on you to associate with Me in My Divinity any	وَوَصَّيْنَا ٱلْإِنسَـٰنَ بِوَٰلِدَيْهِ حُسْنًا ۖ وَإِن جَـٰهَدَاكَ لِتُشْرِكَ بِى

whole being can do good deeds. The good deeds of a man's heart and mind are that his thought and intention be pure and sound. The good deeds of his tongue consist of abstention from uttering evils and saying only that which accords with truth and justice. As for the good deeds of the limbs of the body, they consist of devoting his life to obeying and serving God and following His laws and commands. A person's belief and good deeds are mentioned as being instrumental in bringing about the following results: (i) that he will be purged of his evil deeds, and (ii) that he will be rewarded according to the best of his deeds and receive compensation that will be well in excess of his good actions.

Purging a person of his evil deeds means that whatever sins he might have committed before embracing the true faith will be forgiven as soon as he enters Islam's fold. Moreover, his lapses, which were not committed out of wilful rebellion, will be overlooked in consideration of his good deeds. Furthermore, when he adopts the life of faith and good deeds he will attain self-development and overcome many of his weaknesses.

Coming to the rewards for believing and doing good deeds, the Qur'ān promises the following: "We shall reward them according to the best of their deeds." This statement is, however, open to two meanings. First, that people will be rewarded in consideration of their best deeds. Secondly, that they will be granted a better reward than what they strictly deserve on the basis of their good deeds. This latter idea is also expressed in other places. Consider, for example, the following verses:

> Whoever will come to Allah with a good deed shall have ten times as much. (*al-Anʿām* 6:160)

> He who shall bring a good deed shall be rewarded with what is better. (*al-Qaṣaṣ* 28:84)

> Indeed Allah wrongs none, not even as much as an atom's weight. Whenever a man does good, He multiplies it two-fold. (*al-Nisā'* 4:40)

that you do not know (to be My associate), do not obey them.[11] To Me is your return, and I shall let you know all	مَا لَيْسَ لَكَ بِهِۦ عِلْمٌ فَلَا تُطِعْهُمَآ إِلَىَّ مَرْجِعُكُمْ فَأُنَبِّئُكُم

11. According to Muslim, Tirmidhī, Aḥmad, Abū Dāwūd and Nasā'ī, this verse was revealed with regard to Saʿd ibn Abī Waqqāṣ. Saʿd had accepted Islam when he was only 18 or 19 years old. When his mother, Ḥamnah bint Sufyān ibn Umayyah, Abū Sufyān's niece, came to know of it she swore that she would neither eat, drink nor sit under the shade until her son recanted his belief in the Prophet Muḥammad (peace be on him). Now, God Himself commands every believer to fulfil his obligations towards his mother. So if Saʿd would not listen to her, she contended, he would be guilty of disobeying God. The very thought that he would be disobeying his mother greatly upset Saʿd and he mentioned the matter to the Prophet (peace be on him). It was on this occasion that this verse was revealed. (See Muslim, *K. Faḍā'il al-Ṣaḥābah, Bāb: Fī Faḍl Saʿd ibn Abī Waqqāṣ*; Tirmidhī, *K. Tafsīr al-Qur'ān, Bāb: Wa min Sūrat al-ʿAnkabūt* and Aḥmad ibn Ḥanbal, *Musnad*, vol. 1, pp. 181 and 185 – Ed.) It is likely that in the early days of Islam other Makkan youths also went through similar experiences after their acceptance of Islam. Hence, why this subject is forcefully repeated in verse 15 of *Sūrah Luqmān*.

The verse makes it emphatically clear that obligation towards one's parents takes the highest priority. Yet, if parents compel their offspring to associate others with God in His Divinity, then they should not be obeyed. The verse states this point in very forceful terms, saying that even if "they exert pressure" in this respect, "do not obey them". Since this verse directs one to disregard even one's parents' pressure to associate others with God in His Divinity, obviously non-parental pressure should be disregarded all the more.

Equally significant, is another point the verse makes. It says: "If they exert pressure on you to associate with Me in My Divinity any that you do not know (to be My associate), do not obey them." This verse contains a weighty argument as to why one should not obey a parental command to engage in polytheism. It is the parents' right that their offspring serve them, take good care of them, show them due respect, and obey them in all lawful matters. However, they have no right to compel their children to blindly follow them in matters of faith. No one is obliged to follow a

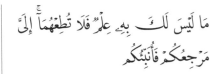

بِمَا كُنتُمْ تَعْمَلُونَ ۝٨ وَٱلَّذِينَ ءَامَنُوا۟
وَعَمِلُوا۟ ٱلصَّٰلِحَٰتِ لَنُدْخِلَنَّهُمْ فِى
ٱلصَّٰلِحِينَ ۝٩ وَمِنَ ٱلنَّاسِ مَن يَقُولُ
ءَامَنَّا بِٱللَّهِ فَإِذَآ أُوذِىَ فِى ٱللَّهِ جَعَلَ فِتْنَةَ

that you have done.[12] (9) As for those who believed and acted righteously, We shall certainly admit them among the righteous.

(10) Among people there are some who say: "We believe in Allah."[13] But when such a person is made to endure suffering in Allah's cause, he reckons the persecution he suffers

---

particular religious faith simply because it happens to be their parents' faith. If offspring know their parents' faith to be false, they should abandon it and embrace the true faith. In this connection, the same applies to everyone else as well. In other words, it is not lawful to follow anyone until one knows that they are on the right path.

12. Ties of kinship and obligations one owes to one's kin are confined to the life of this world. Eventually everyone, parents and children alike, has to return to the Creator and will then be held accountable in their individual capacity. If parents are guilty of misleading their offspring, they will be taken to task. By the same token, if the offspring persist in error out of deference to their parents, they too will be punished. However, if children choose to follow the Straight Way and at the same time do not neglect their obligations towards their parents, and they are still harassed by their parents for not joining them in their error, such parents will not escape God's punishment.

13. Although the speaker in the above instance is a single individual, he employs a plural pronoun for himself and says: "We believe in Allah." Imām Rāzī makes an insightful comment about this. According to him, a hypocrite always tries to parade himself as part of the believers' community. He mentions his faith to be the same as the believers'. In so doing, his behaviour is similar to that of a coward who accompanies

ٱلنَّاسِ كَعَذَابِ ٱللَّهِ وَلَئِن جَآءَ نَصْرٌ مِّن
رَّبِّكَ لَيَقُولُنَّ إِنَّا كُنَّا مَعَكُمْ ۚ أَوَلَيْسَ ٱللَّهُ
بِأَعْلَمَ بِمَا فِى صُدُورِ ٱلْعَٰلَمِينَ ﴿١٠﴾
وَلَيَعْلَمَنَّ ٱللَّهُ

at the hands of people as though it is a chastisement from Allah.[14] But if victory comes from your Lord, the same person will say "We were with you."[15] Does Allah not know whatever is in the hearts of the people of the world? (11) Allah will

an army on expedition. Valiant members of that army fight with such determination that the enemy is forced to flee. Now although the coward takes no part in the battle itself, once all return from the expedition he counts himself among the brave who established their valour on the battlefield.

14. A person should abjure disbelief in and disobedience of God out of fear of chastisement from God. The case cited here, however, sharply contrasts with this. Filled with fear of persecution by Islam's enemies, the person concerned recants the true faith and gives up righteous acts. After being subjected to threats, physical manhandling, arrest and incarceration at the unbelievers' hands he thinks that this persecution is of the same order as will be the punishment in Hell set up by God, the punishment that he must suffer after death on account of unbelief. He, therefore, decides to undergo punishment in the Afterlife rather than endure sufferings in the present life. Driven by this he recants his belief in Islam and rejoins the unbelievers' camp. In doing so, his only concern is to lead a happy, trouble-free life in this world.

15. This person returned to the fold of unbelief in order to save his skin and so doing he also betrayed the believers. He did so because he was not prepared to suffer even a minor loss or injury in the cause of the true faith. However, when God will grant victory to the true believers who staked their lives and their belongings in His cause, he will once again return to the believers' camp and claim a share in the spoils of war. He will then assure the Muslims that in his heart of hearts he was always with them, that he prayed throughout for their victory and held their striving and sacrifices in the highest esteem.

It should be made clear at this point that it is permissible to make a statement indicating one's disbelief when one is confronted with unendurable torment, losses or extreme fear, provided one adheres to the true faith within one's heart. However, there is a world of difference between the following two persons' situations: one is a sincere believer who resorts to expressing unbelief in order to save his life, and the other is a self-seeking opportunist who recognises Islam as the truth and yet joins hands with the unbelievers because he dreads the risks and dangers involved in adhering to the true faith. Ostensibly, there is not much difference between the two. However, what sets the two totally apart is that the sincere Muslim not only remains loyal to Islam as a faith but his true sympathies also lie with Islam and the Muslims. Thus, the success of the Muslims always fills him with joy and when they suffer any reverse, he is agonised intensely. Even when he acts under duress, he makes the most of every possible opportunity to help and support the Muslims. In fact, he always remains on the look-out for an opportune moment to join the Muslims' ranks as soon as the enemy's grip over him is relaxed.

In sharp contrast to this, an opportunist carefully weighs the pros and cons of the two options, of following his faith or joining the unbelievers' camp. When he encounters hardships in adhering to the true faith and realises that benefits will accrue to him by joining the unbelievers' camp, he abandons his faith and gels with the unbelievers so as to ensure his own safety as also to derive material benefits from it. In seeking to achieve his selfish ends, he never shrinks from doing anything that openly violates Islamic principles and is hurtful to Muslims' interests. At the same time, he is shrewd enough not to totally exclude the possibility that some day Islam might gain ascendancy. So, whenever he gets the chance to interact with the Muslims, he lavishly praises their beliefs, claims that he considers their doctrines to be true and pays glowing tributes to their sacrifices in the cause of Truth. So doing, he makes a kind of investment, hoping to cash it in at an appropriate moment. The following Qur'ānic passage lays bare this calculating, business-like mentality of hypocrites:

> These hypocrites watch you closely: if victory is granted to you by Allah, they will say: "Were we not with you?" And were the unbelievers to gain the upper hand, they will say: "Did we not have mastery over you, and yet we protected you from the believers?"
>
> (*al-Nisā'* 4:141)

ٱلَّذِينَ ءَامَنُوا۟ وَلَيَعْلَمَنَّ ٱلْمُنَٰفِقِينَ ﴿١١﴾
وَقَالَ ٱلَّذِينَ كَفَرُوا۟ لِلَّذِينَ ءَامَنُوا۟ ٱتَّبِعُوا۟
سَبِيلَنَا وَلْنَحْمِلْ خَطَٰيَٰكُمْ وَمَا هُم
بِحَٰمِلِينَ مِنْ خَطَٰيَٰهُم مِّن شَىْءٍ ۖ إِنَّهُمْ
لَكَٰذِبُونَ ﴿١٢﴾

surely ascertain who are the believers and who are the hypocrites.[16]

(12) The unbelievers say to the believers: "Follow our way and we will carry the burden of your sins."[17] (They say so even though) they are not going to carry any part of their sins.[18] Surely they are lying.

16. God regularly provides occasions for such trials so that the true faith of the Muslims and the insincerity of the hypocrites become manifest. In this way, everyone reveals their true colours. *Āl ʿImrān* 3:179 reiterates the same truth: "Allah will not let the believers stay in the state they are: He will set the wicked apart from the good."

17. The Makkan unbelievers' contention was that doctrines such as Life after Death, Resurrection, the Grand Assembly and Reckoning were all a farce. They also asserted that if the Afterlife did turn out to be a reality and people were indeed subjected to a Reckoning, then they would be ready to bear the burden of others' sins. They asked the converts to recant their faith and return to their ancestral one for they, the unbelievers, would assume all responsibility for the consequences that might ensue. Traditions mention several Quraysh chiefs saying the kind of things mentioned here to those who had converted to Islam. For example, it is related that Abū Sufyān and Ḥarb ibn Umayyah ibn Khalaf said the same to ʿUmar when he embraced Islam. (See Ṭabarī, *Tafsīr*, and Abū Ḥayyān, *al-Baḥr al-Muḥīt*, comments on *al-ʿAnkabūt* 29:12 – Ed.)

18. First of all, it is out of the question that anyone will bear the burden of others' sins in the Hereafter, or that a sinner will be exonerated because some other person owns the latter's sins. Instead, everyone will be recompensed in the Hereafter for their own deeds. As the Qur'ān says: "Everyone will bear the consequences of what he does, and no one shall

(13) They will certainly carry their own burdens and other burdens besides their own.[19] They will assuredly be called to account on	وَلَيَحْمِلُنَّ أَثْقَالَهُمْ وَأَثْقَالًا مَّعَ أَثْقَالِهِمْ ۖ وَلَيُسْـَٔلُنَّ

bear the burden of another", (*al-Anʿām* 6:164). Let us suppose though for argument's sake that some people will be allowed to bear the burden of others' sins. Yet once anyone has even a glimpse of Hell's scorching fire as recompense for unbelief and polytheism, he will certainly shrink from taking on board another's such sin. For this would mean, on the one hand, that he who forsook the true faith should be pardoned and admitted to Paradise. On the other hand, he who had made the offer to carry another's punishment will be cast into Hell as punishment for his own unbelief as also for the unbelief of the person who embraced this on account of his assurance.

19. True, the unbelievers will not carry the burden of others' sins. At the same time, they will not escape receiving double punishment. Not only will they be punished for straying from the Truth, but they will also be taken to task for misleading others. This point may be better illustrated by the following example. Let us consider that someone commits a theft and asks someone else to be his accomplice in the crime. Now, the latter will not be acquitted on the mere plea that he so thieved at someone else's behest. He will, in any case, be duly punished for his crime, for it is against the dictates of justice that he be exonerated and the instigator be punished in his place. The instigator, however, will receive a double punishment – for his own misdeed as well as for leading another astray. The Qur'ān states this principle in the following words: "[They say so] that they may bear the full weight of their burdens on the Day of Resurrection and also of the burdens of those whom they misled on account of their ignorance", (*al-Naḥl* 16:25). The Prophet (peace be on him) reaffirmed the same principle in the following statement: "Whoever invites [someone] to right guidance will receive a reward for him who followed right guidance [on account of his invitation] without the reward of either of them being decreased, and whoever invites [someone] to error will incur sin equal to the sins of those who follow him, without the sin of any of them being decreased the least." (Muslim, *K. al-ʿIlm, Bāb: Wa man Sanna Sunnah Ḥasanah aw Sayyi'ah* – Ed.)

the Day of Resurrection concerning the fabrications which they contrived.[20]

(14) We did indeed send Noah to his people[21] and he lived among them a

يَوْمَ ٱلْقِيَـٰمَةِ عَمَّا كَانُوا۟ يَفْتَرُونَ ﴿١٣﴾ وَلَقَدْ أَرْسَلْنَا نُوحًا إِلَىٰ قَوْمِهِۦ فَلَبِثَ فِيهِمْ

20. Their fabrications lay, for example, in the false statement: "The unbelievers say to the believers: 'Follow our way and we will carry the burden of your sins'," (verse 12). This statement rests on two premises: one, that the polytheistic creed which they follow is true whereas the Prophet's monotheistic faith is false. Hence, it would not be intrinsically wrong to give it up. Two, that there will be no second life. The very notion of the Hereafter to which the Muslims subscribe and because of which they are fearful of embracing the unbelievers' polytheistic cult is absolutely baseless. Because of these presuppositions, the unbelievers approached the Muslims with virtually the following proposition: "If you believe that abjuring Islam is a sin and if indeed an Afterlife does take place where you will be held accountable for abjuring Islam, then we will bear the burden of that sin. So, abandon Muḥammad's faith at our responsibility and revert to the faith of your forefathers."

To this they added two other untruths. First, the notion that if someone commits a crime at someone else's behest, the former will be exonerated on the grounds that he committed the sin at someone else's instigation and, hence, the latter will be made to bear the entire burden of the sin. Secondly, they falsely promised that they would bear responsibility on behalf of those who reverted from true faith to unbelief. On the Day of Judgement when, contrary to their expectations, they will come face to face with Hell, they will not be at all willing to suffer for the sins of those whom they misled in this world in addition to suffering for their own unbelief.

21. For further details regarding the Prophet Noah's story see *Āl ʿImrān* 3:33-34; *al-Nisā'* 4:163; *al-Anʿām* 6:84; *al-Aʿrāf* 7:59-64; *Yūnus* 10:71-73; *Hūd* 11:25-48; *al-Anbiyā'* 21:76-77; *al-Mū'minūn* 23:23-30; *al-Furqān* 25:37; *al-Shuʿarā'* 26:105-123; *al-Ṣāffāt* 37:75-82; *al-Qamar* 54:9-15; *al-Ḥāqqah* 69:11-12 and *Nūḥ* 71:1-28.

thousand years save fifty.[22] Eventually the Flood overtook them while they	أَلْفَ سَنَةٍ إِلَّا خَمْسِينَ عَامًا فَأَخَذَهُمُ ٱلطُّوفَانُ وَهُمْ

These stories about the Prophets may be better appreciated if they are read against the backdrop of the opening verses of this *sūrah*. On the one hand, they apprise Muslims that the believers of yore had also been subjected to similar tests and trials. On the other hand, they warn the wrong-doing unbelievers that they should not entertain the illusion that they will ever get the better of God or elude His grasp. This history of ancient nations and of their Messengers is narrated to press home these truths.

22. This does not mean that the Prophet Noah (peace be on him) was 950 years old. What the Qur'ān specifically states is that commencing from his designation as a Prophet until the Flood, Noah strove for a period of 950 years to reform his evil and wayward nation. Although he endured their excesses for such a long time, he did not lose heart. This truth is stated here in order to impress upon the early Makkan Muslims, who faced opposition and persecution, that they had only been exposed to such adamance and obstinacy for a few years. They were reminded of Noah's undaunting resolve, courage and perseverance for he put up with severe hardships for a full 950 years.

The Biblical and Qur'ānic versions of Noah's story are at variance with one another. The Bible puts Noah's age at 950 years. Further, it states that he was 600 years old when the Flood struck his people and that he lived for 350 years after the Flood, (*Genesis* 7:6; 9:28-29). However, if one takes into account Qur'ānic statements about Noah, one would think that he must have lived for at least a thousand years. This because he spent 950 years calling his people to the Truth after assuming the office of Prophethood. It goes without saying that he must have been appointed to this august office at a reasonably mature age and that he must also have lived at least for some time after the Flood.

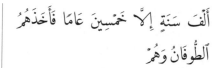

Noah's extraordinarily long age appears to some people as incredible. However, there is no dearth of wonders in God's creation. No matter in which direction one looks, one will observe wonders that are quite out of the ordinary. The appearance of a phenomenon as a matter of routine does not mean that it cannot appear in some other extraordinary form. Indeed,

were engaged in wrong-doing.[23] (15) Then We rescued Noah together with the people in the Ark[24] and made it (that is, the Ark) a lesson for all people.[25]

ظَٰلِمُونَ ﴿١٤﴾ فَأَنجَيْنَٰهُ وَأَصْحَٰبَ
ٱلسَّفِينَةِ وَجَعَلْنَٰهَآ ءَايَةً لِّلْعَٰلَمِينَ ﴿١٥﴾

---

a long list of events points to extraordinary and exceptional happenings in every part of the Universe and among all species of creation. Anyone who clearly knows that God has and exercises absolute power cannot be troubled by the statement that He granted someone the age of a thousand years. Since He is God of both life and death, He may grant anyone a span of age He wills. The fact is that a man cannot live even for one moment merely because he so desires. However, if God so wills, He can grant him a very, very long life.

23. The Flood overtook Noah's people while they were engrossed in wrong-doing. Had they given up their wrong-doing before the Flood, God would not have afflicted them with that scourge.

24. This refers to those who had professed faith in the Prophet Noah (peace be on him) and whom God had allowed to board the Ark. This is evident from the following passage:

> Thus it was until Our command came to pass and the oven boiled over. We said: "Take into the Ark, a pair of every species; and take your own family except those who have already been declared (as unworthy); and also take everyone who believes." But those who, along with him, had believed were indeed just a few. (*Hūd* 11:40)

25. This could also mean that this horrendous calamity or this great event was made a Sign for coming generations to derive a lesson from. However, the wording of this verse and of verses 13-15 of *al-Qamar* suggest that Noah's Ark itself, which remained anchored on the mountain top for centuries, was the Sign demonstrating to people that it was stationed there as a result of the Flood. This Ark is also mentioned elsewhere in the Qur'ān in the following words:

(16) We sent Abraham[26] and he said to his people: "Serve Allah and fear Him.[27] This is better for you if you only knew. (17) Those that you worship instead of Allah are merely idols, and you are simply inventing lies (about them).[28] Indeed those whom you worship

وَإِبۡرَٰهِيمَ إِذۡ قَالَ لِقَوۡمِهِ ٱعۡبُدُواْ ٱللَّهَ
وَٱتَّقُوهُۖ ذَٰلِكُمۡ خَيۡرٞ لَّكُمۡ إِن كُنتُمۡ
تَعۡلَمُونَ ١٦ إِنَّمَا تَعۡبُدُونَ مِن دُونِ ٱللَّهِ
أَوۡثَٰنٗا وَتَخۡلُقُونَ إِفۡكًاۚ إِنَّ ٱلَّذِينَ تَعۡبُدُونَ

> And We bore Noah on the Ark built of planks and nails, which sailed on under Our supervision: a reward for him who had been shown ingratitude. And We left the Ark as a Sign. Is there, then, any who will take heed? (*al-Qamar* 54:13-15)

Explaining these verses, Ibn Jarīr al-Ṭabarī reports on the authority of Qatādah, that when the Muslims reached al-Jazīrah in the time of the Companions, they saw the Ark perched on Mount Jūdī; and according to another tradition, near a town called Bāqirwā. (Cf. Ṭabarī, *Tafsīr*, comments on *al-Qamar* 54:15 – Ed.) In our own times, too, reports occasionally appear about expeditions dispatched to trace the Ark. This because, while flying over Mount Arārāṭ, an object resembling the Ark was sighted. (For further details see *Towards Understanding the Qur'ān*, Vol. III, *al-Aʿrāf* 7: n. 47, pp. 37-38 and Vol. IV, *Hūd* 11: n. 46, pp. 102-104.)

26. Cf. *al-Baqarah* 2:122-141; *Āl ʿImrān* 3:64-71; *al-Anʿām* 6:71-82; *Hūd* 11:69-83; *Ibrāhīm* 14:35-41; *al-Ḥijr* 15:45-60; *Maryam* 19:41-50; *al-Anbiyā'* 21:51-75; *al-Shuʿarā'* 26:69-104; *al-Ṣāffāt* 37:75-113; *al-Zukhruf* 43:26-35 and *al-Dhāriyāt* 51:22-46.

27. They were exhorted to fear God and give up associating others with Him in His Divinity. They were to eschew disobedience of God.

28. When they set up idols, they were in fact guilty of inventing falsehoods. This, because the idols themselves were an embodiment of falsehood. The same applies to the baseless notions they cherished about these idols: that they were gods or goddesses, God's incarnations,

beside Allah have no power to provide you with any sustenance. So seek your sustenance from Allah and serve only Him and give thanks to Him alone. It is to Him that you will be sent back.[29] (18) And if you give

مِن دُونِ ٱللَّهِ لَا يَمْلِكُونَ لَكُمْ رِزْقًا
فَٱبْتَغُوا۟ عِندَ ٱللَّهِ ٱلرِّزْقَ وَٱعْبُدُوهُ وَٱشْكُرُوا۟
لَهُۥٓ ۖ إِلَيْهِ تُرْجَعُونَ ﴿١٧﴾ وَإِن

His offspring or favourites, or that they had the power to intercede with God, to heal the sick, or grant people a livelihood. The unbelievers and polytheists fabricated these notions: in other words, they resorted to conjecture. The only truth about them was that they were idols – lifeless, powerless, and resourceless.

29. These few sentences of the Prophet Abraham (peace be on him) enshrine a great number of cogent arguments against idolatry. It goes without saying that there must be a convincing reason to take someone as one's Lord. One such reason could be that He is intrinsically worthy of worship. The second reason could be that He is man's Creator to whom he owes his existence. A third reason could be that He is man's Sustainer and provides him with the means to exist. A fourth reason could be that He exercises control over man's destiny and, out of fear, man worships Him lest he incur His displeasure and thus ruin his future.

The Prophet Abraham (peace be on him), however, contends that none of these considerations support idolatry; rather, all four provide reasons for devotion to the One True God. Abraham's plain statement that the objects of idolaters' worship are "merely idols" demolished the first of the four possible reasons to regard them as deities. Moreover, by saying that the idols were their own inventions further highlighted why idols could not be considered worthy of man's worship. Thus, the second possible basis for regarding them as deities was destroyed. The third possible basis for their godhead is dismissed by saying that idols do not provide man's sustenance. Then, last of all, it was stated that man is ultimately destined to return to God rather than to any idol. Hence idols have no role in making or marring man's prospects in the Hereafter, which will,

the lie (to the Messenger),[30] then many nations before you also gave the lie (to their Messengers). The Messenger is charged with no other duty than to deliver the Message in clear terms."

(19) Have they never observed[31] how Allah creates for the first time and then repeats it? Indeed (to repeat the creation of a thing) is even easier for Allah (than creating it for

تُكَذِّبُوا۟ فَقَدْ كَذَّبَ أُمَمٌ مِّن قَبْلِكُمْ ۖ وَمَا عَلَى ٱلرَّسُولِ إِلَّا ٱلْبَلَٰغُ ٱلْمُبِينُ ﴿١٨﴾
أَوَلَمْ يَرَوْا۟ كَيْفَ يُبْدِئُ ٱللَّهُ ٱلْخَلْقَ ثُمَّ يُعِيدُهُۥٓ ۚ إِنَّ ذَٰلِكَ عَلَى ٱللَّهِ

in any case, be decided by God alone. Hence every basis for associating others with the One True God in His Divinity was refuted and Abraham established overwhelmingly that there was no reason for man to hold anyone other than the One True God as his deity.

30. If Abraham's people rejected his call to monotheism and his warning that eventually they will return to God and if they regarded the very idea of His reckoning as false, there was nothing novel about this. For earlier Prophets, such as Noah, Hūd and Ṣāliḥ (peace be on them), had expounded the same message to their respective peoples but it was rejected and the Prophets labelled as liars. It is now for Abraham's people to decide whether these earlier nations, by giving the lie to God's Prophets, had caused any harm to those Prophets or brought destruction upon themselves.

31. The Qur'ānic passage under study (vv. 19-23) constitutes a parenthetical statement, marking a break from the Prophet Abraham's story. This is directly addressed to the unbelieving Makkans. The reason why it is directed specifically at them is that they were guilty of committing

the first time).[32] (20) Say: "Go about the earth and see how He created for the first time, and then Allah will recreate life." Surely, Allah has power over everything.[33] (21) He chastises whom He will and forgives whom He will. To Him all of you will be sent back. (22) You cannot overpower Allah, neither on the

يَسِيرٌ ﴿١٩﴾ قُلْ سِيرُوا۟ فِى ٱلْأَرْضِ فَٱنظُرُوا۟
كَيْفَ بَدَأَ ٱلْخَلْقَ ۚ ثُمَّ ٱللَّهُ يُنشِئُ ٱلنَّشْأَةَ
ٱلْـَٔاخِرَةَ ۚ إِنَّ ٱللَّهَ عَلَىٰ كُلِّ شَىْءٍ قَدِيرٌ ﴿٢٠﴾
يُعَذِّبُ مَن يَشَآءُ وَيَرْحَمُ مَن يَشَآءُ ۖ وَإِلَيْهِ
تُقْلَبُونَ ﴿٢١﴾ وَمَآ أَنتُم بِمُعْجِزِينَ فِى

---

two major errors: one, polytheism and idolatry and two, denial of the Hereafter. The evil consequences of the former were graphically recounted in the above discourse to do with the Prophet Abraham (peace be on him). As for denial of the Hereafter, God adds a few words in its refutation here so that both errors stand refuted at one and the same time.

32. It is a common spectacle that countless objects are continually being created out of nothing. Likewise, one also observes that as all sorts of people disappear, others of the same kind come into being, replacing the former ones. The polytheists conceded that this spectacle was related to God's creative power. In other words, they did not deny that God was the Creator. In this respect, they did not essentially differ from present-day polytheists. Thus, an argument is developed on the basis of a premise which they themselves recognised. It is pointed out here that they themselves accept that God is constantly creating objects *ex nihilo* before their very eyes. In view of this, what makes them believe that God cannot resurrect human beings after they die? (For further discussion see *Towards Understanding the Qur'ān*, Vol. VII, *al-Naml* 27, n. 80, pp. 174-176.)

33. Since they witness God's creative power in His initial creation of everything, they should have no difficulty in believing that He can create them again after they die. It is quite evidently within His power to do so.

earth nor in the heaven.[34] None can protect you from Allah nor come to your aid against Him.[35] (23) Those who disbelieved in Allah's signs and in meeting Him, it is they who have despaired of My Mercy;[36] it is they for whom a painful chastisement lies ahead.

ٱلْأَرْضِ وَلَا فِى ٱلسَّمَآءِ ۖ وَمَا لَكُم مِّن
دُونِ ٱللَّهِ مِن وَلِىٍّ وَلَا نَصِيرٍ ﴿٢٢﴾ وَٱلَّذِينَ
كَفَرُوا۟ بِـَٔايَٰتِ ٱللَّهِ وَلِقَآئِهِۦٓ أُو۟لَٰٓئِكَ
يَئِسُوا۟ مِن رَّحْمَتِى وَأُو۟لَٰٓئِكَ لَهُمْ عَذَابٌ
أَلِيمٌ ﴿٢٣﴾

34. Man cannot flee to some far-away place, whether it be the deepest recesses of the earth or the greatest heights of the sky, to escape God's wrath. He will be seized wherever he might be and will be made to stand before Him for reckoning. A similar challenge is thrown to the *jinn* and human beings elsewhere in the Qur'ān in the following words:

> O company of *jinn* and men, if you have the power to go beyond the bounds of heaven and the earth, go beyond them! Yet you will be unable to go beyond them for that requires infinite power. (*al-Raḥmān* 55:33)

35. The believers are plainly told that they neither have the power to elude God's grasp, nor will any powerful patron or guardian protect them against God or enable them to escape His punishment. No one in the entire Universe has any authority to protect those who committed unbelief and polytheism, refused to obey God's commands, audaciously defied God and spread injustice and corruption on earth. No one has the power to prevent the enforcement of God's punishment against them. Nor will anyone dare plead with God for forgiveness on their behalf.

36. This means that obdurate unbelievers will have no portion of God's mercy; in fact, they have no reason to entertain any such expectation. The fact is that the unbelievers deny the Hereafter. They do not even recognise that a Day will come when they will have to stand before God for His judgement. This clearly means that, to start with, they do not even look forward to receiving any reward in the Next Life and that they entertain

(24) The people (of Abraham) had no other answer than to say:[37] "Kill him or burn him."[38] But Allah delivered him from the fire.[39] There are many Signs in this for those who

فَمَا كَانَ جَوَابَ قَوْمِهِۦٓ إِلَّآ أَن قَالُوا۟
ٱقْتُلُوهُ أَوْ حَرِّقُوهُ فَأَنجَىٰهُ ٱللَّهُ مِنَ ٱلنَّارِ ۚ إِنَّ
فِى ذَٰلِكَ لَءَايَٰتٍ لِّقَوْمٍ

no expectation of God's forgiveness and mercy. However, on the Day of Judgement when they will be brought back to life – which is, in any case, altogether contrary to their expectations – they will have no opportunity to receive any portion of God's mercy. Moreover, when they open their eyes in the Hereafter, they will come face to face with the Divine Signs which they had rejected in this world as utterly false and which they will then come to know were true. There will, therefore, be no reason for them to look forward to God's mercy.

37. This marks the resumption of the Prophet Abraham's story.

38. The Prophet Abraham's people had no reasonable response to his weighty arguments. Their only answer was: "Kill him or burn him." They said this because they were not ready to listen to the person who spoke the truth, who pointed out their errors, and asked them to distance themselves from them. It is clear from their response that they were all united about putting the Prophet Abraham (peace be on him) to death. They differed only as regards the mode of killing. Some suggested that he be murdered while others preferred that he be burned alive. In the end, the latter option was chosen in an attempt to make an example of Abraham that would deter others from championing the Truth with such zeal and single-mindedness.

39. The wording of the verse implies that they finally decided to burn the Prophet Abraham (peace be on him) alive and that he was so hurled into a fire. The Qur'ān, however, confines itself to stating that he was rescued. Elsewhere, the Qur'ān clarifies that by God's command the fire became cool and safe for Abraham: "We said: 'O fire, become coolness and safety for Abraham'," (*al-Anbiyā'* 21:69). Had Abraham not actually been thrown into the fire, this command would be meaningless.

believe.[40] (25) He said:[41] "You have taken up idols instead of Allah as a bond	يُؤْمِنُونَ ﴿٢٤﴾ وَقَالَ إِنَّمَا ٱتَّخَذْتُم مِّن دُونِ ٱللَّهِ أَوْثَٰنًا

The truth that emerges from this incident is that all things owe their properties to God's command. He may alter the property of a thing as and when He wills. In the normal course of things, fire's property is to burn and when a combustible object is cast into it, it is reduced to ashes. This property to burn is part of a system that God has instituted. This fact does not, however, prevent God from ever issuing a command in violation of the normal pattern that He has devised. Being the Lord of fire, as of everything else, He can command fire to cease burning. It is within His power to transform an inferno into a blooming garden. True, such things are out of the ordinary and are a deviation from the normal order of things and happen only rarely. Moreover, when they do take place they do so for some overriding reason. Nevertheless, there is no basis to believe that God's power is circumscribed by the bounds of normal occurrences or to think that nothing beyond the ordinary can ever take place by God's command.

40. There are Signs for the believers in the Prophet Abraham's example. Rather than cling to the false religion of his family, his people and his country, Abraham (peace be on him) opted to follow the Truth as soon as it dawned upon him that polytheism was nothing but falsehood whereas monotheism was the quintessence of Truth. Once Abraham (peace be on him) realised this, he ceaselessly preached that people should give up polytheism and embrace monotheism. He did so in utter disregard of the obduracy and bigotry of his people. So deep was his devotion to monotheism that he refused to relinquish it even when hurled into a blazing fire. There are also God's Signs in the fact that He made His Prophets, including Abraham (peace be on him), undergo certain tests so as to establish their mettle. There is also God's Sign in the fact that after Abraham had successfully passed through the tests to which God had subjected him, He assisted Abraham so gloriously that the cauldron of fire into which he had been hurled was miraculously made cool.

41. It appears from the context that the Prophet Abraham (peace be on him) would have addressed his people in these words only after he was miraculously saved from the fire.

of love among yourselves in the present life,[42] but on the Day of Resurrection you will disown and curse one another.[43] Your refuge shall be the Fire, and none will come to your aid."

مَّوَدَّةَ بَيْنِكُمْ فِي ٱلْحَيَوٰةِ ٱلدُّنْيَا ثُمَّ
يَوْمَ ٱلْقِيَـٰمَةِ يَكْفُرُ بَعْضُكُم بِبَعْضٍ
وَيَلْعَنُ بَعْضُكُم بَعْضًا وَمَأْوَىٰكُمُ ٱلنَّارُ
وَمَا لَكُم مِّن نَّـٰصِرِينَ ﴿٢٥﴾

42. The nucleus of their collective life was devotion to idols rather than to God. The fact is that even devotion to idols can provide a workable basis for bringing about worldly cohesion among a people. This because people can be brought together by any cause, gathering around both true and false beliefs as they do. Moreover, any kind of cohesion and unity, even if it is founded on a false proposition, can serve as a means to foster and sustain friendships, family ties and vocational bonds, as also provide a basis for religious, social, cultural, economic and political fellowship.

43. The unbelievers are told that their social structure, based as it is on a false proposition, will not endure in the Hereafter. The only bonds that will endure – bonds of friendship, cooperation, kinship, and reverential discipleship – will be those based on servitude to the One True God and on righteous conduct and piety. In the Next World, bonds rooted in unbelief, polytheism, misguidance and waywardness will cease to be; in fact, friendships in this world will turn into enmity. All those who are bound in devotion to those they revere will become enemies to one another. Father and son, husband and wife, and teacher and disciple will curse each other. Each of them will blame the other for his error and demand that the latter be given double the punishment for having misguided him. The Qur'ān states this at several places. The following are illustrative:

> On that Day even bosom friends shall become enemies to one another, all except the God-fearing. (*al-Zukhruf* 43:67)
>
> As a nation enters Hell, it will curse the one that went before it, and when all are gathered there, the last of them shall say of the first: "Our Lord! These are the ones who led us astray. Let their torment be doubled in Hell-Fire." (*al-Aʿrāf* 7:38)

(26) Then did Lot believe him,[44] and Abraham said: "I am emigrating unto my Lord.[45] He is All-Powerful,	۞ فَـَٔامَنَ لَهُۥ لُوطٌ ۘ وَقَالَ إِنِّى مُهَاجِرٌ إِلَىٰ رَبِّىٓ ۖ إِنَّهُۥ هُوَ ٱلْعَزِيزُ

They will say: "Our Lord, we obeyed our chiefs and our great ones, and they turned us away from the Right Way. Our Lord, mete out to them a double chastisement and lay upon them a mighty curse." (*al-Aḥzāb* 33:67-68)

44. The sequence of the discourse indicates that the Prophet Abraham (peace be on him) made these remarks after he was miraculously delivered from the fire. Among those present, however, Lot was the only one to come forward and declare his belief in Abraham (peace be on him) and pledge to follow him. Presumably, many others, too, were persuaded to believe in the truth of Abraham's message. However, the hostility that the whole nation as well as the state generally displayed towards Abraham's teaching was ferocious. Thanks to that, no one other than Lot, the Prophet Abraham's nephew, could muster the courage to follow his way, which seemed beset with risks. It was Lot's unique privilege that he publicly accepted his uncle Abraham's message and later accompanied his uncle and aunt, Sarah, when they migrated for God's cause.

We should stop here for a moment to dispel one misperception whereby some people are bound to ask: did Lot indulge in unbelief and polytheism before witnessing the Prophet Abraham's rescue from the fire? Did he embrace faith only after this miraculous incident? If this were the case, can anyone who once committed polytheism be designated to the august office of Prophethood? The Qur'ān only says the following about Lot: "Then did Lot believe him." These words do not necessarily mean that before this miraculous event Lot disbelieved in God or associated others with God in His Divinity. What is stated here is simply that after Abraham's rescue from the fire Lot testified to the truth of his mission and pledged to follow him. It is also likely that he was then only a youth who, for the first time, came to know about his uncle's mission and his exalted status as God's Messenger.

45. Abraham migrated for the sake of his Lord and expressed his readiness to go wherever God wanted him to.

All-Wise,"[46] (27) and We bestowed upon him (offspring like) Isaac and Jacob,[47] and bestowed prophethood and the Book on his descendants[48] and granted him his reward in this world; he will certainly be among the righteous in the Hereafter.[49]

ٱلْحَكِيمُ ﴿٢٦﴾ وَوَهَبْنَا لَهُۥٓ إِسْحَـٰقَ وَيَعْقُوبَ
وَجَعَلْنَا فِى ذُرِّيَّتِهِ ٱلنُّبُوَّةَ وَٱلْكِتَـٰبَ
وَءَاتَيْنَـٰهُ أَجْرَهُۥ فِى ٱلدُّنْيَا ۖ وَإِنَّهُۥ فِى
ٱلْـَٔاخِرَةِ لَمِنَ ٱلصَّـٰلِحِينَ ﴿٢٧﴾

46. Abraham reiterated his conviction that God, being All-Powerful and All-Wise, will protect him in the best possible manner and, in His infinite wisdom, will choose for him the land to which he should migrate.

47. The Prophets Isaac and Jacob (peace be on them) were respectively Abraham's son and grandson. His other sons are not mentioned here because only the Prophet Shuʿayb (peace be on him) was raised as God's Messenger among the Midianite branch of Abraham's descendants. As for the Ishmaelite branch, no Messenger was raised among them for another 2,500 years until the advent of the Prophet Muḥammad (peace be on him). In contrast, Isaac's descendants continued to be favoured with Messengers and Scriptures until the advent of the Prophet Jesus (peace be on him).

48. This includes all Prophets raised among the various branches of the Prophet Abraham's descendants.

49. The purpose of the statement is to stress that the rulers, the clergy and the polytheists of Babylon, who sought to degrade the Prophet Abraham's call and blindly followed the wrong-doers in opposing it, had all disappeared, and no trace of them could be found. However, the Prophet Abraham (peace be on him) whom they had tried to burn alive for his "crime" of upholding God's Word, and who was also forced into exile in a state of utter helplessness, was immensely exalted by God. This is borne out by the fact that for the last four thousand years he has remained a highly renowned figure in world history, a position he will enjoy till the

(28) We sent Lot[50] and he said to his people: "You commit the abomination that none in the world ever committed before you. (29) What! Do you go to men (to satisfy your lust),[51] engage in highway robbery, and commit evil deeds in your gatherings?"[52] Then they had no answer to offer other than to say: "Bring Allah's chastisement upon us if you are truthful." (30) Lot said: "My Lord, aid me against these mischievous people."

وَلُوطًا إِذْ قَالَ لِقَوْمِهِۦٓ إِنَّكُمْ لَتَأْتُونَ
ٱلْفَـٰحِشَةَ مَا سَبَقَكُم بِهَا مِنْ أَحَدٍ مِّنَ
ٱلْعَـٰلَمِينَ ﴿٢٨﴾ أَئِنَّكُمْ لَتَأْتُونَ ٱلرِّجَالَ
وَتَقْطَعُونَ ٱلسَّبِيلَ وَتَأْتُونَ فِى نَادِيكُمُ
ٱلْمُنكَرَ ۖ فَمَا كَانَ جَوَابَ قَوْمِهِۦٓ إِلَّآ أَن
قَالُوا۟ ٱئْتِنَا بِعَذَابِ ٱللَّهِ إِن كُنتَ مِنَ
ٱلصَّـٰدِقِينَ ﴿٢٩﴾ قَالَ رَبِّ ٱنصُرْنِى عَلَى
ٱلْقَوْمِ ٱلْمُفْسِدِينَ ﴿٣٠﴾

end of time. All Jews, Christians and Muslims unanimously regard him as their patriarch and religious guide. His message has been instrumental in providing direction to mankind for the last four thousand years. Besides the invaluable rewards that will be his in the Hereafter, Abraham's renown in this world too is unrivalled, being quite incomparable to those who hanker after material gain and fame.

50. Cf. *al-Aʿrāf* 7:80-84; *Hūd* 11:69-83; *al-Ḥijr* 15:57-79; *al-Anbiyā'* 21:71-75; *al-Shuʿarā'* 26:160-175; *al-Naml* 27:54-58; *al-Ṣāffāt* 37:133-138, and *al-Qamar* 54:33-40.

51. They made males a means for the gratification of their sexual desires. This point is also made elsewhere in the Qur'ān as follows: "You approach men lustfully in place of women", (*al-Aʿrāf* 7:81).

52. Not only did they commit shameful acts, they did so publicly. The same reproach against them features in another verse, whereby: "We sent Lot, and recall when he told his people: 'Do you commit shameless acts with your eyes open?'" (*al-Naml* 27:54).

(31) When Our emissaries brought the good news to Abraham,[53] and said (to him): "We are surely going to destroy the inhabitants of this city;[54] its inhabitants are immersed in wrong-doing." (32) Abraham said: "But Lot is there."[55] They

وَلَمَّا جَآءَتۡ رُسُلُنَآ إِبۡرَٰهِيمَ بِٱلۡبُشۡرَىٰ قَالُوٓاْ
إِنَّا مُهۡلِكُوٓاْ أَهۡلِ هَٰذِهِ ٱلۡقَرۡيَةِۖ إِنَّ أَهۡلَهَا
كَانُواْ ظَٰلِمِينَ ۝٣١ قَالَ إِنَّ فِيهَا لُوطٗاۚ

53. In *Sūrahs Hūd* and *al-Ḥijr* it is stated that the angels deputed to destroy the Prophet Lot's people first went to the Prophet Abraham (peace be on him). They gave him the good news of the birth of his son, Isaac, and of his grandson, Jacob. The angels also informed him that they were on their way to destroy the Prophet Lot's people.

54. "This city" here alludes to the territory in which Lot's people lived. The Prophet Abraham (peace be on him) at that time lived in the city of Hebron in Palestine, presently known as al-Khalīl. A few miles to the southeast of the city lies that part of the Dead Sea which was once inhabited by Lot's people and which is now submerged by the sea. This is a low-lying area and is easily visible from the hill-tops of Hebron. It is for this reason that the angels pointed in the direction of the city, saying to the Prophet Abraham: "We are surely going to destroy the inhabitants of this city." (See also *Towards Understanding the Qur'ān*, Vol. VII, *al-Shuʿarā'* 26: n. 114, pp. 108-109.)

55. The opening part of this story is narrated in *Sūrah Hūd*. The Prophet Abraham (peace be on him) was disconcerted when he observed that angels had appeared in human form, for this usually indicates that they are on some ominous mission. He was relieved, however, when they gave him the good news of the birth of his son. When he also came to know that they were on their way to destroy the Prophet Lot's people, he pleaded fervently that mercy be shown them. In the words of the Qur'ān: "He began to dispute with Us concerning the people of Lot. Surely Abraham was forbearing, tender-hearted and oft-turning to Allah." Abraham's plea, however, was not accepted: "Thereupon (our angels) said to him:

replied: "We are well aware of those who are there. We shall save him and all his household except his wife." His wife is among those who will stay behind.[56]

(33) When Our emissaries came to Lot he was distressed and embarrassed on their account.[57] They said: "Do not

قَالُواْ نَحْنُ أَعْلَمُ بِمَن فِيهَا لَنُنَجِّيَنَّهُۥ وَأَهْلَهُۥٓ
إِلَّا ٱمْرَأَتَهُۥ كَانَتْ مِنَ ٱلْغَٰبِرِينَ ۝٣٢
وَلَمَّآ أَن جَآءَتْ رُسُلُنَا لُوطًا سِيٓءَ بِهِمْ
وَضَاقَ بِهِمْ ذَرْعًا وَقَالُواْ لَا

'O Abraham! Desist from this, for indeed your Lord's command has come; and a chastisement which cannot be averted is about to befall them'," (*Hūd* 11:74-76). It was then that the Prophet Abraham (peace be on him) realised that Lot's people were doomed to suffer Divine scourge. He was also inevitably concerned about the Prophet Lot (peace be on him), as mentioned in the verse: "But Lot is there." The safety of the latter and his family worried Abraham for if the scourge were to strike Lot's people while he was in their midst, how could Lot and his family remain safe?

56. We learn from *al-Taḥrīm* 66:10 that the Prophet Lot's wife was not sincere towards her husband. It was, therefore, decided that notwithstanding her being the wife of a Prophet, she too should be afflicted with God's scourge. It is likely that when the Prophet Lot (peace be on him) settled in Jordan after his migration, he might have married a woman from among the local populace. However, even after spending many years in a Prophet's company, she did not sincerely embrace faith and her allegiance to her unbelieving people endured. God, of course, does not accord any weight to ties of kinship in judging people; rather, He judges everyone on the basis of faith and conduct. Therefore, her marital tie with one of His Prophets could not save her from punishment. Her fate was tied with that of her people's with whom she had religious and moral bonds rather than with her husband.

57. The reason for the Prophet Lot's anxiety and discomfort was that the angels had come to him in the form of handsome young men. (The fact

fear nor be distressed.[58] We shall save you and all your household except your wife who is among those that will stay behind. (34) We shall bring down upon the people of this city a scourge from the heaven because of their evil-doing." (35) And We have left a vestige of it

تَخَفۡ وَلَا تَحۡزَنۡۖ إِنَّا مُنَجُّوكَ وَأَهۡلَكَ
إِلَّا ٱمۡرَأَتَكَ كَانَتۡ مِنَ ٱلۡغَٰبِرِينَ ٣٣ إِنَّا
مُنزِلُونَ عَلَىٰٓ أَهۡلِ هَٰذِهِ ٱلۡقَرۡيَةِ رِجۡزٗا مِّنَ
ٱلسَّمَآءِ بِمَا كَانُواْ يَفۡسُقُونَ ٣٤ وَلَقَد
تَّرَكۡنَا مِنۡهَآ

that they were angels was not initially known to Lot.) Now Lot was well aware of his people's moral corruption. The angels' visit, in the form of handsome young men therefore presented him with a difficult problem, namely, the protection of his guests from the immoral onslaughts of his community. He could not turn his guests away for that would be an act inconsistent with hospitality. Furthermore, if he did not offer them his hospitality, they would be obliged to spend the night in the town, which would amount to leaving his visitors to the tender mercy of hungry wolves. The Qur'ānic passage here does not narrate any further details of the story but an extensive account of it appears in *Sūrahs Hūd, al-Ḥijr* and *al-Qamar.* (See *Hūd* 11:76-83; *al-Ḥijr* 15:60-77, and *al-Qamar* 54:33-39.) According to these, on learning of these handsome men's visit, many people barged into the Prophet Lot's house, demanding that the guests be handed over to them so that they might satisfy their unbridled lust.

58. The visitors assured the Prophet Lot (peace be on him): "Do not fear nor be distressed." In other words, Lot's people would not be able to cause them the slightest harm. At this moment they revealed their identity, telling Lot that they were angels who had been sent down to inflict God's scourge upon his people. It is stated in *Sūrah Hūd* that on observing his people rushing to his house, and realising that he could not save his guests, Lot (peace be on him) exclaimed: "Would that I had the strength to set you straight, or could seek refuge in some powerful support." Thereupon the angels said: "O Lot! We indeed are Messengers of your Lord. And your people will in no way be able to hurt you", (*Hūd* 11:80-81).

in that city as a Clear Sign[59] for a people who use their reason.[60]

(36) And We sent to Midian their brother Shuʿayb.[61] He said: "My people, serve Allah and look forward to the Last Day[62]

ءَايَةً بَيِّنَةً لِّقَوْمٍ يَعْقِلُونَ ۝٣٥ وَإِلَىٰ مَدْيَنَ
أَخَاهُمْ شُعَيْبًا فَقَالَ يَٰقَوْمِ ٱعْبُدُوا۟ ٱللَّهَ
وَٱرْجُوا۟ ٱلْيَوْمَ ٱلْءَاخِرَ

---

59. "A Clear Sign" here refers to the Dead Sea which, owing to its association with Lot, is also called the Sea of Lot. Time and again the Qur'ān impressed on the Makkan unbelievers that a Sign of the chastisement that had visited those wicked people could still be seen. This was observable both in the morning and night along the highway in the course of people's commercial journeys to Syria. The relevant Qur'ānic verses are as follows: "The place (where the rain of stones occurred) lies along a known route" (*al-Ḥijr* 15:76), and "You pass by their desolate habitations in the morning and at night", (*al-Ṣāffāt* 37:137-138).

It is now almost universally recognised that what is presently the southern part of the Dead Sea became so transformed as a result of a terrible earthquake, which caused the land mass to cave in. It was in this part that the capital of the Prophet Lot's people, Sodom, was located. One can still find ruins of some submerged towns in the sea. Aided with the latest diving and archaeological devices, expeditions are presently in progress to study these ruins. The results of these studies, however, are still to be obtained. (For further details see *Towards Understanding the Qur'ān*, Vol. VII, *al-Shuʿarā'* 26: n. 114, pp. 108-109.)

60. On the punishment laid down for sodomy in the *Sharīʿah* see *Towards Understanding the Qur'ān*, Vol. III, *al-Aʿrāf* 7: n. 68, pp. 52-53.

61. For further details see *al-Aʿrāf* 7:85-93; *Hūd* 11:84-96 and *al-Shuʿarā'* 26:177-191.

62. This is open to the following interpretations: (i) They should be assured that the Afterlife will inevitably come to pass. They should not, therefore, consider the life of this world to be an end in itself. They should

and do not go about the earth committing mischief." (37) But they denounced him as a liar.[63] So a mighty earthquake overtook them, and by the morning they lay overturned in their houses.[64]

(38) And We destroyed ʿĀd and Thamūd, whose dwellings you have observed.[65] Satan had embellished their deeds for them and had turned them away from the Right Path although they were a people of clear perception.[66]

وَلَا تَعْثَوْا۟ فِى ٱلْأَرْضِ مُفْسِدِينَ ﴿٣٦﴾
فَكَذَّبُوهُ فَأَخَذَتْهُمُ ٱلرَّجْفَةُ فَأَصْبَحُوا۟ فِى
دَارِهِمْ جَٰثِمِينَ ﴿٣٧﴾ وَعَادًا وَثَمُودَا۟ وَقَد
تَّبَيَّنَ لَكُم مِّن مَّسَٰكِنِهِمْ ۖ وَزَيَّنَ لَهُمُ
ٱلشَّيْطَٰنُ أَعْمَٰلَهُمْ فَصَدَّهُمْ عَنِ
ٱلسَّبِيلِ وَكَانُوا۟ مُسْتَبْصِرِينَ ﴿٣٨﴾

---

be certain that the present life will be followed by the Hereafter wherein they will be held to account and receive reward or punishment. (ii) They are urged to do good deeds that might improve their prospects in the Hereafter.

63. They did not accept the Prophet Shuʿayb as God's Messenger or his teachings to be from God. As a consequence of their rejection of these truths, they were afflicted with God's scourge.

64. That is, the whole territory they inhabited was destroyed.

65. The Arabs of the Prophet's time were familiar with the lands of ʿĀd and Thamūd. The former lived in southern Arabia, which is presently known as Aḥqāf, Yaman and Ḥaḍramawt. The ruins of Thamūd are found to this day in northern Ḥijāz covering the region from Rābigh to ʿAqabah, from Madyan and Khaybar to Taymā' and Tabūk. At the time the Qur'ān was revealed, these ruins would have been even more prominent.

66. They were not ignorant fools; rather, they were a shrewd people, well-skilled in the management of worldly affairs. It cannot, therefore,

(39) And We destroyed Qārūn (Korah) and Pharaoh and Hāmān. Moses came to them with Clear Signs but they waxed arrogant in the land although they could not have outstripped (Us).[67] (40) So We seized each for their sin. We let loose upon some a violent tornado with showers of stones;[68] some were overtaken by a mighty Cry;[69] some were caused to be swallowed up by the earth,[70] and some We drowned.[71] Allah

وَقَـٰرُونَ وَفِرْعَوْنَ وَهَـٰمَـٰنَ ۖ وَلَقَدْ جَآءَهُم
مُّوسَىٰ بِٱلْبَيِّنَـٰتِ فَٱسْتَكْبَرُوا۟ فِى ٱلْأَرْضِ
وَمَا كَانُوا۟ سَـٰبِقِينَ ﴿٣٩﴾ فَكُلًّا أَخَذْنَا
بِذَنۢبِهِۦ ۖ فَمِنْهُم مَّنْ أَرْسَلْنَا عَلَيْهِ حَاصِبًا
وَمِنْهُم مَّنْ أَخَذَتْهُ ٱلصَّيْحَةُ وَمِنْهُم مَّنْ
خَسَفْنَا بِهِ ٱلْأَرْضَ وَمِنْهُم مَّنْ أَغْرَقْنَا ۚ

---

be said that Satan had cast a spell on them, made them blind to facts, robbed them of their ability to think rationally, or that he forced them to follow his way. The fact is that they knowingly chose the way shown to them by Satan because it contained the promise of many benefits and much pleasure. They, therefore, deliberately rejected the way shown by the Prophets for they found it hard and unattractive in view of its many stringent moral interdictions.

67. That is, they could neither escape God's grip nor frustrate His plans.

68. This refers to the 'Ād who were continuously subjected to a storm for seven nights and eight days. (See also *al-Ḥāqqah* 69:7.)

69. This refers to the Thamūd.

70. This refers to Korah.

71. This refers to Pharaoh and Hāmān.

would not wrong them, but it is they who wronged themselves.[72]

(41) The case of those who took others than Allah as their protectors is that of a spider who builds a house; but the frailest of all houses is the spider's house; if they only knew.[73]

وَمَا كَانَ ٱللَّهُ لِيَظْلِمَهُمْ وَلَٰكِن كَانُوٓاْ
أَنفُسَهُمْ يَظْلِمُونَ ۝٤٠ مَثَلُ ٱلَّذِينَ ٱتَّخَذُواْ
مِن دُونِ ٱللَّهِ أَوْلِيَآءَ كَمَثَلِ ٱلْعَنكَبُوتِ
ٱتَّخَذَتْ بَيْتًا ۖ وَإِنَّ أَوْهَنَ ٱلْبُيُوتِ لَبَيْتُ
ٱلْعَنكَبُوتِ ۖ لَوْ كَانُواْ يَعْلَمُونَ ۝٤١

72. The stories recounted here are addressed both to the Muslims and to the Makkan unbelievers. They were narrated so that the Muslims would not give in to despair and demoralisation and so that they would remain patient and resolute in upholding the Truth even in the face of very severe hardships. These stories should also instil in them full trust in God and make them assured that His aid will ultimately come and that He will see to it that their oppressors are humbled and God's Word is exalted.

On the other hand, these stories were also narrated to impart an important lesson to the Makkan wrong-doers who were bent upon obliterating Islam. They were thereby warned not to mistake God's forbearance. Since they had not been seized for a long time for their wrong-doing and rebellion, they had fallen prey to the delusion that they would never be brought to justice. Rather, they believed that they were free to act as they wanted, believing that this world was not subject to moral laws. Such mistaken notions would eventually bring upon them the same scourge which smote the unbelieving nations of the Prophets Noah, Lot, and Shuʿayb, for the ʿĀd and Thamūd. Korah and Pharaoh also met the same horrendous fate.

73. All these nations had been guilty of indulging in polytheism. They looked upon their idols as guardians and patrons who could make or mar their destiny. They presented offerings to them and worshipped them so as to procure their protection. They believed that by doing so their idols would help, support and protect them against every calamity. However, it is unmistakably evident from history, as related in the Qurʾān, that such false

(42) Surely Allah knows fully what they call upon apart from Him. He is the Most Powerful, the Most Wise.[74] (43) These are the parables that We set forth to make people understand. But only those endowed with knowledge will comprehend them.

إِنَّ ٱللَّهَ يَعۡلَمُ مَا يَدۡعُونَ مِن دُونِهِۦ
مِن شَيۡءٍۚ وَهُوَ ٱلۡعَزِيزُ ٱلۡحَكِيمُ ﴿٤٢﴾
وَتِلۡكَ ٱلۡأَمۡثَٰلُ نَضۡرِبُهَا لِلنَّاسِۖ
وَمَا يَعۡقِلُهَآ إِلَّا ٱلۡعَٰلِمُونَ ﴿٤٣﴾

---

beliefs and superstitions proved of no avail to them when God ordained their annihilation. No god or goddess, no *avtār,* saint or spirit, no *jinn* or angel whom they used to worship, came to their rescue. When they came face to face with this reality, they felt remorseful about having cherished false notions, but nonetheless they met their doom and were obliterated.

By relating these stories, the Qur'ān issues a dire warning to the Makkan polytheists: their expectations about receiving help and support from imaginary lords, idols, that are themselves helpless, will prove as frail as a spider's web. In the same way that a spider's web cannot withstand the mere touch of a finger, their polytheistic notions will be demolished as soon as the Divine scourge smites them. The fact is that ignorance alone accounts for their false beliefs and superstitions. Had they reflected on reality, their worldview would not have been erected on baseless foundations. The truth is that God, the One True Lord of the Universe, alone has all power and authority. It is He, as the Qur'ān says, in Whom man can place his reliance:

> He who rejects the evil ones and believes in Allah has indeed taken hold of the firm, unbreakable handle. And Allah (whom he has held for support) is All-Hearing, All-Knowing. (*al-Baqarah* 2:256)

74. God, of course, fully knows the truth about those whom the polytheists have chosen to be their deities and whom they call upon for help. Notwithstanding their misplaced devotion, these deities are absolutely powerless for all power lies with God alone. It is He alone Who governs the Universe by dint of His power and wisdom.

(44) Allah has created the heavens and the earth in Truth.[75] Certainly there is a Sign in this for those who believe.[76]

(45) (O Prophet), recite the Book that has been

خَلَقَ ٱللَّهُ ٱلسَّمَـٰوَٰتِ وَٱلْأَرْضَ بِٱلْحَقِّ ۚ
إِنَّ فِى ذَٰلِكَ لَـَٔايَةً لِّلْمُؤْمِنِينَ ﴿٤٤﴾ ٱتْلُ
مَآ أُوحِىَ إِلَيْكَ مِنَ ٱلْكِتَـٰبِ

This verse can also be translated as follows: "Surely Allah knows fully that what they call upon apart from Him is nothing (in reality) and He alone is the Most Powerful, the Most Wise."

75. The order of the Universe is based on truth rather than falsehood. Whoever ponders the workings of the Universe with an open mind realises that the heavens and the earth have nothing to do with imaginary musings and conjectures. They are rooted instead in the bedrock of truth and reality. It is simply impossible for a person to weave a philosophy out of his conjecture and imagination that adequately fits the scheme of the Universe, a scheme wherein only that which is anchored in truth and reality works and strikes root. Any system of ideas and presuppositions incongruent with reality will of necessity collide with it and be shattered into pieces.

The order of the Universe testifies to the fact that none other than the One True God is its Creator, Lord and Regulator. Suppose someone were to disregard this vital fact and proceed on the assumption that the Universe is without God or that there is a multiplicity of gods that provide security to their devotees in return for the offerings they make. Such baseless notions would not alter the truth at all. On the contrary, at one time or another, the victim of such false notions will face a rude shock.

76. The creation of the heavens and the earth provides testimony verifying the truth of monotheism and the falsity of polytheism and atheism. This testimony, however, can only be perceived by those who believe in the Prophets' teachings. As for those who reject the Prophets, they are unable to see the manifest truth that is evident to everyone.

revealed to you and establish Prayer.[77] Surely Prayer forbids indecency	وَأَقِمِ ٱلصَّلَوٰةَ ۖ إِنَّ ٱلصَّلَوٰةَ تَنْهَىٰ عَنِ ٱلْفَحْشَآءِ

77. This is apparently addressed to the Prophet (peace be on him), but in fact is meant for all believers. The believers were then facing immense hardship in their effort to follow their faith. In the earlier verses of this *sūrah* (see vv. 1-42), the believers were continually urged to remain patient and resolute and place all their trust in God. They are now being directed to adopt certain practical measures – to recite the Qur'ān and establish Prayer. The underlying idea is that these will equip them with firm character and such remarkable qualities that they will be able to withstand all onslaughts from evil forces. Once they are so equipped, the believers will have acquired the ability to turn the tide of the forces of evil pitted against them. It is evident, though, that one can only derive strength from reciting the Qur'ān when one correctly comprehends its teachings and when one's heart and soul absorb them. This is not the case, however, when Qur'ān-recitation is merely a mechanical repetition of the Qur'ān's text. Likewise, offering Prayer should not be confined to a set of bodily acts; rather, it should instil in the reciter's heart the message of the Qur'ān and make it the driving force of his character and conduct. What kind of impact Prayer should have on a man's conduct is clearly outlined in this very verse. (For elaboration see n. 78 below.)

As for recitation of the Qur'ān, if this does not go beyond the reciter's throat to reach his heart, it will certainly not provide him with the strength to withstand the tempestuous onslaughts of the forces of unbelief. In fact, it will hardly enable him even to sustain his faith. It is pertinent in this regard to bear in mind the following *ḥadīth* about a group of people who used to recite the Qur'ān: "They will recite the Qur'ān the while it will not go beyond their throats. They will go out of the fold of faith as an arrow goes out of the bowstring". (See Bukhārī, *K. Aḥādīth al-Anbiyā', Bāb: Qawl Allāh: Ammā 'Ādun fa uhlikū*; Muslim, *K. al-Zakāh, Bāb: Dhikr al-Khawārij wa Ṣifātihim*; Mālik, *Muwaṭṭa', K. al-Nidā' li al-Ṣalāh, Bāb*: *Mā jā'a fī al-Qur'ān* – Ed.) If one's mind, heart, character and conduct are not transformed after reciting the Qur'ān, and one still persists in doing what the Qur'ān forbids, this is not a true believer's recitation of the Qur'ān. The Prophet (peace be on him) characterised such people in these terms: "He who treats the prohibitions of the Qur'ān as lawful does not [truly]

and evil.[78] And Allah's remembrance is of even	وَٱلْمُنكَرِ ۗ وَلَذِكْرُ ٱللَّهِ

believe in the Qur'ān", (See Tirmidhī, *K. Faḍā'il al-Qur'ān, Bāb: Mā jā'a fī man qara'a Ḥarfan min al-Qur'ān mā lahū min al-Ajr* – Ed.) Such recitation does not reform a person's life or strengthen his spirit. In fact, it makes him all the more brazen with God and even more shameless before his own conscience so that no vestige of good character is left in him. Such a person is even more guilty than he who does not recite the Qur'ān. For the person who believes the Qur'ān to be the Book of God but who then violates its directives after becoming acquainted with them, as a result of reading the Qur'ān, is like a criminal who violates the law not out of ignorance, but with full knowledge of what he is doing. The following statement from the Prophet (peace be on him) applies fully to such people: "The Qur'ān is a witness either for you or against you", (Muslim, *K. al-Ṭahārah, Bāb*: *Faḍl al-Wuḍū'* – Ed.)

In other words, if one faithfully follows the message of the Qur'ān, one will benefit from it immensely. Whenever one is asked about one's conduct, whether in this world or in the Next, one can refer to the Qur'ān and plead that one acted according to it. If one's deeds are in accord with it, one need not fear any punishment from the courts in this world or any punishment in the Hereafter. However, if someone receives the message of the Qur'ān and knows what God expects him to do and what to avoid and still acts contrary to the Qur'ān's directives, this will be a witness against him. It will strengthen the case against him in God's court. For at this stage no one will be able to plead ignorance as a reason for exoneration nor will he be let off with a lighter punishment.

78. This is one among the many important attributes of Prayer that is highlighted here in sync with the context. At the time it was revealed, the early Muslims of the Makkan period encountered fierce hostility. To be able to withstand this, the Muslims stood in much greater need of moral rather than material strength. Two things were earlier indicated in order to generate moral strength among them and to ensure its growth – reciting the Qur'ān and establishing regular Prayers. The Muslims are now being told that by establishing Prayer they will be able to purge themselves of the evils in which they, as well as the *jāhilī* society of Arabia and the neighbouring lands, were enmeshed before their acceptance of

Islam. The establishment of Prayer has the power to help them overcome the evils that mar their lives.

A little reflection will make it clear why this particular attribute of Prayer is emphasised here. It goes without saying that purification from vice is beneficial both in the present world and in the Next. It gives one an edge over those who are engrossed in vice and who have pitted themselves in a battle against good in a bid to preserve the corrupt *jāhilī* system. The words *faḥshā'* and *munkar* used here refer to indecent and evil actions that are instinctively repulsive to human nature and which have always been known to be evil by all nations and societies. In fact, even those who are themselves enmeshed in corruption look upon evil as evil. Arabian society at the time the Qur'ān was revealed was no exception to this. The Arabs of the time recognised what was morally right to be right and what was wrong to be wrong and distinguished between good and evil. None of them branded good deeds to be evil or *vice versa*.

Against this backdrop, the emergence of a movement in a society that was immersed in evil and its ability to bring about a moral transformation among those influenced by it gave that movement a moral edge over others. This was bound to have an impact. The Arabs could not simply disregard a movement that extirpated evil and made those whom it influenced become conspicuously upright and pious in comparison with their contemporaries. It was impossible for ordinary Arabs not to feel the moral weight of the movement that was eradicating evils in their society and transforming people into virtuous and upright human beings. It was also difficult for them to extend their support, merely under the influence of the hollow slogans of *jāhilī* bigotry, to those who were themselves steeped in moral vice and who were striving to keep intact the *Jāhilīyah* corruption that had been extant for centuries. Therefore, rather than ask the Muslims to equip themselves with material resources, the Qur'ān urged them to establish Prayer, which would infuse moral excellence in them. This, in turn, would help this handful of people win over the hearts and minds of those around them and enable them, ultimately, to prevail over their opponents.

The merit of Prayer outlined in this verse, *viz.* that it forbids indecency and evil, has two aspects. The first is its essential characteristic, whereby it prevents man from indecency and evil. The second is, in fact, its required characteristic, whereby he who observes Prayer should actually desist from all acts of indecency and evil. As for restraining man from evil and indency, Prayer is undoubtedly a powerful means to this end.

Of all the possible restraints against committing evil, Prayer is the most effective. What could be more effective than summoning man five times a day to remember God and to refresh in him the fact that he has no right to act with unfettered freedom for he is the servant of an All-Knowing God, One Who is aware even of the desires and intentions that lie hidden in his heart. Furthermore, He it is to Whom man will one day have to render an account of all his deeds.

Prayer not only serves as a reminder of all these truths, but it also practically trains man not to disobey any of God's commands even when no one is watching him. This because from the moment a person rises to pray until he finishes it, God alone knows whether that person has or has not observed all the commands prescribed by Him for offering Prayer. For example, if someone joins the Prayer while he is not in a state of *wuḍū'*, this fact is known to none except himself and God. Likewise, someone might apparently join the Prayer and perform all the physical acts of which it consists while within himself he might have no intention of praying at all. It is also possible that instead of reciting what is required in Prayer, the person instead recites amorous songs. In such cases who else but the person themselves or God knows that, in reality, Prayer has not been offered at all? However, when someone offers Prayers five times a day, duly observing all its requirements, ranging from ritual cleanliness of body and clothing to recitations as laid down by Divine Law, this exercise constantly rejuvenates his conscience, awakens in him a sense of accountability to God, and transforms him into a responsible, duty-conscious person. Thereby, he is trained to willingly adhere to the dictates of faith, both in public and in private, regardless of whether he is subjected to supervision by any external authority and regardless of whether or not others are aware of his deeds.

Seen in this light, one reaches the inevitable conclusion that Prayer does indeed restrain man from committing acts of indecency and evil. In fact, there is no scheme of training aimed at dissuading people from evil as effective as Prayer. As for the question of whether someone will really refrain from evil after following the regime of regular daily Prayers, the result will obviously vary from one participant in this scheme of self improvement to another. If someone is sincerely interested in deriving benefit from Prayer and takes the required steps in that direction, his way of life will doubtlessly be reformed. As for the person who is not ready to mend his ways or who deliberately deprives himself of the benefits of Prayer, it is clear that no scheme of reform is going to help him. The following analogy illustrates this. Food is essential for the nutrition and growth of the body. However, food can perform this function only when one lets it do so. If someone were to immediately vomit the food after

greater merit.[79] Allah knows all that you do.	أَكۡبَرُۗ وَٱللَّهُ يَعۡلَمُ مَا تَصۡنَعُونَ ﴿٤٥﴾

eating it, even the most nutritious food will do him no good. Obviously, the situation of such a person is not a good basis to conclude that food is not nutritious for them. Following the same analogy, the example of someone who prays regularly and yet commits evil does not prove that Prayer fails to forbid indecency and evil. Rather, it is more apt to say that the person concerned does not truly offer Prayers. His likeness is that of the person who vomits after taking food and thus becomes weaker by the day.

This potential of Prayer to prevent people from indecency and evil features in several traditions from the Prophet (peace be on him) and from some leading Companions and Successors. ʿImrān ibn Ḥuṣayn narrates that the Prophet (peace be on him) said: "He whose Prayer does not deter him from indecency and evil is, in fact, one whose Prayer takes him further away from God." (Ibn Abī Ḥātim and Ṭabarī, *Tafsīr*, comments on *al-ʿAnkabūt* 29:45 and Ṭabarānī, *al-Muʿjam al-Kabīr,* tradition 10862 – Ed.) Ibn ʿAbbās narrates the following saying of the Prophet (peace be on him): "Anyone whose Prayer does not forbid him from indecency and evil (is a Prayer that) further removes from God", (Ibn Abī Ḥātim, *Tafsīr*, comments on *al-ʿAnkabūt* 29:45 and Ṭabarānī, *al-Muʿjam al-Kabīr,* tradition 10862 – Ed.) Ḥasan al-Baṣrī narrated a tradition directly from the Prophet (peace be on him) which enshrines the same idea. Ibn Jarīr al-Ṭabarī and al-Bayhaqī narrated a tradition from ʿAbd Allāh ibn Masʿūd, that the Prophet (peace be on him) said: "The Prayer of someone who does not obey the imperatives of Prayer and who does not refrain from indecency and evil, is not taken into account", (Ibn Jarīr al-Ṭabarī and Ibn Abī Ḥātim). Several traditions of similar import are related on the authority of ʿAbd Allāh ibn Masūd, ʿAbd Allāh ibn ʿAbbās, Ḥasan al-Baṣrī, Qatādah and al-Aʿmash. Imām Jaʿfar al-Ṣādiq says: "If one wants to ascertain whether one's Prayer has been accepted by God or not, one should assess how far one has abstained from indecency and evil. If one has stopped committing evil under the influence of Prayer, one's Prayer has been accepted", (al-Ālūsī, *Rūḥ al-Maʿānī* and Qurṭubī, *al-Jāmiʿ li Aḥkām al-Qur'ān*, comments on *al-ʿAnkabūt* 29:45 – Ed.).

79. This may be interpreted variously. First, God's remembrance, that is Prayer, is greater and of much higher value than merely its potential to

(46) Argue not with the People of the Book[80] except in the fairest manner,[81] unless it be those of them

۞ وَلَا تُجَـٰدِلُوٓا۟ أَهْلَ ٱلْكِتَـٰبِ
إِلَّا بِٱلَّتِى هِىَ أَحْسَنُ إِلَّا ٱلَّذِينَ

prevent acts of indecency and evil. Far from being only a force to restrain people from evil, observance of Prayer also prompts them to do good and excel others in so doing. Secondly, remembrance of God is an act of great intrinsic merit; it is, in fact, the best of deeds. Man cannot do anything better than engage in God's remembrance. Thirdly, that God's remembrance of man is of an even higher value than man's remembrance of God. The idea that God remembers man occurs in the Qur'ān as follows: "So remember Me and I shall remember you", (*al-Baqarah* 2:152). Prayer represents man's remembrance of God. When God's servant remembers Him, He too remembers His servant. Apart from these three interpretations, there is also the subtle interpretation offered by Abū al-Dardā's wife who said that: "Remembrance of God does not consist only of Prayer. Its range is very wide. As one observes fasting or pays *zakāh* or does any other good act, he is in fact remembering God. Likewise, when anyone avoids committing evil, he is prompted to do so by his remembrance of God. Thus remembrance of God embraces every aspect of a believer's life."

80. It is pertinent to mention that the Muslims were asked in the latter part of the *sūrah* to migrate (see v. 56). At that time, Abyssinia, the only safe haven for the Muslims was under Christian sway. Accordingly, the Muslims are being instructed as regards the norms they should observe in their religious discussions with People of the Book.

81. That is, if a discussion takes place with the People of the Book it should consist of putting forward reasonable arguments, be couched in decent and refined language, and be animated by a spirit of mutual understanding. The main concern in this respect should be to make sure, as far as possible, that the other party remains in a proper frame of mind to reconsider its ideas. If someone preaches Islam, his aim should be to win the hearts and minds of his addressees so as to bring them around to the Straight Way. However, if he engages in acrimonious argument, as though he were having an intellectual bout aimed at inflicting humiliating defeat on his enemy, this would be a self-defeating exercise. Instead, one should deal with the other party sympathetically and sensitively just as a

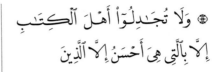

that are utterly unjust.[82] Say to them: "We believe in what was revealed to us and what was revealed to you. One is our God and

ظَلَمُواْ مِنْهُمْۖ وَقُولُوٓاْ ءَامَنَّا بِٱلَّذِىٓ أُنزِلَ إِلَيْنَا وَأُنزِلَ إِلَيْكُمْ وَإِلَٰهُنَا

physician deals with a patient. For obviously the physician has to be on guard lest any indiscretion on his part aggravates the patient's sickness. A physician's attention is always focused on one point: how best to heal his patient while causing him minimal pain. Seen in this context, it is evident that while this directive was given in connection with religious discussions with the People of the Book, its application is not confined to discussions with them alone. It is, in fact, a directive of universal import as regards preaching Islam, so much so that one frequently encounters the same in the Qur'ān:

> (O Prophet!) Call men to the way of your Lord with wisdom and goodly exhortation, and reason with them in the best manner possible. (*al-Naḥl* 16:125)

> (O Prophet!) Good and evil are not equal. Repel (evil) with that which is good, and you will see that he, between whom and you there was enmity, shall become as if he were a bosom friend (of yours). (*Ḥā' Mīm Sajdah* 41:34)

> (O Prophet!) Repel evil in the best manner. We are well aware of all that they say about you. (*al-Mu'minūn* 23:96)

> (O Prophet!) Show forgiveness, enjoin equity and avoid the ignorant. And if it happens that a prompting from Satan should stir you up, seek refuge with Allah. (*al-A'rāf* 7:199-200)

82. This means that the attitude one should adopt in dealing with the "utterly unjust" depends on the kind of wrong they actually inflict, which varies from situation to situation. What is stressed here is that the Muslims need not observe gentleness and leniency towards all their enemies, at all times, and in all circumstances, for this might cause them to mistake such gracious behaviour for weakness and timidity. Islam certainly teaches its followers to be gracious, affable and kind in their dealings with others. At the same time, however, it does not teach its exponents to resign themselves to humiliation and degradation.

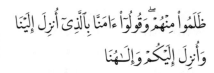

your God; and we are those who submit ourselves to Him."[83] (47) (O Prophet), thus have We bestowed the	وَإِلَٰهُكُمْ وَٰحِدٌ وَنَحْنُ لَهُۥ مُسْلِمُونَ ﴿٤٦﴾ وَكَذَٰلِكَ أَنزَلْنَآ

83. Here God indicates to the expounders of Truth how they can engage in refined religious discussions with others by offering an example. They are told not to make the erroneous position of the other party the starting point of such a discussion. Rather, the discussion should commence with identifying and highlighting the elements of truth that are common to both parties. In other words, commonalties rather than differences should be taken up first. As for contentious matters, an effort should be made to point out to the other party that the standpoint of the believers in regard to these matters is in conformity with that which is common to both parties whereas the standpoint of the other party is in conflict with what is commonly agreed.

It is also pertinent to remember that the People of the Book, unlike the Arabian polytheists, did not deny revelation, messengership and the Hereafter. Rather, they affirmed these truths as did the Muslims. Now, had there been any dispute between the Muslims and the People of the Book on these questions and had Muslims denied the latter's Scriptures and asked them to believe only in their Scripture, the Qur'ān, and had they declared the People of the Book to be unbelievers on that account this would certainly have caused serious discord. But the position of Muslims was quite different for they themselves affirmed belief in the Scriptures of the People of the Book as well as in the Revelation that had been made to the Prophet Muḥammad (peace be on him). Hence, it was for the People of the Book to explain why they accepted one of God's Scriptures and rejected others. The Muslims were, therefore, directed that if they encountered the People of the Book they should expound their standpoint: that they believed in the same God in Whom they believed, and that they too were committed to obeying Him. They were also to make it clear that they were bound to follow all the directives and commands that came from God, be they those that came to the People of the Book or to the Muslims. They were also required to clarify that they were devout servants of God rather than worshippers of any particular country, nation or race. This notion is repeatedly stressed in the Qur'ān in the context of the Muslims' encounter with the People of the Book. See,

Book on you.[84] So those on whom We had bestowed the Book before believe in it,[85] and of these (Arabs) too a good many believe in it.[86] It is none but the utter unbelievers who deny Our Signs.[87]

إِلَيْكَ ٱلْكِتَـٰبَ ۚ فَٱلَّذِينَ ءَاتَيْنَـٰهُمُ ٱلْكِتَـٰبَ يُؤْمِنُونَ بِهِۦ ۖ وَمِنْ هَـٰٓؤُلَآءِ مَن يُؤْمِنُ بِهِۦ ۚ وَمَا يَجْحَدُ بِـَٔايَـٰتِنَآ إِلَّا ٱلْكَـٰفِرُونَ ﴿٤٧﴾

---

for example, *al-Baqarah* 2: vv. 4, 136, 177 and 285; *Āl 'Imrān* 3:84; *al-Nisā'* 4:14, 61, 150-152, 162-164 and *al-Shūrā* 42:13.

84. This can be interpreted in two ways. First, that in the same manner that God had revealed Scriptures to other Prophets in the past, He has now revealed a Scripture to the Prophet Muḥammad (peace be on him). Secondly, that God has revealed this Book, the Qur'ān, and has directed people to believe in it in addition to believing in the earlier Scriptures.

85. The context clearly indicates that here the expression "those on whom We had bestowed the Book" is not applicable to all People of the Book. It rather applies only to those who were endowed with true knowledge and understanding of the Scriptures and were, thus, its recipients in the true sense of the expression rather than those who simply carried the Scriptures as donkeys carry a huge load of books. Hence when the Scripture revealed to the Prophet Muḥammad (peace be on him) was presented to such people – a Scripture that confirmed the truth of the earlier Scriptures – they displayed no prejudice or stubbornness in attesting to its truth. Rather, they accepted it with the same sincerity that they had displayed in accepting the earlier Scriptures.

86. The words "of these" refers here to the people of Arabia. The purpose being to stress that lovers of the Truth everywhere – People of the Book as well as others – had begun to embrace the Book revealed to the Prophet Muḥammad (peace be on him).

87. Hence the word "unbelievers" refers to those who were not ready to pay heed to the Truth. These were they who would not disregard their

(48) (O Prophet), you did not recite any Book before, nor did you write it down with your hand; for then the votaries of falsehood would have had a cause for doubt.[88]

وَمَا كُنتَ تَتْلُواْ مِن قَبْلِهِۦ مِن كِتَٰبٖ
وَلَا تَخُطُّهُۥ بِيَمِينِكَۖ إِذٗا لَّٱرۡتَابَ
ٱلۡمُبۡطِلُونَ ۝٤٨

biases and prejudices, who would not accept constraints on their lusts, and who were uncomfortable about reining in their unfettered freedoms. It is for reasons such as these that they were inclined to deny the Truth.

88. The same argument in support of the Prophet Muḥammad's designation to that office also occurs in *Sūrahs Yūnus* and *al-Qaṣaṣ*. (See *Towards Understanding the Qur'ān*, Vol. IV, *Yūnus* 10: n. 21, pp. 19-21; Vol. VII, *al-Qaṣaṣ* 28: nn. 64 and 109, pp. 224-226 and 250-253. See also Vol. IV, *al-Naḥl* 16: n. 107, pp. 366-367; Vol. V, *Banī Isrā'īl* 17: n. 105, pp. 71-72; Vol. VI, *al-Mu'minūn* 23: n. 66, pp. 112-113 and Vol. VII, *al-Furqān* 25: n. 12, pp. 7-10.)

The argument proffered in the present verse rests on the fact that the Prophet Muḥammad (peace be on him) was an unlettered person. His compatriots, his fellow tribesmen, his relatives and those in whose midst he had spent his whole life knew only too well that he had never read a single book, nor had he ever learned to write. After referring to this fact, God mentions it as conclusive proof that the Prophet's deep knowledge of the teachings of the earlier Scriptures, of the events relating to the lives of the Prophets, of the beliefs held by different religions, of the history of ancient nations and of matters relating to culture, morality and economy could have no other source than revelation from Him. Had the Prophet (peace be on him) been a literate person, been engaged in academic pursuits and been adept at reading and writing, the unbelievers would at least have some basis to cast doubt on the Divine provenance of his teachings. Indeed, they could have ascribed it to the Prophet's own studies rather than to revelation. However, the fact that he was unlettered struck at the roots of all such doubts and objections. So stubbornness was the reason for their rejection of his Prophethood, for no other grounds could be deemed as being even minimally reasonable.

(49) But it is a set of Clear Signs in the hearts of those who have been endowed with knowledge.[89] None except the utterly unjust will deny Our Signs. (50) They say: "Why were Signs from his Lord not sent down upon him?"[90] Say: "The Signs are only with Allah. As for me, I am no more than a plain warner."

بَلْ هُوَ ءَايَٰتٌۢ بَيِّنَٰتٌ فِى صُدُورِ
ٱلَّذِينَ أُوتُوا۟ ٱلْعِلْمَ ۚ وَمَا يَجْحَدُ بِـَٔايَٰتِنَآ
إِلَّا ٱلظَّٰلِمُونَ ﴿٤٩﴾ وَقَالُوا۟ لَوْلَآ أُنزِلَ عَلَيْهِ
ءَايَٰتٌ مِّن رَّبِّهِۦ ۖ قُلْ إِنَّمَا ٱلْءَايَٰتُ عِندَ
ٱللَّهِ وَإِنَّمَآ أَنَا۠ نَذِيرٌ مُّبِينٌ ﴿٥٠﴾

---

89. That is, the Qur'ān provides clear, luminous Signs to people of knowledge and wisdom in support of the Prophet Muḥammad's Messengership. The reason was that this wonderful Book, the Qur'ān, had begun to pour forth from the lips of an unlettered person. Furthermore, this person had all of a sudden begun to display astounding qualities and accomplish prodigious achievements even though in the early years of his life there was no evident basis to expect all this from him.

If one examines the biographies of illustrious historical personalities, one can identify in their milieu factors that contributed to the formation of their characters and which prepared them for their spectacular achievements. This is understandable because there is a clear correspondence between man's milieu and the main elements of his personality. However, the stark fact in the case of the Prophet Muḥammad (peace be on him) is that one cannot find anything in his milieu to explain his marvellous accomplishments. There was nothing in the Arabian environment or even in adjoining lands that could have shaped or moulded his extraordinary personality. The Qur'ān refers to this truth by asserting that the Prophet's personality is not simply a Sign but "a set of Clear Signs". While those who are ignorant may not perceive these Signs, those endowed with knowledge are convinced that his ways are no different from those of a Messenger from God.

90. This refers to miracles which inspire faith and vindicate the truth of the Prophet Muḥammad's Messengership.

(51) Does it not suffice for them (as a Sign) that We revealed to you the Book that is recited to them?[91] Surely there is mercy and

أَوَلَمْ يَكْفِهِمْ أَنَّآ أَنزَلْنَا عَلَيْكَ ٱلْكِتَٰبَ
يُتْلَىٰ عَلَيْهِمْ ۚ إِنَّ فِى ذَٰلِكَ لَرَحْمَةً

---

91. Is the revelation of a Scripture like the Qur'ān to an unlettered person not enough of a miracle to persuade people to believe in Muḥammad's Messengership? Is any further proof needed? Moreover, tangible miracles are effective for those who directly experience them, and, hence, their impact has a temporal dimension. This, however, does not apply to the Qur'ān. This living miracle is and will always remain before people's eyes. Furthermore, it is recited to them day in and day out.

In face of this explicit Qur'ānic statement about the unletteredness of the Prophet Muḥammad (peace be on him), one can only express astonishment at the audacity of those who seek to project him as literate. They do so while the Qur'ān specifically identifies him as unlettered precisely because this is a powerful argument in support of his Messengership's genuineness. As for reports that claim that he was literate or that he had acquired literacy at a later stage, these too should be dismissed out of hand. Any report contrary to the Qur'ān is not even worth considering. Furthermore, such reports are also too defective and weak as regards their authenticity to serve as the basis of any serious argument. Bukhārī, for instance, records the following: When the Treaty of Ḥudaybīyah was being drafted, the representative of the Makkan unbelievers raised his objection to the use of the title "Messenger of Allah" for Muḥammad (peace be on him). Thereupon the Prophet (peace be on him) directed 'Alī, his scribe, to strike it out and replace it with Muḥammad ibn 'Abd Allāh. 'Alī declined to do so. It was then that the Prophet (peace be on him) took the pen from his hand and struck out the title, "Messenger of Allah", and inscribed the words Muḥammad ibn 'Abd Allāh. (See Bukhārī, *K. al-Ṣulḥ, Bāb: Kayfa yuktabu mā Ṣālaḥa Fulān ibn Fulān …*; idem, *K. al-Jizyah, Bāb: al-Muṣālaḥah 'alā Thalāthat Ayyām aw Waqt Ma'lūm*; idem, *K. al-Maghāzī, Bāb: 'Umrat al-Qaḍā'*; Muslim, *K. al-Jihād wa al-Siyar, Bāb: Ṣulḥ al-Ḥudaybīyah fī al-Ḥudaybīyah* – Ed.)

This report, narrated by Barā' ibn 'Āzib, was variously recorded four times by Bukhārī and twice by Muslim. In each instance, the report contains different wording.

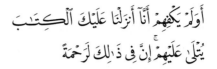

i. The report, as it occurs in Bukhārī's *Kitāb al-Ṣulḥ*, is as follows: "He [to wit, the Prophet (peace be on him)] said to 'Alī: 'Strike it out.' He replied: 'I am not the one who will strike it out.' Then the Prophet (peace be on him) struck it out with his own hand."
ii. Another report in the same work states: "He [to wit, the Prophet (peace be on him)] told 'Alī: 'Strike out the [words] 'Messenger of Allah'. He replied: 'By God, I will never strike you out.' Finally, the Prophet (peace be on him) took the text and wrote: 'This is the treaty concluded by Muḥammad ibn 'Abd Allāh'."
iii. The same narrator, Barā' ibn 'Āzib, is credited with the following report in Bukhārī's *Kitāb al-Jizyah*: "The Prophet (peace be on him) could not write on his own. He asked 'Alī to strike out the [words] 'Messenger of Allah'. 'Alī said: 'By God, I will never strike out [these words].' Then the Prophet (peace be on him) asked 'Alī to indicate the location where these words were inscribed, whereupon 'Ālī did so. The Prophet (peace be on him) then struck out those words with his own hand."
iv. However, in Bukhārī's *Kitāb al-Maghāzī*, the following version appears: "The Prophet (peace be on him) took the text, though he did not know how to write, and then wrote: 'This is the treaty concluded by Muḥammad ibn 'Abd Allāh'."
v. Barā' ibn 'Āzib reports in another version, as recorded in Muslim's *Kitāb al-Jihād*, that after 'Alī declined to strike out those words, the Prophet (peace be on him) struck out the words 'Messenger of Allah' with his own hand.
vi. Muslim also has the same narrator, Barā' ibn 'Āzib, reporting that the Prophet (peace be on him) asked 'Alī to indicate the words 'the Messenger of Allah' in the text. 'Alī did so and the Prophet (peace be on him) struck out those words and replaced them with "Ibn 'Abd Allāh".

The discrepancies in these reports clearly show that secondary narrators were unable to faithfully recount the actual words of Barā' ibn 'Āzib. Thus one cannot affirm with absolute certainty, on the basis of any of these reports, that the Prophet (peace be on him) himself wrote the words 'Muḥammad ibn 'Abd Allāh'. It is possible that after 'Alī declined to remove the words 'Messenger of Allah', the Prophet (peace be on him) himself removed them after 'Alī had indicated their location. It is also possible that after removing those words, the Prophet (peace be on him) might have asked 'Alī or some other scribe to write 'Ibn 'Abd Allāh' in their

good counsel in it for those who believe.[92] (52) Say (O Prophet): "Allah suffices as a witness between me and you. He knows whatever

وَذِكْرَىٰ لِقَوْمٍ يُؤْمِنُونَ ﴿٥١﴾ قُلْ كَفَىٰ بِٱللَّهِ
بَيْنِى وَبَيْنَكُمْ شَهِيدًا ۖ يَعْلَمُ

place. In fact, some reports indicate that the treaty had been committed to writing by two scribes, 'Alī and Muḥammad ibn Maslamah. (See Ibn Ḥajar al-'Asqalānī, *Fatḥ al-Bārī, K. al-Ṣulḥ, Bāb: al-Shurūṭ fī al-Jihād wa al-Muṣālaḥah*, Beirut: Dār al-Ma'rifah, 1379, vol. 5, 343.) It is not unlikely, therefore, that what one scribe declined to do was done by the other scribe. Even if the Prophet (peace be on him) wrote his name with his own hand, this should not come as a big surprise. For there are many illiterate people in the world who know only how to sign their own name. Beyond that, they cannot read or write anything.

The earliest authority of another report which is cited to support the claim that the Prophet (peace be on him) was literate is that of Mujāhid, a report that was narrated from him by Ibn Abī Shaybah and 'Umar ibn Shabbah. According to this report, the Prophet (peace be on him) had acquired literacy before his demise. In the first place, this report is quite weak according to the criteria of *isnād*. In fact, as Ibn Kathīr says: "it is weak and without any foundation". Secondly, its weakness is also evident from the fact that if the Prophet (peace be on him) had acquired the skill of reading and writing, this would have made news all around and have been known to a very large number of people. Such an event would, therefore, have been reported by a large number of Companions. Thus, it would also have become known who was or who were the people from whom the Prophet (peace be on him) learned such skills. Now, no one except 'Awn ibn 'Abd Allāh, from whom Mujāhid heard this, transmits this information. It is also noteworthy that 'Awn was not a Companion; rather, he was a Successor. Furthermore, 'Awn does not name the Companion(s) from whom he came to know this. It is obvious that one cannot dismiss a known incident on the basis of such weak traditions.

92. The sending down of the Qur'ān represents a great blessing from God for all mankind for it is the Book of guidance and admonition for all. However, only those who believe in it can benefit from it.

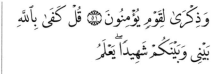

is in the heavens and the earth. As for those who believe in falsehood and are engaged in infidelity with Allah, it is they who will be the losers."

(53) They ask you to hasten in bringing chastisement upon them.[93] Had there not been an appointed term for it, the chastisement would have already visited them; in fact it will come down upon them all of a sudden (at its appointed time) while they will not be aware of it. (54) They ask you to hasten the chastisement upon them although Hell encompasses the unbelievers. (55) (They will become aware of it) the Day when the chastisement will overwhelm them from above and from under their feet, and He will say to them: "Taste now the consequence of the deeds that you used to commit."

مَا فِي ٱلسَّمَٰوَٰتِ وَٱلْأَرْضِ ۗ وَٱلَّذِينَ
ءَامَنُوا۟ بِٱلْبَٰطِلِ وَكَفَرُوا۟ بِٱللَّهِ أُو۟لَٰٓئِكَ هُمُ
ٱلْخَٰسِرُونَ ﴿٥٢﴾ وَيَسْتَعْجِلُونَكَ بِٱلْعَذَابِ ۚ
وَلَوْلَآ أَجَلٌ مُّسَمًّى لَّجَآءَهُمُ ٱلْعَذَابُ
وَلَيَأْتِيَنَّهُم بَغْتَةً وَهُمْ لَا يَشْعُرُونَ ﴿٥٣﴾
يَسْتَعْجِلُونَكَ بِٱلْعَذَابِ وَإِنَّ جَهَنَّمَ
لَمُحِيطَةٌۢ بِٱلْكَٰفِرِينَ ﴿٥٤﴾ يَوْمَ يَغْشَىٰهُمُ
ٱلْعَذَابُ مِن فَوْقِهِمْ وَمِن تَحْتِ أَرْجُلِهِمْ
وَيَقُولُ ذُوقُوا۟ مَا كُنتُمْ تَعْمَلُونَ ﴿٥٥﴾

93. The unbelievers repeatedly challenged the Prophet (peace be on him) to bring on the chastisement he warned them about. If he were a genuine Messenger and if they were guilty of rejecting the Truth, why did he not have them struck down with that chastisement?

(56) O My servants who believe, verily My earth is vast; so serve Me alone.[94] (57) Every being shall taste death, then it is to Us that you shall be sent back.[95]

يَـٰعِبَادِىَ ٱلَّذِينَ ءَامَنُوٓا۟ إِنَّ أَرْضِى
وَٰسِعَةٌ فَإِيَّـٰىَ فَٱعْبُدُونِ ۝٥٦ كُلُّ نَفْسٍ ذَآئِقَةُ
ٱلْمَوْتِ ۖ ثُمَّ إِلَيْنَا تُرْجَعُونَ ۝٥٧

94. This is an allusion to *Hijrah.* The purpose of the verse is to impress on the believers that their supreme duty is to serve God. Now, if it was difficult to do so in Makkah, God's earth was immensely vast and not confined to any particular place. Since the believers were devotees of God rather than of any particular country or nation, they should migrate to some other land where it would be possible to live freely as God's servants. Their priority should be to serve and worship their Lord rather than their people or country.

Whenever there is a clash between loyalty to one's country and people on the one hand, and loyalty to God on the other, a believer's faith is truly tested. Whenever a true believer is put to such a test, he is bound to spurn all other loyalties that conflict with his loyalty to God. As for those who falsely claim to be believers, they are likely to give up their faith and remain loyal to their country or nation. The unmistakable upshot of this verse is that while a true believer can be the lover of his people and country, he cannot be their worshipper, making his country and his people the locus of his ultimate loyalty. This is because he cherishes devotion to God above everything else. A believer can sacrifice everything for the sake of devotion to God, but he cannot sacrifice devotion to God for anything else.

95. That is, man should not be obsessive about his life. After all he has to die some day as no one is immortal. A man's thoughts, therefore, should not be focused on how to keep himself alive. The true matter of concern should be how he can preserve his faith and fulfil his obligations towards God. For, it is to God that he will return. If one suffers the loss of one's faith for the sake of survival, this leads to consequences quite different from losing any other thing, including one's own life in order to keep faith intact. Thus the question on which a person's thinking should be centred is: what is it that man carries with him when he returns to his Lord? Is it his life for whose sake he sacrificed his faith or his faith for whose sake he sacrificed his life?

(58) We shall house those who believed and acted righteously in the lofty mansions of Paradise beneath which rivers flow. There they shall remain for ever. How excellent a reward it is for those who acted (in obedience to Allah),[96] (59) who remained steadfast[97] and put their trust in their Lord![98] (60) How many

وَٱلَّذِينَ ءَامَنُواْ وَعَمِلُواْ ٱلصَّٰلِحَٰتِ لَنُبَوِّئَنَّهُم مِّنَ ٱلْجَنَّةِ غُرَفًا تَجْرِى مِن تَحْتِهَا ٱلْأَنْهَٰرُ خَٰلِدِينَ فِيهَا ۚ نِعْمَ أَجْرُ ٱلْعَٰمِلِينَ ﴿٥٨﴾ ٱلَّذِينَ صَبَرُواْ وَعَلَىٰ رَبِّهِمْ يَتَوَكَّلُونَ ﴿٥٩﴾ وَكَأَيِّن

96. It is possible that someone remains deprived of all worldly bounties on account of having followed the course of faith and righteousness and, thus, apparently has had an unsuccessful worldly life. This, however, should not be something about which to worry for this person will certainly be fully compensated for all the losses he has suffered. Furthermore, he will also receive an excellent reward for his performance.

97. That is, true believers adhered to their faith in the face of all manner of hardships, sufferings and losses. They put up with all this and patiently faced all dangers that came their way never once turning their backs on their duty. They were well aware of the worldly benefits that might accrue to them if they abandoned faith, yet that option held no appeal. They saw the unbelievers around them flourishing, but they did not cast even a passing glance at their wealth and affluence.

98. True believers put their trust in their Lord rather than in their properties and businesses or family and tribal affinities. They are the ones who resolve to face every risk and take on any opposing power in their faith's cause as a result of putting their faith in God and disregarding all possible material considerations. When the need arises, they abandon their hearths and homes. They do so trusting that God will never deprive those who have such unflinching faith in Him and who adhere to faith and righteousness of their due reward. They do so knowing that God will

an animal there is that does not carry about its sustenance. Allah provides sustenance to them and to you. He is All-Hearing, All-Knowing.[99]

مِّن دَآبَّةٍ لَّا تَحْمِلُ رِزْقَهَا ٱللَّهُ يَرْزُقُهَا وَإِيَّاكُمْ ۚ وَهُوَ ٱلسَّمِيعُ ٱلْعَلِيمُ ﴿٦٠﴾

not disappoint his believing and righteous servants, and that He will aid them in this world as also amply reward them in the Next.

99. While migrating in the cause of God the believers should not be overly concerned with questions about how they will obtain their sustenance, just as they are not concerned about the safety of their lives. Before their very eyes, they observe innumerable animals and birds going about on land, sea and air. They do not carry their sustenance, yet God sustains them. Wherever they go, they receive their sustenance. Therefore, mundane considerations should not deter the believers from migrating in the cause of faith. God will provide them with their livelihood from the same treasure-house of resources from which He provides all His countless creatures.

The same truth was taught by the Prophet Jesus (peace be on him) to his disciples:

> No one can serve two masters; for either he will hate the one and love the other, or he will be devoted to the one and despise the other. You cannot serve God and mammon.
>
> Therefore I tell you, do not be anxious about your life, what you shall eat or what you shall drink, nor about your body, what you shall put on. Is not life more than food, and the body more than clothing? Look at the birds of the air: they neither sow nor reap nor gather into barns, and yet your heavenly Father feeds them. Are you not of more value than they? And which of you by being anxious can add one cubit to his span of life? And why are you anxious about clothing? Consider the lilies of the field, how they grow; they neither toil nor spin; yet I tell you, even Solomon in all his glory was not arrayed like one of these. But if God so clothes the grass of the field, which today is alive and tomorrow is thrown into the oven, will he not much more clothe you, O men of little

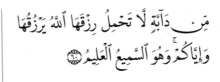

(61) If you[100] were to ask them: "Who created the heavens and the earth and Who has kept the sun and the moon in subjection?" they will certainly say: "Allah." How come, then, they are being deluded from the Truth? (62) Allah enlarges the sustenance of

وَلَئِن سَأَلْتَهُم مَّنْ خَلَقَ ٱلسَّمَٰوَٰتِ
وَٱلْأَرْضَ وَسَخَّرَ ٱلشَّمْسَ وَٱلْقَمَرَ لَيَقُولُنَّ
ٱللَّهُ ۖ فَأَنَّىٰ يُؤْفَكُونَ ﴿٦١﴾ ٱللَّهُ يَبْسُطُ ٱلرِّزْقَ

---

faith? Therefore do not be anxious, saying, 'What shall we eat?' or 'What shall we drink?' or 'What shall we wear?' for the Gentiles seek all these things; and your heavenly Father knows that you need them all. But seek first his kingdom and his righteousness, and all these things shall be yours as well.

Therefore do not be anxious about tomorrow, for tomorrow will be anxious for itself. Let the day's own trouble be sufficient for the day. (*Matthew* 6:24-34).

The background to both the Qur'ānic verse and the Biblical passages is the same. Inevitably, there comes a stage in the struggle for the cause of Truth when, irrespective of all other factors, Truth's devotee is left with no other option but to place all his trust in God and stake all that he has, including his life, for His cause. In such circumstances, those who are excessively occupied with calculating the different possibilities available to them in the future will be able to do nothing. This because when they take one step forward they will try to make sure that their lives and livelihoods are fully guaranteed. It is only those who have revolutionary fervour and are willing to take risks and even imperil their lives that can make any impact and bring about change. It is through the heroic efforts and sacrifices of such people that the Word of God will eventually be exalted and those doctrines opposed to it will be reduced to ineffectuality.

100. This marks the resumption of the discourse addressed to the Makkan unbelievers.

any of His servants whom He will, and straitens the sustenance of whom He will. Surely Allah has knowledge of everything. (63) If you were to ask them: "Who sent down water from the sky and therewith revived the earth after its death?" they will certainly say: "Allah." Say: "To Allah alone be praise and thanks."[101] But most people do not understand.

(64) The present life is nothing but sport and amusement.[102] The true life is in the Abode of the

لِمَن يَشَآءُ مِنْ عِبَادِهِۦ وَيَقْدِرُ لَهُۥٓ ۚ إِنَّ ٱللَّهَ
بِكُلِّ شَىْءٍ عَلِيمٌ ﴿٦٢﴾ وَلَئِن سَأَلْتَهُم مَّن نَّزَّلَ
مِنَ ٱلسَّمَآءِ مَآءً فَأَحْيَا بِهِ ٱلْأَرْضَ مِنۢ
بَعْدِ مَوْتِهَا لَيَقُولُنَّ ٱللَّهُ ۚ قُلِ ٱلْحَمْدُ لِلَّهِ ۚ بَلْ
أَكْثَرُهُمْ لَا يَعْقِلُونَ ﴿٦٣﴾ وَمَا هَٰذِهِ
ٱلْحَيَوٰةُ ٱلدُّنْيَآ إِلَّا لَهْوٌ وَلَعِبٌ ۚ وَإِنَّ ٱلدَّارَ

101. The words *al-ḥamdu li Allāh* (for God alone be praise and thanks) here suggest two things. First, praise and thanks for all the great tasks – the creation of the heavens and the earth, the harnessing of the sun and the moon, the bestowal of sustenance on all creatures, and the sending down of water from the sky and therewith the revival of the earth after it had become dead. If all this is so, then quite obviously God alone deserves praise and thanks. Secondly, God should also be thanked for the fact that even the unbelievers recognised that all these tasks were performed by Him alone.

102. This present worldly life is no more than child's play, which soon comes to an end and once such play does end, the child heads towards his home. Even a king, who acts as a king in the world, is in reality not so. At an appointed hour his reign ends and he leaves the stage of the world empty-handed. He is reduced to the same resourcelessness which characterised him at birth. No one, irrespective of the position he holds,

Hereafter; if only they knew.[103] (65) When they embark in the ships they call upon Allah, consecrating their faith to Him. But when He rescues them and brings them to land, they suddenly begin to associate others with Allah in His Divinity (66) that they may be ungrateful for the rescue that We granted them, and that they may revel in the pleasures (of the present life).[104] Soon they shall come to know. (67) Do they not see that We have given them a

ٱلْـَٔاخِرَةَ لَهِىَ ٱلْحَيَوَانُ ۚ لَوْ كَانُوا۟
يَعْلَمُونَ ﴿٦٤﴾ فَإِذَا رَكِبُوا۟ فِى ٱلْفُلْكِ دَعَوُا۟
ٱللَّهَ مُخْلِصِينَ لَهُ ٱلدِّينَ فَلَمَّا نَجَّىٰهُمْ
إِلَى ٱلْبَرِّ إِذَا هُمْ يُشْرِكُونَ ﴿٦٥﴾ لِيَكْفُرُوا۟ بِمَآ
ءَاتَيْنَٰهُمْ وَلِيَتَمَتَّعُوا۟ ۖ فَسَوْفَ يَعْلَمُونَ ﴿٦٦﴾
أَوَلَمْ يَرَوْا۟ أَنَّا جَعَلْنَا

will live in this world for ever. Everyone is here for a short, pre-ordained term. Those who are swayed by worldly matters and even barter their faith and conscience to obtain worldly glory in fact commit a childish act. For they will enjoy this world for no more than a few years, at best for around 60-70 years. In any case, they are bound to die one day and enter the Next World where they will be able to carry nothing; rather, their excessive worldliness will prove to be their bane. So viewed, this life is no more than sport and amusement.

103. Had people realised that this worldly life is no more than a term of trial and that the Next Life is everlasting, they would not have wasted the time allocated to them on senseless play and amusement. On the contrary, they would have utilised each and every moment to engage in acts that would improve their prospects in the unending life of the Hereafter.

104. For an explanation of this see *Towards Understanding the Qur'ān*, Vol. II, *al-Anʿām* 6: nn. 29 and 41, pp. 231-233 and 239-240; Vol. IV, *Yūnus* 10: nn. 29 and 31, pp. 26-27 and 28; Vol. V, *Banī Isrā'īl* 17: n. 84, p. 60.

sanctuary of safety whereas people around them are being snatched away?[105] So, do they believe in falsehood and ungratefully deny Allah's bounties? (68) Who can be more unjust than he who foists a lie on Allah or gives the lie to the Truth after it has come to him?[106] Is Hell not the resort of the unbelievers? (69) As for those who strive in Our cause, We shall surely guide them to Our Ways.[107] Indeed Allah is with those who do good.

حَرَمًا ءَامِنًا وَيُتَخَطَّفُ ٱلنَّاسُ مِنْ
حَوْلِهِمْ ۚ أَفَبِٱلْبَٰطِلِ يُؤْمِنُونَ وَبِنِعْمَةِ ٱللَّهِ
يَكْفُرُونَ ﴿٦٧﴾ وَمَنْ أَظْلَمُ مِمَّنِ ٱفْتَرَىٰ عَلَى
ٱللَّهِ كَذِبًا أَوْ كَذَّبَ بِٱلْحَقِّ لَمَّا جَآءَهُۥٓ ۚ
أَلَيْسَ فِى جَهَنَّمَ مَثْوًى لِّلْكَٰفِرِينَ ﴿٦٨﴾
وَٱلَّذِينَ جَٰهَدُوا۟ فِينَا لَنَهْدِيَنَّهُمْ سُبُلَنَا ۚ وَإِنَّ
ٱللَّهَ لَمَعَ ٱلْمُحْسِنِينَ ﴿٦٩﴾

---

105. The unbelievers are asked to consider: who is it who brought about the wonderful peace and security that prevailed in Makkah? Was it an idol such as al-Lāt or Hubal that had made it happen? Was it possible for anyone other than God to keep Makkah secure against all kinds of violence and disorder for a period of approximately 2,500 years despite its location in the strife-ridden Arabian Peninsula? If it was not God, then who maintained Makkah's sanctity across the ages?

106. They rejected the Prophet's claim to Messengership, decrying it as false. This will have either of the following two consequences. If the Prophet (peace be on him) made a false claim and invoked God's name in that regard, he will be reckoned the worst wrong-doer. However, if the Prophet's claim to Messengership is true, then it will be the rejecters who will be judged as wrong-doers for they dubbed a true Messenger a liar.

107. The expression *mujāhadah* is explained in note 8 of this *sūrah*: "Whosoever strives (in the cause of Allah) does so to his own good" (see verse 6). As for the present verse, it contains a note of assurance.

Great indeed is the assurance that God extends here to those who sincerely strive in His cause and expose themselves to clashes and conflicts with the rest of the world. God assures such people that He is not wont to leave them to their fate. Instead, He helps and guides such people at every step and constantly opens up new avenues for them that will help them to proceed to Him. He instructs them at every turn as to what the ways are through which they can achieve His good pleasure. He also constantly illuminates the right way for them, making it distinct from the meandering labyrinths of error. The greater the sincerity of the believers, the greater is the support, guidance and succour that God bestows upon them.

Sūrah 30

Al-Rūm

(The Romans)

(Makkan Period)

Title

The word *al-Rūm* occurs at the very outset of the *sūrah*. Hence the *sūrah*'s title derives from this.

Period of Revelation

The historical event to which the *sūrah* refers at the very outset enables us to establish with certainty the period of its revelation. Verses 2-3 read: "The Romans have been defeated in the neighbouring land."

At the time the *sūrah* was revealed, Jordan, Syria and Palestine – the lands adjacent to Arabia – were under Roman control. However, in 615 C.E. the Persians defeated the Romans and completed their occupation of these lands. It can, therefore, be safely said that this *sūrah* was revealed in 615 C.E. The Muslims' migration to Abyssinia also took place in the same year.

Historical Background

The prophecy made in the opening part of the *sūrah* – namely, that the Romans would prevail in the course of just a few years – constitutes a conclusive piece of evidence that the Qur'ān is the Word of God. It is also among the most outstanding testimonies to the truthfulness of the Prophet Muḥammad (peace be on him) as God's Messenger. In order to have a better understanding of this prophecy, it is necessary to take into consideration the historical events pertinent to these verses.

Some eight years before the proclamation of Muḥammad (peace be on him) as a Prophet, the Roman emperor, Maurice, (r. 582-602 C.E.) was confronted with rebellion as a result of which he was overthrown by Phocas who seized the throne. After gaining victory, Phocas (r. 602-610 C.E.) first had five of Emperor Maurice's sons put to death with their father as witness, and some time later Maurice himself was also executed. Not only that, Phocas also had their severed heads hung in the empire's capital, Constantinople. A few days thereafter, he also ordered that the empress and her three daughters be put to death. This provided Khusraw II [r. 590-628], the Sasanid emperor of Persia, with a moral pretext to invade the Roman Empire. This, because Maurice was his benefactor and it was with his support that Khusraw II had been able to accede to the Persian throne. No wonder he used to address Maurice as his father. Accordingly, he declared that he would take revenge on Phocas for the blood of Maurice and his family. In 603 C.E., he commenced his war against Persia.

Within a few years, having inflicted a series of successive defeats on Phocas's army, Khusraw II made his way up to Edessa, (presently known as Urfa), in Asia Minor and up to Aleppo and Antioch in Syria. The Roman chiefs, realising that Phocas was in no position to defend the state, requested the African governor to provide military aid. The governor despatched a powerful fleet to Constantinople under the leadership of his son, Heraclius. Soon after Heraclius reached Constantinople, Phocas was deposed and Heraclius was sworn in as emperor. On ascending to the throne, Heraclius (r. 610-641 C.E.) treated Phocas exactly as the latter had treated his predecessor, Maurice. This happened in 610 C.E., the year in which God entrusted Prophethood to Muḥammad (peace be on him).

The moral grounds on which Khusraw II had declared war against the Romans were no longer valid after the overthrow and assassination of Phocas. Had his only objective been to punish the usurper Phocas, this had already been achieved and Khusraw II should have entered into a peace agreement with the new emperor. However, instead, Khusraw II continued his military onslaught. In fact, he projected this war as a fight between Zoroastrianism and Christianity. The sympathy of some Christian sects, namely the Neostrians and Jacobites, which had been excommunicated and had suffered persecution for years at the hands of the Roman ecclesiastical authority, lay with the Zoroastrian invaders. The Jews too extended their support to the invaders so much so that the number of Jews enlisted in Khusraw II's army totalled 26,000.

Heraclius could not stem the tide of Khusraw II's advancing army. Soon after his ascension to the imperial throne, he received the news that Antioch had fallen to the enemy. Damascus fell in 613 C.E. In 614 C.E., the Persians gained control of Jerusalem and wreaked havoc on the Christians. In this respect, 90,000 Christian inhabitants of Jerusalem were slain. Furthermore, the *Sanctum Sanctorum*, the Holy Sepulchre, was destroyed. The Persians seized the True Cross which the Christians believed to be the one on which the Prophet Jesus (peace be on him) had been crucified, and transported it to Ctesiphon (Madā'in). The chief priest, Zecharias was taken prisoner and all the important churches of the town were razed to the ground. Khusraw II was totally inebriated by this victory as is evident from the letter he wrote to Heraclius from Jerusalem:

> Khusraw, greatest of gods and master of the whole earth, to Heraclius his vile and insane slave. You say that you trust in your god. Why, then, has he not delivered Jerusalem out of my hands? (Percy Sykes, *A History of Persia*, London: Macmillan, 1958, Vol. I, p. 483.)

Within a year of this victory, the Persian army had established its control over Jordan, Palestine and the entire Sinai Peninsula and even began to knock at Egypt's gates. Around the same period, a clash of more far-reaching consequence took place in Makkah. Of these two forces, one was led by the Prophet Muḥammad (peace be on him) who championed the cause of monotheism, and the other was led by the Quraysh chiefs who stood for polytheism. Things had come to such a pass that a large number of Muslims had had to leave their hearth and home and take refuge in the Christian kingdom of Abyssinia, an ally of the Roman Empire. In those days, news of the Persians' victory over the Romans was on everyone's lips in Makkah. The Makkan polytheists rejoiced at the Persians' victory, taunting the Muslims that the fire-worshippers of Persia had subdued the Christians who, like the Muslims, believed in revelation and prophecy. They also ominously predicted that they – the idolaters of Arabia – would gain a similar victory against the Muslims, obliterating not only them but their faith, Islam, as well.

It was against such a backdrop that this *sūrah* was revealed. Contrary to the dominant trend at the time, the *sūrah* categorically prophesied that:

> The Romans have been defeated in the neighbouring land; but after their defeat they shall gain victory in a few years… On that day will the believers rejoice at the victory granted by Allah (*al-Rūm* 30:2-5).

This passage in fact contains two prophecies: one, that the Romans would gain ascendancy over the Persians, and two, that it would be around the same time that the Muslims would emerge victorious. There was nothing in the objective conditions obtaining at that time to provide any reasonable basis for the hope that these prophecies would come true within a few years. For, on the one hand, there was only a handful of Muslims in Makkah and these were being remorselessly persecuted and relentlessly pursued by their tormentors. In fact, it was not until eight years after this prophecy that there was any indication that the Muslims would grow into a force formidable enough to achieve a convincing victory against their enemies. On the other hand, the Romans were being increasingly routed at the hands of the Persians, so much so that by

619 C.E. the whole of Egypt had fallen to them. Indeed, the Persian army had continued to force its way as far as the vicinity of Tripoli, strutting abroad as victors. The same story was repeated in Asia Minor where the Persian army rampaged. In 619 C.E. it reached the shores of the Bosphorus and captured Chalcedon (presently called Kadiköy), in the vicinity of Constantinople. The Roman emperor sent his emissary to Khusraw II, imploring him, in utter servility, to conclude a peace treaty, and expressing his desire to do so at every cost. Khusraw II, however, contemptuously spurned the offer, saying: "I shall not grant protection to the emperor until he is brought in chains before me, abjures obeisance to his crucified god, and pledges allegiance to the fire-god."

In utter frustration, Heraclius planned to abandon Constantinople and move to Carthage, presently called Tunis. According to the British historian, Edward Gibbon:

> At the time when this prediction is said to have been delivered, no prophecy could be more distant from its accomplishment, since the first twelve years (AD 610-622) of Heraclius announced the approaching dissolution of the empire. (Edward Gibbon, *Decline and Fall of the Roman Empire*, 5th ed. London: Methuen, 1924, p. 74.)

When the Qur'ānic verses embodying the above prophecies were revealed, the Makkan unbelievers made them the butt of their ridicule. Ubayy ibn Khalaf had a bet with Abū Bakr that if the Romans gained victory within three years, he would give him ten camels; and *vice versa*. When the Prophet (peace be on him) came to know of this, he asked Abū Bakr to stipulate a period of ten years and to increase the bet from ten to a hundred camels. This, because the expression used in the verse (*biḍʿa sinīn*) covers a period of up to ten years. Abū Bakr, therefore, revised the terms of the bet with Ubayy. Under the new terms, the loser was required to pay one hundred camels to the winner. (See Tirmidhī, *K. al-Tafsīr*, *Bāb*: *Wa min Sūrat al-Rūm;* Ṭabarī, *Tafsīr*, comments on *al-Rūm* 30:40 – Ed.)

In 622 C.E. the Prophet (peace be on him) migrated to Madīnah. It was around the same time that Heraclius quietly left Constantinople along the Black Sea route and made necessary preparations to attack Persia from the rear. To launch this counterattack, Heraclius appealed to the Church for money. In response, Pope Sergius lent him the wealth that the Church had accumulated through the offerings it had received from its followers. (The Pope, however, lent this money, which was meant to rescue Christianity from the clutches of Zoroastrianism, on interest.) Heraclius launched his attack in 623 C.E., Armenia being his first target. The following year, in 624 C.E., he was able to penetrate into Azerbaijan and destroy Clorumia, the birthplace of Zoroaster, ravaging in his course the Persians' largest fire-temple. It was part of Divine dispensation that at the same time the Muslims achieved their first victory, quite a decisive one, against the polytheists at Badr. Thus the two prophecies made in *Sūrah al-Rūm* came true almost simultaneously and before the expiry of ten years after their revelation.

Subsequently the Romans continued their onward march, crushing the Persians in every encounter, not least in the crucial Battle of Nineveh, in 627 C.E. Then they ravaged Dastagird which housed the Persian royalty. Soon thereafter Heraclius marched triumphantly to Ctesiphon, the Persian Empire's capital. In 628 C.E., an internal revolt broke out in Khusraw's own palace. Khusraw himself was taken captive and his 18 sons were put to death before his own eyes. After a few days, he too died unable to withstand the severe hardships of captivity. This coincided with the signing of the Ḥudaybīyah Treaty, which the Qur'ān terms as a "clear victory" (*Sūrah al-Fatḥ* 48:1). In the same year, Khusraw's son, Kavad II, concluded peace with the Romans and returned to them all the conquered territories and further, in 629 C.E., travelled all the way to Jerusalem to restore the Holy Cross at its original site. It was in the same year that the Prophet (peace be on him) entered Makkah for the first time after the *Hijrah* to perform *'Umrah* which he had postponed earlier in keeping with one of the conditions of the Treaty of Ḥudaybīyah.

Following all these developments there remained no doubt that the Qur'ānic prophecies had come true. As a result, a large number of Arabian polytheists embraced Islam. The heirs of Ubayy ibn Khalaf conceded defeat in the bet that Ubayy had made with Abū Bakr and, in consequence, they paid him a hundred camels. Abū

Bakr presented these to the Prophet (peace be on him) who directed that they be given in charity. It should be remembered that the bet had been made at a time when gambling had not yet been declared unlawful. By the time the Romans had regained the ascendency, gambling had, however, been prohibited. Hence the Prophet (peace be on him) allowed Abū Bakr to receive a hundred camels from the unbelievers who were in a state of war with the Muslims. However, he also directed him to give his gains to charity.

Subject Matter and Themes

The *sūrah* opens with the statement that the Romans had been defeated. Yet, contrary to popular perception at the time that the days of the Roman Empire were numbered, it was asserted that a sea change would occur in a matter of only a few years. The Romans, who had just then been subdued and overpowered, would emerge as triumphant and prevail.

These introductory remarks imply that man, superficial as he is, is prone to draw inferences merely on the basis of what he observes. He cannot, however, see what lies behind appearances. This often leads to misperceptions and miscalculations. Man is prone to err as he is incapable of knowing what will happen in the future. This handicap makes him susceptible to miscalculations. This being so, how catastrophic it is for man to risk the very capital of his life, basing himself merely on his own superficial knowledge.

The discourse on the confrontation between the Roman and Persian Empires is, however, placed later in the broader context of the Hereafter. Quite a number of verses (see vv. 1-27) of this *sūrah* impress, in a variety of ways, that the Next Life definitely lies within the range of the possible, that its occurrence eminently stands to reason, that it is in fact imminently essential. Furthermore, belief in the Hereafter is also necessary to keep human life on a sound keel. Were man to plan for his life without firmly believing in the Next Life, he would inevitably land himself in the same mire that ensues from being carried away by mere appearances.

While advancing arguments in support of the Hereafter, the Qur'ān invokes the testimony of the same phenomena of the

Universe that also confirms monotheism. Accordingly, from verse 28 onwards the *sūrah* turns to an affirmation of monotheism and a refutation of polytheism. It stresses that the religious faith rooted in man's nature consists of exclusively consecrating service and worship to the One True God. As for polytheism, it is opposed both to the nature of the Universe and to man's own inherent nature. Besides, its adoption always gives rise to corruption and evil. Attention is then drawn to the colossal evils resulting from the conflict between the Roman and Persian Empires, the two rival powers of the time. These evils, too, had their roots in polytheism. The fact rather is that all communities in human history that had succumbed to evil were immersed in polytheism.

At the conclusion of this discourse, a parable is invoked. The rain that God suddenly sends down renews the dead earth which is instantly revived and begins to flush with life and blossom. The same happens when Messengers are raised and through them revelation is communicated to mankind, causing a revival in human life. Like rainfall, Prophethood and revelation also represent God's mercy and compassion for humanity for they bring about fresh life and growth and give rise to goodness and well-being all around.

Should the Arabs avail themselves of the blessings of revelation, God's mercy will cause their desolate land to blossom with every kind of good. But if they fail to do so, they will only hurt themselves. Thereafter, even if they grieve over their mistakes, this will do them no good and the time to make amends will already have passed.

In the name of Allah, the Most Merciful, the Most Compassionate.	بِسْمِ ٱللَّهِ ٱلرَّحْمَٰنِ ٱلرَّحِيمِ
(1) *Alif. Lām. Mīm.* (2) The Romans have been defeated (3) in the neighbouring land; but after their defeat they shall gain victory in a few years.[1] (4) All power	الٓمٓ ﴿١﴾ غُلِبَتِ ٱلرُّومُ ﴿٢﴾ فِىٓ أَدْنَى ٱلْأَرْضِ وَهُم مِّنۢ بَعْدِ غَلَبِهِمْ سَيَغْلِبُونَ ﴿٣﴾ فِى بِضْعِ سِنِينَ

1. It is evident from the statements of ʿAbd Allāh ibn ʿAbbās and other Companions and Successors that in this war between the Roman and Persian Empires, the Muslims' sympathies lay with the former whereas the Makkan unbelievers sympathised with the latter.

This was so for several reasons. First, the Persians had portrayed this war as a war between Zoroastrianism and Christianity. They were trying to use the war not only for territorial expansion, but also as a means to spread their faith. The letter that Khosrau wrote to Caesar after the conquest of Jerusalem carries this unmistakable note for he interpreted his victory as a proof of the truth of his faith, Zoroastrianism. Moreover, in substantive terms, Zoroastrianism bore some resemblance with the religion of the Makkan polytheists. Common to both was the rejection of monotheism. The Zoroastrians believed in a duality of gods and worshipped fire. The Makkan unbelievers, being polytheists, naturally felt a degree of affinity with the Zoroastrians.

At the other end of the spectrum were the Christians. Notwithstanding the polytheistic elements that might have penetrated their religious beliefs and practices in the course of time, in principle they subscribed to God's unity and considered it to be the quintessence of the true faith. They also believed in the Hereafter and regarded revelation and prophecy as the main source of guidance. Thus, the core of their belief system resembled the Islamic faith. The Muslims, therefore, had a natural sympathy for the monotheistic Christians and an uncomfortable distaste for the Zoroastrian polytheists.

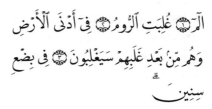

The second reason why the Muslims had a certain sympathy with the Christians had to do with the fact that the adherents of every Prophet are reckoned as Muslims until a new Prophet is raised. However, if they reject the new Prophet after receiving his message, they are no longer

belongs to Allah both before and after.[2] On that day will the believers rejoice[3] (5) at the victory granted by Allah. He grants victory to whomsoever He pleases. He is the Most Mighty, the Most Compassionate.

لِلَّهِ ٱلْأَمْرُ مِن قَبْلُ وَمِنۢ بَعْدُ ۚ وَيَوْمَئِذٍ يَفْرَحُ
ٱلْمُؤْمِنُونَ ﴿٤﴾ بِنَصْرِ ٱللَّهِ ۚ يَنصُرُ مَن يَشَآءُ ۖ وَهُوَ
ٱلْعَزِيزُ ٱلرَّحِيمُ ﴿٥﴾

---

considered believers. (See *Towards Understanding the Qur'ān*, Vol. VII, *al-Qaṣaṣ* 28: n. 73, pp. 229-232.) It was some five or six years after the Prophet Muḥammad's advent that the Romans suffered their defeat at the hands of the Persians. By then, the Prophet's message had not found its way beyond the confines of Arabia. The Muslims, therefore, did not consider the Christians as unbelievers. Their attitude towards them though was distinct from that they held towards the Jews whom they counted as unbelievers for their rejection of Jesus's Prophethood.

The third reason behind this solicitude for the Christians can be attributed to the kind and sympathetic treatment the Muslims received from them during the early days of Islam, as mentioned in *al-Qaṣaṣ* 28:52-55 and *al-Mā'idah* 5:82-85. Not only that, but quite a number of Christians had begun to accept Islam with open hearts. The Muslims also had goodwill for the Christians because the Christian emperor of Abyssinia, Negus, had provided a safe haven for Muslim migrants to his realm and had rejected the Makkan unbelievers' demand that they be handed over to them.

2. The fact that the Persians gained a considerable victory did not at all mean that God was weak and had been overpowered. Nor did the subsequent victory of the Romans mean that God's dominion had thereby been restored. For sovereignty in any case belongs exclusively to God. It was God Who had granted victory to one party earlier and later to the other. No one can gain the upper hand against anyone merely by dint of power alone. It is God Who ultimately decides who should rise and who should fall.

3. According to ʿAbd Allāh ibn ʿAbbās, Abū Saʿīd al-Khudrī, Sufyān al-Thawrī, al-Suddī and others, the Romans' victory over the Persians coincided with the Muslims' victory over the Makkan polytheists in the Battle of Badr. (See *Tafsīr*, comments on *al-Rūm* 30:41 – Ed.) The Muslims'

(6) This is Allah's promise and He does not go back on His promise. But most people do not know.

(7) People simply know the outward aspect of the worldly life but are utterly heedless of the Hereafter.[4] (8) Do they not reflect on themselves?[5] Allah created

وَعۡدَ ٱللَّهِۖ لَا يُخۡلِفُ ٱللَّهُ وَعۡدَهُۥ وَلَٰكِنَّ
أَكۡثَرَ ٱلنَّاسِ لَا يَعۡلَمُونَ ﴿٦﴾ يَعۡلَمُونَ
ظَٰهِرٗا مِّنَ ٱلۡحَيَوٰةِ ٱلدُّنۡيَا وَهُمۡ عَنِ ٱلۡأٓخِرَةِ
هُمۡ غَٰفِلُونَ ﴿٧﴾ أَوَلَمۡ يَتَفَكَّرُواْ فِيٓ أَنفُسِهِمۗ
مَّا خَلَقَ ٱللَّهُ

---

rejoicing, therefore, was twofold. This is corroborated by both Persian and Roman records of the time. It was in 624 C.E. that the Battle of Badr took place and it was in the same year that Caesar razed the largest fire temple of the Zoroastrians to the ground and ravaged Zarathustra's birthplace.

4. There are myriad signs and evidences which confirm the imminence of the Hereafter. If the unbelievers disregard these signs – and there is no good reason for them to do so – they themselves are to blame. It is their own fault if they fix their gaze on the outward appearances of worldly life and become oblivious to what lies behind it and which is bound to overtake them. Such negligence is strange in view of the repeated warnings they received at God's behest.

5. This in itself is persuasive proof of the imminence of the Hereafter. Were the unbelievers only to reflect on themselves, they would have found convincing proofs that the Next Life will follow the present one. Man is, after all, distinguished from all other creatures by the following three features:

i. Innumerable objects on earth and its environs have been yoked to man's service and man has been vested with a wide range of abilities so that he can make use of these.
ii. Man has been granted freedom to choose his course in life. He is free to believe or to disbelieve, to obey or to disobey, to do good or evil. He may opt for truth or falsehood, for right or wrong. But once he makes the choice, he is enabled, by the nature of things, to pursue his choice and, in so doing, can use the resources which

the heavens and the earth and whatever lies between them in Truth and for an appointed term.[6] Yet many people deny that they will

ٱلسَّمَٰوَٰتِ وَٱلْأَرْضَ وَمَا بَيْنَهُمَآ إِلَّا بِٱلْحَقِّ وَأَجَلٍ مُّسَمًّى ۗ وَإِنَّ كَثِيرًا مِّنَ ٱلنَّاسِ

God has created regardless of whether he wants to use them in obeying God or disobeying Him.

iii. Man has been inherently endowed with moral consciousness. Thanks to this, he instinctively differentiates between voluntary and involuntary acts and judges some voluntary acts to be good and others to be evil. He also concludes that good acts merit reward and evil acts merit punishment.

These innate traits indicate that at some point in time man should be called to account; that he should be asked how he used the abilities, power and authority that were granted to him in the world and how he exercised his free-will to choose between good and evil. These traits also require that man's voluntary acts should be appraised and that he should be rewarded or punished for his good and bad acts respectively. It is also evident that the appraisal of man's performance is possible only after the term granted to him to act comes to an end. Furthermore, this can only happen when the actions of not just one individual or nation, but of all human beings, come to a final end. This, because an individual's death or even the disappearance of a whole nation does not bring about an end to the total effects of a person's actions. In fact, all the good and evil effects of a person's actions should be taken into account when passing the final judgement on him. For until the full impact of a person's actions materialise, how can he be judged and requited in keeping with the strict requirements of justice?

Thus, man's own being and the position he enjoys in this world require that there should be an Afterlife in which everyone will be judged in the light of his life's record and be recompensed in accordance with his performance.

6. Two additional arguments in support of the Hereafter are adduced in this verse. If man looks carefully at the order of the Universe external to himself, the following two facts emerge:

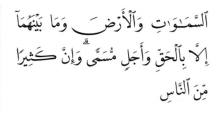

i. This Universe has been created in truth. It is not a child's play crafted for the mere fun of it. Creation did not take place for sheer amusement. The Universe is not a child's play house of sand or clay devoid of any serious meaning and purpose, a play house about which it could be said that it would be all the same whether it was made or destroyed. On the contrary, the Universe is characterised by the prevalence of an order actuated with profound purpose. Every atom of the Universe bears witness that it has been created for a definite end, that a well-defined law permeates all its objects, and that everything in it serves a definite purpose.

This is evident from the whole gamut of human culture and economy and the entire accumulation of human knowledge and expertise. Man has been able to make advancements in various domains only after identifying the laws of nature that govern the operation and purpose of everything. Had he been a mere puppet in this vast yet meaningless spectacle, no advancement could have been accomplished either in the domains of science, culture or civilisation. Given this, how can the unbelievers entertain the preposterous notion that God created man without any purpose? How can anyone be led to such a belief when it is evident that the All-Wise God ingrained a sense of purpose in the whole of creation and also equipped man with the highest intellectual and physical faculties? Moreover, God has imbued man with a moral sense, has granted him free-will, and has placed innumerable objects and forces of the Universe at his disposal. How is it even conceivable that God would do all this and yet endow man's existence with no purpose? How can it stand to reason that man, after doing much that is good or evil, just or unjust, and right or wrong, will simply be reduced to dust after he dies without facing the consequences for any of his deeds? The fact is that man's every action affects the lives of thousands upon thousands of human beings like himself as well as upon innumerable objects in the Universe. How is it possible that no sooner than a person dies the whole record of his deeds will be reduced to naught without him bearing any responsibility for them?

ii. Another fact that becomes evident by studying the order of the Universe is that nothing in it is everlasting. There is an appointed term for everyone and everything. Upon the expiry of that term, it comes to an end. The same holds true for the Universe as a whole. All the forces that are at work in it are finite. At a given point in time, all of them will finish and the present order will cease.

In the past, owing to lack of knowledge some people were taken in by the contentions of those philosophers and scientists who claimed that this world neither had a beginning nor an end. However, modern science has almost definitively cast its vote in favour of the position of those who believe that the world will some day come to an end. It has,

meet their Lord.[7] (9) Have they not travelled through the earth that they may observe what was the end of their predecessors[8] who were far mightier and tilled

بِلِقَآيِ رَبِّهِمْ لَكَـٰفِرُونَ ۝ أَوَلَمْ يَسِيرُوا۟
فِى ٱلْأَرْضِ فَيَنظُرُوا۟ كَيْفَ كَانَ عَـٰقِبَةُ
ٱلَّذِينَ مِن قَبْلِهِمْ ۚ كَانُوٓا۟ أَشَدَّ مِنْهُمْ قُوَّةً

---

thus, resolved the long drawn-out debate between atheists and theists regarding whether this Universe has existed from eternity or was created in time. Atheists can no longer invoke reason and logic to claim that the world has always been and will always be.

The contention of the materialists of ancient times rested on the notion that matter is imperishable and that it only changes its form, that the total quantum of it always remains the same. Consistent with this notion, it was held that this material world is without a beginning and an end. The discovery of atomic energy has dealt a severe blow to this. It is now fairly clear that there is a permanent nexus between matter and energy. Matter changes into energy, and *vice versa*, and neither retains a fixed form or structure. The second law of thermodynamics has demonstrated that this material world has neither always been nor will always be; it necessarily had a beginning in time and at some point is bound to end. One can, therefore, no longer invoke science to deny the Afterlife. That being the position, it is obvious that philosophy, unsupported by science, is in no position to deny Afterlife.

7. The unbelievers reject the idea that after death they will have to return to and stand before their Lord for His judgement.

8. This argument in support of the Hereafter is drawn from history. Throughout history a large number of people denied the notion of the Hereafter. There have been a very large number of people, in fact whole nations, who either denied the Hereafter or altogether disregarded it. There have also been others who fabricated totally false notions about it, seeking to reduce it to an absurdity.

It is noteworthy, however, that all through history whenever the Hereafter was denied it always led to moral corruption. It made people consider themselves as devoid of all responsibility, thus making them unfettered brutes. They intermittently committed evil and brazenly perpetrated injustice and oppression. It was this which inexorably led many nations to be decimated. Does this lesson from history down the

the land[9] and built upon it more than these have ever built?[10] And Allah's Messengers came to them with Clear Signs.[11] It was	وَأَثَارُوا۟ ٱلْأَرْضَ وَعَمَرُوهَآ أَكْثَرَ مِمَّا عَمَرُوهَا وَجَآءَتْهُمْ رُسُلُهُم بِٱلْبَيِّنَـٰتِ ۖ فَمَا كَانَ

ages not prove that the Afterlife is an incontrovertible reality, a reality whose denial entails disastrous consequences for mankind? Man was persuaded to accept the law of gravity because he has invariably observed material objects gravitate to the earth. Likewise, man has considered poison to be fatal because he has witnessed its deadly effect. By the same token, when it is a proven fact that the rejection of the Afterlife has always led to man's moral impairment, this should be a sufficient basis to affirm belief in the Afterlife and to conclude that man cannot live a wholesome life without believing in it.

9. The Qur'ānic expression *"athārū al-arḍ"* may refer to a range of activities such as ploughing farms, digging the earth to draw subterranean water, constructing over ground and subterranean canals, and mining, etc.

10. This is a rejoinder to those who regard the material prosperity of a community as proof of the rectitude of its behaviour. Such people contend that it is absolutely inconceivable that God would make those who had been conspicuously successful in the world, who had skilfully exploited natural resources on a wide scale, carried out massive construction works, and established a glorious civilisation the fodder of Hell-fire. The Qur'ānic view on the issue, however, is that these constructive tasks were also accomplished by many communities in the past. Now, it is common knowledge that those communities, which had once boasted flourishing cultures and civilisations, were destroyed by God's scourge and all their architectural accomplishments razed to the ground. Divine scourge seized those nations that had attained material prosperity but that had done so without adhering to right beliefs and following the norms of good conduct. This is how God's Law of Retribution operates in the world. Such being the case, how can wicked people escape God's Retribution in the World-to-Come?

11. The Messengers brought with them Clear Signs that were sufficient to establish their veracity. Mention of the advent of Messengers in

not Allah Who wronged them, but it is they who wronged themselves.[12] (10) Evil was the end of those evil-doers, for they gave the lie to Allah's Signs and scoffed at them.

(11) Allah creates in the first instance and will later repeat it.[13] Thereafter it is to Him that you shall

ٱللَّهُ لِيَظۡلِمَهُمۡ وَلَٰكِن كَانُوٓاْ أَنفُسَهُمۡ
يَظۡلِمُونَ ۝٩ ثُمَّ كَانَ عَٰقِبَةَ ٱلَّذِينَ أَسَٰٓـُٔواْ
ٱلسُّوٓأَىٰٓ أَن كَذَّبُواْ بِـَٔايَٰتِ ٱللَّهِ وَكَانُواْ
بِهَا يَسۡتَهۡزِءُونَ ۝١٠ ٱللَّهُ يَبۡدَؤُاْ ٱلۡخَلۡقَ ثُمَّ
يُعِيدُهُۥ ثُمَّ إِلَيۡهِ

---

this context means, on the one hand, that evidence for the Afterlife is found in man's own being, in the workings of the Universe, and in the record of human history. On the other hand, God's Messengers were raised in succession and were endowed with those Signs and miracles which confirmed their Prophethood. They too warned mankind of the impending Afterlife.

12. When these communities failed to respond to the call of the Messengers who came to them with Clear Signs from God, they were utterly destroyed. This was certainly not an act of God's injustice and cruelty to them; rather, it is these communities themselves that had invited destruction upon themselves. If an individual or a community does not see reason and pays no heed to the admonitions of those who sincerely warn and counsel them to follow the Straight Way, it is not God but they themselves who are to blame for the disastrous end that overtakes them. This, because God has made true guidance available to mankind through His Books and Prophets. Additionally, He has endowed man with knowledge and intellect wherewith he can ascertain the soundness of the knowledge imparted by the Prophets and Scriptures. Had God not made such guidance available to mankind or had He not endowed man with these capacities, there would have been at least some basis to aver that God had engaged in wrong-doing.

13. This statement is couched in terms of an assertion. However, the assertion is also inclusive of its supportive argument. For common sense

be sent back. (12) On that Day when the Hour[14] will come to pass, the criminals shall be dumbfounded.[15] (13) None whom they had associated with Allah in His Divinity will intercede on

تُرۡجَعُونَ ۝١١ وَيَوۡمَ تَقُومُ ٱلسَّاعَةُ يُبۡلِسُ
ٱلۡمُجۡرِمُونَ ۝١٢ وَلَمۡ يَكُن لَّهُم مِّن شُرَكَآئِهِمۡ
شُفَعَٰٓؤُاْ

---

requires that He Who was able to bring all His creatures into existence in the first instance will definitely be able to recreate them. The initial act of creation is obviously a fact that is recognised by all. In fact, even the unbelievers and polytheists acknowledge this to be God's act, the act of the Supreme Deity. It would be absolutely puerile, then, to contend that God, Who in their own belief is the initial Creator of all, lacks the power to recreate them.

14. That is, the Hour when everyone will be returned to God to face His reckoning.

15. The verb used here is derived from the verbal noun *iblās* which denotes puzzlement caused by the shock of grief, utter perplexity in the face of total despair, bewilderment at the inability to explain one's conduct. When this verb is used in the context of a culprit, it brings out the image of a criminal caught red-handed. Such is his predicament that there is no way for him either to flee or to obtain his release by satisfactorily explaining his conduct. He is thus left speechless in a state of utter despair and quandary.

It would be pertinent to clarify at this stage what is meant by the word *mujrimūn* (criminals). The significance of this term is not confined to those who are guilty of murder, theft, robbery and other crimes of the kind. The term also applies to those who are guilty of rebellion against God, who disown the teachings and guidance of His Messengers, who deny or are heedless of accountability in the Next Life, who serve others rather than the One True God, and who worship their own carnal desires. Such people are criminals in God's sight regardless of whether their basically erroneous attitude is combined with what is designated in common parlance as "crime" or not. The term "criminals" is also applicable to those who, despite affirming belief in God, in the Messengers, and in the Hereafter, deliberately disobey God and persist in this disobedience till their very last breath.

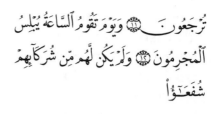

their behalf;[16] rather, they will disown those whom they had set up as Allah's associates in His Divinity.[17] (14) On that Day when the Hour will come to pass,	وَكَانُوا۟ بِشُرَكَآئِهِمْ كَـٰفِرِينَ ﴿١٣﴾ وَيَوْمَ تَقُومُ ٱلسَّاعَةُ

16. Three types of beings are usually associated with God in His Divinity. To the first category belong angels, Prophets, saints, martyrs and pious people whom the polytheists invest with Divine attributes, and for whom they consecrate worship rituals. On the Day of Judgement, these beings will plainly tell their devotees that the latter had engaged in polytheistic acts without the consent of the objects themselves; rather, that they had done so in violation of their teachings. They will thus disown them altogether. They will also make it quite clear that they will not intercede with God on their behalf.

The second category is comprised of objects that are devoid of consciousness or even life – the sun, the moon, the planets, trees, stones and animals. Polytheists elevated these objects to Godhead, worshipped them, and addressed prayers to them. Those objects, however, are totally unaware that human beings, whom God designated as His vicegerent, are engaged in such adoration. As things stand, none of these objects will be in a position to intercede with God on behalf of their devotees in the Next Life.

The third category consists of those who are notorious for their evil, those who exerted their efforts, had recourse to deception, falsehood and trickery and did not shrink from using force in order to make God's creatures serve and worship them. These include Satan, false religious leaders and tyrannical and oppressive rulers. In the Next Life they will be absolutely helpless; in fact, they will face severe reckoning and punishment. They will be in no position to speak on behalf of their devotees. If anything, they will rather seek to save themselves or secure relief for themselves by pleading that their devotees were responsible for the crimes that they committed, and that they should not be taken to task for their devotees' waywardness. In sum, on the Day of Judgement the polytheists will receive no help from any quarter.

17. On the Day of Judgement, the polytheists will confess their mistake of associating others with God in His Divinity. It will then be quite evident to them that their false gods do not even have the least share in Divinity.

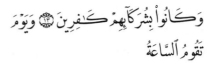

people will be split into groups.[18] (15) Then those who believed and acted righteously will be placed	يَوْمَئِذٍ يَتَفَرَّقُونَ ﴿١٤﴾ فَأَمَّا ٱلَّذِينَ ءَامَنُوا۟ وَعَمِلُوا۟ ٱلصَّـٰلِحَـٰتِ فَهُمْ فِى

They will thus disown in the Next World the very polytheism to which they obdurately cling in the present world.

18. All collective entities that have held people together in the world – entities based on an affinity to a common nation, race, homeland, language, tribe, vocation or community of economic and political interests – will dissolve on the Day of Judgement. Human beings will then be grouped together afresh in consideration of their faith and conduct alone. To one group will belong pious believers from all nations down the ages. The other group will comprise all those who held on to a variety of erroneous beliefs and a whole range of erroneous behaviour. Islam recognises only one legitimate basis for distinguishing between people – their beliefs and their conduct. It recognises this as the primary reason for considering a group of people to belong to one collectivity as distinct from the other in this world as well as in the Next. The votaries of Ignorance, however, vehemently disagree with this view.

From the Islamic viewpoint, faith and morals constitute the core that unifies or divides some people from others. All those who embrace the true faith and seek to mould their lives in accordance with God's Guidance constitute a single community, no matter to which part of the globe they belong. Likewise, those who reject the true faith and disobey God constitute another community, regardless of the territory or race to which they belong.

These two communities are distinct from each other; they cannot be a common entity. The members of these two entities neither have a common way of life in this world nor will they encounter the same end in the Hereafter. Their paths as well as their destiny are different from this world to the Next. However, the devotees of Ignorance have insisted throughout history, as they do now, that human beings should be grouped together on the basis of their affinity to race, country or language. All those who share such commonalities should be considered as one collective entity irrespective of their creed as against people belonging to other collective entities. Such an entity then should have a common pattern of life that is able to accommodate the devotees of the One True God and the polytheists as well as those who do not believe in God and all under one umbrella.

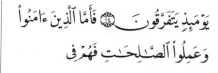

in a Garden[19] and will be happy and jubilant.[20] (16) As for those who disbelieved and gave the lie to Our Signs and to the encounter of the Hereafter,[21] they will be arraigned for chastisement.

رَوْضَةٍ يُحْبَرُونَ ﴿١٥﴾ وَأَمَّا ٱلَّذِينَ كَفَرُوا۟
وَكَذَّبُوا۟ بِـَٔايَـٰتِنَا وَلِقَآئِ ٱلْـَٔاخِرَةِ
فَأُو۟لَـٰٓئِكَ فِى ٱلْعَذَابِ مُحْضَرُونَ ﴿١٦﴾

This was also the view entertained at the time of the Prophet (peace be on him) by people like Abū Jahl and Abū Lahab and the chiefs of the Quraysh. Hence why they reproached the Prophet Muḥammad (peace be on him), contending that he had created division in the ranks of their people. By way of response, the Qur'ān makes it clear that in the Hereafter all false entities that had come into vogue in this world will be dissolved and people will ultimately be grouped together according to their creed and worldview, their character and conduct. This is what Islam seeks to accomplish. The premise being that the ways of life of those who will ultimately have different ends cannot be the same in this world.

19. Here the glory and splendour of the Garden are emphasised. Since this Garden is mentioned as a reward from God, it is not to be interpreted literally to mean that there will only be one Garden in the Next World. Instead, what is really intended by the expression "a Garden" is the unique value of what people will receive as reward – a Garden that will simply make them feel ecstatic with joy.

20. The Qur'ānic expression *yuḥbarūn* encompasses elements of happiness, delight, honour, glory and veneration. Thus, those who will be placed in Paradise will be shown honour, they will be happy and jubilant, and will enjoy all kinds of joy and delight.

21. It is noteworthy that belief is bracketed with acting righteously, and those who possess both are promised immense reward on that account (see v. 15). However, while speaking of the terrible consequences of disbelief, no reference has been made to evil deeds ensuing from it (see v. 16). This indicates that disbelieving will suffice to wreck one's ultimate end, whether one commits other misdeeds along with it or not.

(17) So[22] glorify Allah[23] in the evening and the morning. (18) His is all praise in the heavens and in the earth; (and glorify Him) in the afternoon and

فَسُبْحَـٰنَ ٱللَّهِ حِينَ تُمْسُونَ وَحِينَ
تُصْبِحُونَ ﴿١٧﴾ وَلَهُ ٱلْحَمْدُ فِى ٱلسَّمَـٰوَٰتِ
وَٱلْأَرْضِ وَعَشِيًّا

22. Use of the word *fa* ("so") in the verse signifies the following: they have now come to know that belief coupled with righteous action leads to one kind of end and disbelieving and decrying the true faith as false to another. This should make them glorify God both in the evening and in the morning.

Use of the word *fa* ("so") also has another significance. The unbelievers dismissed the Hereafter as something improbable. In so doing they perceived God as One devoid of absolute power, as One unable to enforce His will. The believers are being told that the way to undermine this false notion is to celebrate God's glory and proclaim that He is free from every weakness. This directive is addressed to the Prophet (peace be on him) and through him to all believers.

23. To glorify God encompasses the declaration that He is above and beyond all the shortcomings, defects and weaknesses which the polytheists attribute to Him; this because of their adherence to polytheism and their denial of the Hereafter.

The best way to glorify God is to observe Prayer. For this reason ʿAbd Allāh ibn ʿAbbās, Mujāhid, Qatādah, Ibn Zayd and some other Qur'ānic scholars maintain that the celebration of God's glory in this verse means to observe Prayer. This interpretation is borne out by the Qur'ānic text itself. For the verse specifies certain hours to celebrate God's glory. Had the intention been merely to state the principle that the believers should look upon God as absolutely perfect and free from every weakness and imperfection, that would not have called for prescribing morning, evening, afternoon and when the sun begins to decline as the scheduled times to celebrate His glory. For evidently to hold on to the belief that God is free from every imperfection and weakness, it would make little sense to tie it with morning, evening, afternoon and with the time when the sun begins to decline. As the verse links glorifying God with these appointed hours the unmistakable reference here is to a definite form in which this act is required to be performed and that can be none other than Prayer.

when the sun begins to decline.[24] (19) He brings forth the living from the dead and brings forth the dead from the living, and revives the earth after it is

وَحِينَ تُظۡهِرُونَ ١٨ يُخۡرِجُ ٱلۡحَيَّ مِنَ
ٱلۡمَيِّتِ وَيُخۡرِجُ ٱلۡمَيِّتَ مِنَ ٱلۡحَيِّ وَيُحۡيِ
ٱلۡأَرۡضَ بَعۡدَ

24. The verse makes a pointed reference to the appointed times of four Prayers that ought to be performed – *Fajr, Maghrib, ʿAṣr* and *Ẓuhr.* Additional allusions to times of Prayers have been made in the following Qur'ānic verses: "Establish Prayer from the declining of the sun to the darkness of the night; and hold fast to the recitation of the Qur'ān at dawn", (*Sūrah Banī Isrā'īl* 17:78). "Establish the Prayer at the two ends of the day and in the first hours of the night", (*Hūd* 11:114). "Glorify your Lord, praising Him before sunrise and before sunset, and glorify Him in the watches of the night and at the ends of the day", (*Ṭā Ḥā* 20:130).

Of these, the verse in *Banī Isrā'īl* (17:78) indicates the time of *Maghrib* Prayer: "from the declining of the sun to the darkness of the night; and hold fast to the recitation of the Qur'ān at dawn". It also indicates the time of *Fajr* Prayer. *Hūd* 11:114 speaks of *Fajr, Maghrib* and *ʿIshā'* Prayers while the verse *Ṭā Ḥā* 20:130, refers to the appointed hours of *Fajr* and *ʿAṣr* Prayers. As to the Prayers "in the watches of the night", they obviously refer to *Maghrib* and *ʿIshā'* Prayers. The three ends of the day are dawn, noon and sunset which allude to the appointed times of *Fajr, Ẓuhr* and *Maghrib* Prayers.

Thus the Qur'ān alludes to the times of all five Prayers that Muslims offer every day the world over. However, it is obvious that were a person to merely read the above Qur'ānic passages, it would not be possible for him to precisely fix the time of these five Prayers unless he were to look to the words and deeds of the Prophet Muḥammad (peace be on him), whom God raised as the teacher of the Qur'ān. By his precept and practice, he further explained and elucidated the appointed times of the five daily Prayers. (For further information see Ṭabarī, *Tafsīr*, comments on *al-Rūm* 30:17 – Ed.)

Let us pause here for a moment and consider the audacity of those who reject *Ḥadīth* as unreliable. They make fun of the Prayers offered by Muslims, claiming that they are not at all what the Qur'ān had commanded. They contend that offering Prayers is quite different from the Qur'ānic command "to establish Prayer" which, in their opinion, means establishing the system of Divine Providence* should this

* Even though the author does not specifically mention the name of the group that expounded this view, it is quite obvious that he is referring here to Mr. Ghulam Ahmad Parwez (d. 1985) who expressed the ideas mentioned here in a great many of his writings but especially in the monthly journal *Ṭulūʿ-i Islām*.

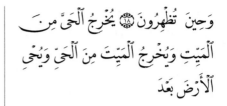

proposition be accepted. One might ask them: what kind of system is it that can be set up before sunrise or from sunset until early night or on Fridays? For the Qur'ān pointedly asks that Friday Prayer be performed: "When the call is made to Prayer on Friday, hasten to the remembrance of Allah", (*Al-Jumuʿah* 62:9). If one were to accept the view that the establishment of Prayer means setting up a system of Divine Providence, it is inexplicable how such a system could be put into effect by washing one's face and hands up to the elbows and feet up to the ankles and wiping over one's head.

It is significant that without this washing ritual, *wuḍū'*, one cannot establish this system! We say so, because the Qur'ān prescribes it as a precondition for Prayer: "When you stand up for Prayer, wash your faces and hands up to the elbows", (*al-Mā'idah* 5:6). Again, what is quite peculiar is that this system cannot be established if one is in a state of ritual defilement whereby one is obliged to take a bath before approaching "this system". "Do not draw near to the Prayer...while you are defiled until you have washed yourselves save when you are travelling", (*al-Nisā'* 4:43). Equally intriguing is the fact that if one has had "contact with women" and is unable to obtain water, one should strike one's hands on clean clay and wipe them over one's face so that one might establish this system! Just consider this verse: "If you have had contact with women and can find no water, then betake yourselves to pure earth, passing with it lightly over your face and your hands", (*al-Nisā'* 4:43). Moreover, were one to accept the above interpretation of establishing Prayer as meaning the establishment of the system of Divine Providence, it is quaint that one is required to establish only half of the system, if one is on a journey! "When you go forth journeying in the land, there is no blame on you if you shorten the Prayer", (*al-Nisā'* 4:101).

It is patently absurd, therefore, to construe the performance of Prayer to mean the establishment of some system. For, the ludicrous implication of this assumption would be that during warfare, half of the soldiers, with their weapons on their persons should remain engaged in establishing the system while the rest should take on the enemy! Then, after the former division of the army performs one prostration, while setting up this system, they should rise and resume fighting the enemy and the latter should replace them and start establishing the system behind the *imām*! Consider the following verse: "(O Messenger!) If you are among the believers and rise (in the state of war) to lead the Prayer for them, let a party of them stand with you to worship, keeping their arms. When they have prostrated, let them go behind you and let another party who have not yet prayed, pray with you, remaining on guard and keeping their arms", (*al-Nisā'* 4:102).

dead. Likewise will you be raised to life (after you die).[25]	مَوْتِهَا ۚ وَكَذَٰلِكَ تُخْرَجُونَ ﴿١٩﴾ وَمِنْ
(20) And of His Signs[26] is that He created you from dust and behold, you	ءَايَـٰتِهِۦٓ أَنْ خَلَقَكُم مِّن تُرَابٍ

It is perfectly clear from all the relevant verses that wherever the expression *"iqāmat al-ṣalāh"* (establishment of Prayer) is used in the Qur'ān, the obvious meaning is the establishment of those same Prayers that Muslims observe across the world. However, it is evident that those who reject the *Ḥadīth*, would fain change the meaning of the Qur'ān rather than try to change themselves in keeping with the imperatives of the Book. It is not until one becomes altogether impudent and audacious with God that one can come up with such a funny view regarding Prayer. Only those who in their heart of hearts do not consider the Qur'ān to be the Word of God can indulge in such preposterous statements. Such people are in fact only exploiting the name of the Qur'ān to mislead others. (In this regard see also n. 50 below.)

25. Man is reminded here of some of God's acts such as bringing forth the living from the dead and the dead from the living and reviving the earth after it is dead (that is, after it has been rendered bereft of all signs of fertility). All these acts of God are observed by everyone day in and day out. How, then, can it even be conceived that God will be unable to revive man after he dies? Let us not forget that it is the same God Who makes living humans and animals regularly discharge waste matter which has apparently no sign of life. At the same time, He infuses life into dead matter and brings into existence countless living beings – animals, plants, and human beings – even though the constituents of which these living beings are composed are devoid of life. God also grants man the opportunity to constantly observe that barren patches of dead land are instantly revived by water and begin to pour out a luxuriant treasure of plant and animal life. Anyone who observes all this and still remains unconvinced that the Omnipotent God Who superintends the entire scheme of existence would be powerless to resurrect human beings after they die certainly suffers from intellectual blindness.

26. Verses 20-26 enumerate several Signs of God. These Signs, in the context of the foregoing, provide, on the one hand, evidence to establish that the Next Life is possible as well as imminent. On the other hand, these

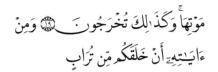

became human beings, and are multiplying around (the earth).[27]

ثُمَّ إِذَآ أَنتُم بَشَرٌ تَنتَشِرُونَ ﴿٢٠﴾ وَمِنْ ءَايَـٰتِهِۦٓ أَنْ خَلَقَ لَكُم مِّنْ أَنفُسِكُمْ أَزْوَٰجًا لِّتَسْكُنُوٓا۟ إِلَيْهَا

(21) And of His Signs is that He has created mates for you from your own kind[28] that you may find

very Signs also corroborate that this Universe is neither devoid of God nor is there a plurality of gods. Instead, there is only One God Who is the sole Creator, Sovereign, Lord and Master of the Universe. As a corollary of this, He alone should be the object of man's worship and service.

27. Man is constituted of some lifeless elements such as traces of carbon, calcium and sodium. Yet that which has been produced from these elements is the wonderful being called man who is possessed of astonishing feeling, emotion, intellection and imagination. Now, none of these traits can be traced to the elements of which he is composed. It is obvious that the creation of man was not coincidental for he was endowed with reproductive power thanks to which billions upon billions of human beings have come into existence. These human beings essentially possess the same structure and endowments and myriad hereditary and individual characteristics. Does it stand to reason that this wonderful feat of creation was accomplished without the creative will of an All-Wise Creator? Or alternatively, can anyone in his right mind believe that the great scheme of man's creation could have been devised and executed and the innumerable forces of heaven and earth yoked to serve man's purposes by the will and power of a multiplicity of gods? Likewise, can anyone believe, unless his rationality has been impaired, that God, Who brought man into existence from nothing, will not have the power to recreate him after he dies?

28. In His immaculate wisdom, God divided mankind into two sexes. Members of both these sexes are identical in their humanity. The basic formula of their physical constitution is the same. And yet the two differ widely in certain aspects of their physical configuration, their mental and psychological characteristics, their emotional and psychic urges. At the same time, they complement each other, each serving as the other's couple. There is an astounding degree of complementarity between the two sexes in so far as the physical make-up, emotional characteristics, and the urges of each complete those of the other.

peace in them[29] and He has set between you love and	وَجَعَلَ بَيۡنَكُم مَّوَدَّةٗ وَرَحۡمَةًۚ

From the very beginning, God in His infinite wisdom has been creating the two in such proportion that each balances out the other. It has never happened – in no age and at no place – that only male or female children have been born. Also, everyone would agree that this phenomenon has nothing to do with any planning or effort on man's part. Nor does man have any role in the fact that males and females are endowed with features that make them complementary to each other. Nor does man have the power to regulate the proportion of male and female births ensuring thereby a degree of balance between the two. Nor would it make sense to regard the birth of billions upon billions of men and women over the ages in the manner mentioned above either as a mere coincidence or as the result of a common scheme devised and executed by a multiplicity of gods. What the phenomenon really indicates is that all this is thanks to the will of an All-Wise Creator, and of only One Creator. It is He Who in His immense wisdom and power initially created an exceedingly appropriate design of the male and the female and then ensured that innumerable males and innumerable females are brought into existence according to the same design with their respective characteristics, and roughly in a given proportion.

29. The arrangement we see around us is that men and women, thanks to their natural instincts, are attracted to one another and when a relationship is established between a male and a female that provides peace and contentment to both of them. This judicious arrangement is designed by God as a means of ensuring procreation of the human species on the one hand, and to bring human civilisation and culture into existence on the other. Had the two sexes been created with their respective varying characteristics the human race would possibly still have multiplied, as we find in the case of sheep and goats. Nevertheless, this multiplication of mankind would not have been productive of culture and civilisation. For it is noteworthy that, as contradistinguished from all animal species, man alone possesses culture and civilisation.

What accounts for this is that the Creator in His wisdom has infused into men and women a strong desire, a thirst, and an urge which draws each to the other. Such is their nature that they remain ill at ease unless a male and a female are unified in an intimate and abiding relationship. It is this thirst for gratification that prompts them to establish, by their mutual effort, a home, a family, and a tribe, which also gives rise to the emergence

mercy.[30] Surely there are Signs in this for those who reflect.

(22) And of His Signs is the creation of the heavens

إِنَّ فِي ذَٰلِكَ لَآيَٰتٍ لِّقَوْمٍ يَتَفَكَّرُونَ ﴿٢١﴾
وَمِنْ ءَايَٰتِهِۦ خَلْقُ ٱلسَّمَٰوَٰتِ

of society, culture and civilisation. These achievements doubtlessly owe themselves to the mental faculties of the human species. Yet the driving force for these achievements was provided by the yearning of each sex for the other, a yearning that is ingrained in their nature which compels them to come together and establish a home. Is it credible that this consummate wisdom was merely an accidental product of the blind forces of nature? Or alternatively, is it credible that a multiplicity of gods sought to achieve this beneficial objective by bringing into being innumerable men and women all endowed with this mutual yearning? The fact is that this phenomenon has only one explanation, that it represents the wisdom of the One All-Wise God. This is far too evident to be denied by any except those who suffer from intellectual myopia.

30. The word *mawaddah* (love) used in the verse denotes sexual love, which is the primary factor that makes a male and a female gravitate towards one another and keeps them bonded together. As for the word *raḥmah* (mercy), it refers to that spiritual relationship which gradually develops among them in the course of their matrimonial life. This is a relationship of cordial mutuality thanks to which the spouses become each other's true well-wishers and sincere co-sharers of each other's joy and sorrow. In fact there comes a time when the passionate ardour of sexual love is relegated to the background and these life-partners become, in their old age, all the more loving, caring and compassionate towards each other.

Love and mercy are thus the two positive forces which the Creator has ingrained in men and women in order to trigger that inherent discontent in them which prompts them to go for its resolution. As a result, they are drawn to each other. In time, these two forces lead to the establishment of a permanent companionship between a couple. Although each of the two might have been brought up in a totally different milieu, they become immensely close to each other and spend their lives in intimacy, rowing together their common boat on the turbulent waters of life. This love and mercy, which have been experienced by millions of human beings in their lives, are not material objects that can be subjected to

and the earth[31] and the diversity of your tongues and colours.[32] Indeed there are Signs in this for the wise.	وَٱلۡأَرۡضِ وَٱخۡتِلَٰفُ أَلۡسِنَتِكُمۡ وَأَلۡوَٰنِكُمۡۚ إِنَّ فِي ذَٰلِكَ لَأٓيَٰتٖ لِّلۡعَٰلِمِينَ ٢٢

weight and measure. Nor can their sources be traced to any of the chemical constituents of which the human body is composed, nor can any laboratory determine how love and compassion come into existence and grow. The only explanation for their existence and growth is that they were judiciously instilled in human nature by the All-Wise Creator for some specific purpose.

31. The heavens and the earth were created *ex nihilo* and were made to function according to an inexorable scheme in which innumerable forces are operating in a state of utter mutual harmony and equilibrium. This definitely indicates that the whole Universe was created and is controlled by a Creator Who is absolutely One.

There is much in the Universe that calls for reflection. In the first place, one ought to reflect on what the source of primary energy was that assumed the form of matter, and how matter split into a multiplicity of elements. Moreover, these elements were made parts of a system that is characterised by amazing balance and equilibrium, giving rise to an awe-inspiring cosmic order that has been in operation for billions of years.

If one considers all this without intellectual bias, one is bound to conclude that this wondrous order could never be the product of mere chance or accident. At the same time, we also see that the entire Universe, from the earth to the most distant planets, is made up of the same elements and is governed by the same laws of nature. It is obvious that anyone who is not utterly tainted by obstinacy is bound to recognise that all this could not have been possible had there been a multiplicity of gods. What has made all this possible is that there is only One God, Who is the Creator and Lord of the entire Universe.

32. Although all human beings have been endowed with the same organs of speech, there being no difference in the structure of their tongues or brains, they speak different languages in different parts of the world. Not only this but even speakers of the same language have different dialects which vary from town to town and region to region. Furthermore, each person has a distinct accent and pronunciation and a mannerism of speech that is markedly different from others. In like manner, even

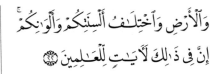

(23) And of His Signs is your sleeping at night and your seeking His Bounty during the day.[33] Indeed there are Signs in this for those who hearken.	وَمِنْ ءَايَـٰتِهِۦ مَنَامُكُم بِٱلَّيْلِ وَٱلنَّهَارِ وَٱبْتِغَآؤُكُم مِّن فَضْلِهِۦٓ ۚ إِنَّ فِى ذَٰلِكَ لَـَٔايَـٰتٍ لِّقَوْمٍ يَسْمَعُونَ ﴿٢٣﴾

though all human beings were created from an identical semen and according to an identical formula of creation, they all differ widely in their complexion. Even offspring of the same parents carry different hues, let alone the fact that different communities are characterised by a variety of complexions.

The Qur'ān mentions variations in language and complexion only for illustrative purposes. Going further along the same line, one observes a mind-boggling variation of different kinds throughout the world. These variations are simply too numerous to be fully spelled out here. Notwithstanding the essential sameness in human beings, animals and plants within their respective species, they differ vastly. Not even one member of a species is quite like any other of the same species, so much so that even two leaves of the same tree are not quite identical.

It is thus fairly clear that the different objects of this world have not been produced by automatic machines geared to mass manufacturing of identical products. On the contrary, the world clearly indicates the role of the All-Powerful Maker and Designer Who pays attention to each and every product, investing each with a unique design and distinctive features, proportions, and traits. As a result, every creation of God is unique in its own right. God's inexhaustible inventiveness accounts for the production of ever new models. It is out of sync with His creative power to repeat any product of His own creation. Anyone who carefully observes the phenomenon of creation can never succumb to the delusion that the Creator, having brought the present cosmic order into being, has withdrawn Himself from His overlordship and into His sleeping chamber. On the contrary, he is bound to conclude that the Creator is ever engaged in His creative task, paying special attention to each and every piece of His creation.

33. The expression "seeking His Bounty" signifies man's effort to seek his livelihood. Man usually sleeps at night and strives during the day to earn his bread. This, however, is not to be taken strictly as a universal rule. For many people indeed sleep during the day and are engaged in seeking their livelihood at night. Significantly, the verse mentions day

and night together, implying that man takes rest and earns his bread both by night and day.

The earning of one's livelihood is yet another manifestation of the All-Wise Creator's Providence. It not only shows His creative power but also His immense mercy and compassion for His creatures. It is evident that He cares for and is benevolently concerned with providing for man's needs and for all that is conducive to His well-being far more than man can care for himself. Let us consider some examples: man has been so constituted that he cannot work continually all the time without interruption. After working for several hours he needs a few hours of rest and relaxation to refresh himself enabling him to resume work for a few more hours.

In order to make this possible God has created in man the disposition to become fatigued and exhausted, which is followed by the urge to take rest. That is not all however. God has also ingrained in man's being the powerful urge to sleep, an urge that involuntarily seizes him after he has remained awake and has exerted himself for a few hours. In fact, this urge to sleep is so powerful that it overpowers man despite his efforts to resist it, forcing him even involuntarily to take a few hours' rest. Once he has taken a rest and is refreshed, his sleep automatically comes to an end.

Man has not yet been able to fathom the nature of sleep and the factors inducing it. All we know about it is that it is innate in human nature, that it is a part of his physiological make-up. The fact that it perfectly attends to man's needs testifies to the fact that it is not merely accidental; rather, it is part of a well thought out scheme devised by the All-Wise Creator. The purposiveness and wisdom underlying it are unmistakable. The phenomenon of sleep also indicates that He Who has ingrained it into the human body certainly cares for man's well-being even more than man himself. For it is possible that had the urge to sleep not been so overpowering, man might have worked continuously and incessantly at the cost of his rest, causing incalculable harm to the life-energy with which he has been endowed.

As for the expression "seeking Allah's Bounty", this points to another genre of Signs. Man's search for livelihood would have been futile had the forces of the Universe not been geared to producing the means of such livelihood, and had man's livelihood not been made readily available. God not only took care of all this, but also bestowed upon man the bodily organs and other physical and mental capacities suitable for seeking his livelihood. Thus, the ability within man to seek his livelihood and the availability of livelihood outside him clearly point to the existence of God Who is Compassionate, Benevolent and Generous to His creatures. Unless a person is puerile it would be hard to consider all this to be merely the outcome of a fortuitous combination of circumstances, or the outcome of

(24) And of His Signs is that He shows you lightning, arousing both fear and hope,[34] and sends down water from the sky and revives the earth after it is dead.[35] Indeed there are Signs in this for those who use their reason.

وَمِنْ ءَايَـٰتِهِۦ يُرِيكُمُ ٱلْبَرْقَ خَوْفًا وَطَمَعًا وَيُنَزِّلُ مِنَ ٱلسَّمَآءِ مَآءً فَيُحْىِۦ بِهِ ٱلْأَرْضَ بَعْدَ مَوْتِهَآ ۚ إِنَّ فِى ذَٰلِكَ لَـَٔايَـٰتٍ لِّقَوْمٍ يَعْقِلُونَ ﴿٢٤﴾

---

the will of a plurality of gods, or that these acts of bounteous generosity owe themselves to some blind, senseless, impersonal force.

34. Thunder and lightning give rise to the hope of rainfall, which in turn helps to produce crops. At the same time, these natural phenomena also evoke dread lest lightning or a thunderstorm cause wide-scale destruction.

35. On the one hand, rainfall indicates that death will be followed by Resurrection. On the other hand, it also indicates that it is the One True God Who manages the affairs of the heavens and the earth. The sustenance of countless earthly creatures rests on the produce of the earth. This, in turn, is contingent upon the fertility of the soil, which depends on rain which might fall directly on earth and accumulate in the form of water reservoirs, or in the form of underground springs, or wells by penetrating the recesses of the earth, or it may assume the form of rivers as a result of snow and ice melting from mountain tops. As for rainfall, it is caused by a number of factors – sunlight, climatic variations, atmospheric temperatures, movements of the wind, and lightning, which causes the clouds to make the rain fall and adds to it a natural fertilizing element.

It is noteworthy that there is perfect equilibrium and harmony among these myriad objects right from the sky down to the earth and that all these objects are geared to innumerable and varied purposes. It is also noteworthy that the equilibrium and harmony obtaining among these numerous objects have been there all along for millions of years. Evidently this cannot be merely accidental. Does it stand to reason that all this is possible without the most careful planning of a Creator possessed of absolute wisdom and power? Does this not conclusively prove that the Creator of the earth, of the sun, of water, of heat and cold, and of all the creatures on earth is the same One True God?

(25) And of His Signs is that the sky and the earth stand firm by His command.[36] Then no sooner than He summons you out of the earth you will come forth.[37] (26) To Him belong all who are in the heavens and all who are on the earth. All are in obedience to Him. (27) It is He Who creates in the first instance and it is He Who will repeat the creation, and that is easier for Him.[38] His is the loftiest attribute in the heavens and the earth. He is the Most Mighty, the Most Wise.

وَمِنْ ءَايَٰتِهِۦٓ أَن تَقُومَ ٱلسَّمَآءُ وَٱلْأَرْضُ
بِأَمْرِهِۦ ۚ ثُمَّ إِذَا دَعَاكُمْ دَعْوَةً مِّنَ ٱلْأَرْضِ
إِذَآ أَنتُمْ تَخْرُجُونَ ﴿٢٥﴾ وَلَهُۥ مَن فِى
ٱلسَّمَٰوَٰتِ وَٱلْأَرْضِ ۖ كُلٌّ لَّهُۥ قَٰنِتُونَ ﴿٢٦﴾
وَهُوَ ٱلَّذِى يَبْدَؤُا۟ ٱلْخَلْقَ ثُمَّ يُعِيدُهُۥ
وَهُوَ أَهْوَنُ عَلَيْهِ ۚ وَلَهُ ٱلْمَثَلُ ٱلْأَعْلَىٰ فِى
ٱلسَّمَٰوَٰتِ وَٱلْأَرْضِ ۚ وَهُوَ ٱلْعَزِيزُ
ٱلْحَكِيمُ ﴿٢٧﴾

---

36. Not only have the sky and the earth come into existence by God's command, but the continuity of their existence also owes itself to His command. But for His command, the whole order of things would have come crashing down within a moment.

37. It is not at all difficult for Him Who created and thereafter manages the affairs of the Universe to resurrect human beings after they die. In order to do so, He will not have to make any elaborate preparations. A single command from Him will suffice to raise to life, from all parts of earth, all those who were ever born and thereafter suffered death.

38. If creation in the first instance was not difficult for God, then why should it be difficult for Him to repeat it? The act of God's creation is before all to see. Evidently, the initial act of creation was not at all difficult for Him. So common sense itself requires that it should be easier for Him to recreate those whom He created once before.

(28) He[39] sets forth for you a parable from your own lives. Do you have among your slaves some who share with you the sustenance that We have bestowed on you so that you become equals in it, all being alike, and then you would hold them in fear as you fear each other?[40] Thus do We make plain

ضَرَبَ لَكُم مَّثَلًا مِّنْ أَنفُسِكُمْ هَل
لَّكُم مِّن مَّا مَلَكَتْ أَيْمَـٰنُكُم مِّن
شُرَكَآءَ فِى مَا رَزَقْنَـٰكُمْ فَأَنتُمْ فِيهِ سَوَآءٌ
تَخَافُونَهُمْ كَخِيفَتِكُمْ أَنفُسَكُمْ ۚ
كَذَٰلِكَ نُفَصِّلُ

---

39. The Qur'ānic discourse up until this point covers the twin subjects of affirming God's unity and the Hereafter. The Signs invoked in the preceding verses also contain evidence to corroborate God's unity. They also indicate that the Afterlife cannot be brushed aside as beyond the range of the possible. From now on until the end of the *sūrah* the discourse focuses on only one subject – an affirmation of God's unity.

40. The polytheists recognised that God is the Creator and Lord of the heavens and the earth and everything therein. In spite of this, they ascribed Divinity to some of God's creatures, declaring them to be associates in His Divinity. They addressed their prayers to these so-called partners, made offerings to them, and took them as their objects of worship.

We have some idea of the Arabian polytheists' belief about these so-called partners of God by the words they used to utter while circumambulating the Ka'bah: "Here we are, O Allah, here we are. You have none as partner except the Partner Who is Yours, he whom You own along with all his possessions." (See Sulaymān b. Aḥmad al-Ṭabarānī, *al-Mu'jam al-Kabīr*, II edn., Mosul: Maktabat al-'Ulūm wa al-Ḥikam, 1401/1982, traditions 12348 and 12883 – Ed.)

In the present verse God refutes this brand of polytheism precisely. The purpose of this parable is to highlight the self-contradiction to which the polytheists had fallen prey. On the one hand, they believed that those human beings who had accidentally become their slaves could not be regarded as co-sharers of their properties. On the other hand, they believed that God had made some of His own creatures partners in His

the Signs for those who use reason. (29) But the wrong-doers follow their desires without any knowledge. Who, then, can show the way to him whom Allah lets go astray?[41] Such shall have no helpers.

(30) (O Prophet[42] and his followers), turn your face single-mindedly[43] to the

ٱلْـَٔايَـٰتِ لِقَوْمٍ يَعْقِلُونَ ۝٢٨ بَلِ ٱتَّبَعَ ٱلَّذِينَ
ظَلَمُوٓا۟ أَهْوَآءَهُم بِغَيْرِ عِلْمٍ ۖ فَمَن يَهْدِى مَنْ
أَضَلَّ ٱللَّهُ ۖ وَمَا لَهُم مِّن نَّـٰصِرِينَ ۝٢٩ فَأَقِمْ
وَجْهَكَ

Godhead. They should better see reason before entertaining such silly notions. (For further elaboration of this point see *Towards Understanding the Qur'ān*, Vol. IV, *al-Naḥl* 16: n. 62, pp. 344-346.)

41. When a man neither exercises his own reason and common sense nor is prepared to give heed to the advice of others, God places a curse on his ability to think straight. After that, whatever ordinarily enables a rational being to arrive at the truth, increasingly drives that obstinate lover of falsehood towards the mire of error. This is the state which has been described by saying: "But the wrong-doers follow their desires without any knowledge. Who, then, can show him the way whom Allah lets go astray?" When a person is disposed to the Truth and seeks God's Guidance, God facilitates his quest commensurate with the extent of his quest's genuineness. By the same token, when a person is disposed to error and insists on following such a course, God grants him the means whereby he might progressively pursue that path. This increasingly drives him away from the Truth.

42. The use of *fa* ("so") here implies that since the truth had been conclusively established and it had become evident to them that God alone is the sole Creator, Master and Lord of the Universe and mankind, it follows that they should turn exclusively to Him in devotion.

43. This refers to the True Faith which the Qur'ān expounds, one whose core is to consecrate one's service, worship and obedience for God alone, recognising none as an associate in His Divinity, His sovereign authority or His claims against His creatures. This is the faith that requires

true Faith[44] and adhere to the true nature on which Allah has created human beings.[45] The mould fashioned by Allah cannot	لِلدِّينِ حَنِيفًاۚ فِطْرَتَ ٱللَّهِ ٱلَّتِى فَطَرَ ٱلنَّاسَ عَلَيْهَاۚ

man to voluntarily commit himself to follow God's guidance and law in all aspects of his life.

44. ".... [T]urning one's face single-mindedly to Allah" implies that after one decides to submit to God, one may not turn one's face in any other direction. Once a person decides to follow this course in his life, he should not pay even scant attention to any other way of life. Once a person has opted for Islam, it should guide his thinking, his likes and dislikes. His values and standards should be derived from Islam, his character and conduct too should bear Islam's stamp, and both his individual and collective life should be subservient to it.

45. All human beings have been created with that true innate nature which prompts them to believe that the One True God alone is the Creator, the Lord and the only object of worship and obedience, requiring them to adhere to that attitude. Should they decide to consider themselves invested with sovereign authority, they would be deviating from their true nature. Likewise, should they decide to submit to the authority of any other than the One True God, they would again be deviating from the true nature with which they were born.

This truth has been elucidated in several traditions narrated from the Prophet (peace be on him). According to both Bukhārī and Muslim, the Prophet (peace be on him) said: "There is no child but is born on his true nature, and then his parents either make him into a Christian or a Jew or a Magian. This is like what happens with an animal who begets an animal with a whole, sound body [and subsequently people slit their ears]. Do you see any born with slit ears?" (See Muslim, *K. al-Qadar, Bāb: Maʿnā kullu Mawlūd yūladu ʿalā al-Fiṭrah*. See also Bukhārī, *K. al-Janā'iz, Bāb: Idhā aslama al-Ṣabī fa māta hal yuṣallā ʿalayh* – Ed.) (It may be noted that the pre-Islamic pagans of Arabia used to slit the ears of new-born animals because of some polytheistic superstition.)

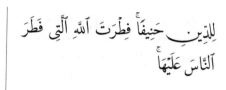

According to another tradition, narrated by Aḥmad ibn Ḥanbal and Nasā'ī, the Muslims killed a large number of their enemies in a battle, including children. On learning this, the Prophet (peace be on him) was infuriated and said: "What happened to people today that they exceeded

be altered.[46] That is the True, Straight Faith,[47] although most people do not know.

لَا تَبۡدِيلَ لِخَلۡقِ ٱللَّهِۚ ذَٰلِكَ ٱلدِّينُ ٱلۡقَيِّمُ
وَلَٰكِنَّ أَكۡثَرَ ٱلنَّاسِ لَا يَعۡلَمُونَ ۝٣٠

all limits in killing so much that they even killed children?" Thereupon someone pointed out that those killed were, after all, the children of polytheists. The Prophet (peace be on him) replied: "The best among you are the children of polytheists. Every living being is born with a true nature until he starts speaking and then his parents turn him into a Jew or a Christian." (See Aḥmad ibn Ḥanbal, *Musnad*, vol. 3, p. 435 and Nasā'ī, *al-Sunan al-Kubrā*, Beirut: Dār al-Kutub al-'Ilmīyah, 1411/1991, *ḥadīth* 8616, Muslim, *K. al-Jannah wa Ṣifat Na'īmihā Bāb: al-Ṣifāt allatī yu'arafū bihā fī al-Dunyā ahl al-Jannah wa ahl al-Nār* – Ed.)

Another tradition in Aḥmad ibn Ḥanbal's *Musnad*, which has been narrated on the authority of 'Iyāḍ ibn Ḥimār al-Mujāshi'ī, mentions that once during the course of his sermon the Prophet (peace be on him) said: "My Lord says: I created all of My servants as *ḥanīf* (worshippers of the One True God alone). Then devils came to them and led them astray from their True Faith: they prohibited what I had made lawful and commanded them to associate others with Me in My Divinity for which I had sent down no sanction." (See Aḥmad ibn Ḥanbal, *Musnad*, vol. 4, p. 162.)

46. God has appointed man to be His servant, having created mankind to serve Him exclusively. No matter what is done, it is impossible to alter the natural pattern inherent in man. Nor can man become anything else than God's servant, nor can any other person or object become his god because of the mere fact that someone has chosen that person or object to be so. Man may make as many deities as he pleases, but the inalterable fact remains that he is the servant of none but the One True God. Out of folly and ignorance, man may invest whomsoever he wishes with God's attributes and authority and regard whomsoever he wants as possessed of the power to make or mar his destiny. The fact is that neither anyone other than God is possessed of Divine attributes nor of the power to determine man's destiny.

As for the present verse, it can also be translated as follows: "Let there be no alteration in the mould fashioned by Allah"; that is, it is not proper for anyone to try to alter, let alone corrupt and distort man's natural mould.

47. That is, to adhere to the true nature on which human beings were created is the right and straight way for mankind.

(31) (Adhere to the True Faith and) turn to Him,[48] and hold Him in awe,[49] and establish Prayer,[50] and do not be of those who associate others with Allah in His Divinity, (32) those who have split up their religion and have become

۝ مُنِيبِينَ إِلَيۡهِ وَٱتَّقُوهُ وَأَقِيمُواْ ٱلصَّلَوٰةَ
وَلَا تَكُونُواْ مِنَ ٱلۡمُشۡرِكِينَ ۝٣١ مِنَ ٱلَّذِينَ
فَرَّقُواْ دِينَهُمۡ وَكَانُواْ

---

48. To turn to God means the following: anyone who opts to act independently of God's directives and thus deviates from the path prescribed for him by God, or whoever betrays God by accepting to serve aught apart from the One True God, should give up that attitude and revert to serving God Whose born servant he is.

49. Man should dread the punishment which he will incur by acting independently of, or worshipping others besides God, despite the fact that it is God Who brought him into being. Man should, therefore, shun all attitudes that lead to God's wrath.

50. Turning to God and holding His wrath in awe are acts of the heart. In order that this state of heart might become manifest and be reinforced, one needs to engage in physical acts which indicate that one has truly returned to the service and worship of the One True God, One Who has no associates in His Divinity. The regular performance of these acts helps develop in man the state of returning to and fearing God. This is why soon after directing man to bring about an attitudinal change, God asks him to engage in an outward, physical act – the establishment of Prayer. As long as an idea is confined purely to the realm of the intellect, it lacks strength and stability. Such an idea might suffer dilution or might change altogether. However, as soon as a person begins to put that idea into effect, it takes root in his personality. Thereafter, as he persists in translating that idea into practice, its hold upon him is further consolidated and then a time comes when the dilution or change of that idea or belief becomes incrementally difficult.

Viewed in this context, the performance of the five daily Prayers at their stated times is the most effective means to develop God-consciousness and God-fearing. No other act is more effective for this purpose than regularly performing the five daily Prayers. These Prayers, as we know,

divided into sects, each party exulting in what they have.[51]	شِيَعًاۖ كُلُّ حِزْبٍۭ بِمَا لَدَيْهِمْ فَرِحُونَ ۝٣٢

are performed regularly after every few hours and are performed in one and the same form. Thanks to this, man rehearses over and over again, at short intervals, the Qur'ān's teaching that man should believe in God and submit to Him in his day-to-day life. All this is repeated on a daily basis in order that man might not forget this imperative.

Observance of prayer also demonstrates to all – believers as well as unbelievers – who has given up defiance of God and committed themselves to obeying Him. This is useful for believers in order that they might become a congregation and a community at the collective level and cooperate with one another in God's cause. Moreover, it also proves useful when any believer slackens in his devotion and others become aware of this in Prayer. This visible display of faith – observance of Prayer – is equally useful for unbelievers because this spectacle of people turning to God might awaken in them their dormant but inherently ingrained God-consciousness. However, even if they do not take heed, the devotional activities of believers are likely to inspire in them a sense of awe. For these purposes too the establishment of Prayer is highly useful.

It ought to be borne in mind that the directive to establish Prayer was given in that phase of the Makkan life of the Prophet (peace be on him) when there were no more than a handful of Muslims. Besides, these Muslims were at that time reeling under the most brutal oppression at the hands of the unbelieving Quraysh, which they continued to endure for the following nine years. At the time when the directive regarding Prayers was given, the possibility that Islam would become a state was hard even to imagine. Had the performance of Prayers been contingent on the existence of the Islamic state, as some ignoramuses have come to fancy, or had the establishment of *Ṣalāh* meant the establishment of a system of Divine Providence as the rejecters of the *Sunnah* claim, it would have been meaningless at this stage to order people to establish Prayer. One also wonders why the Prophet (peace be on him) and other Muslims carried out this command for nine more years of the Makkan period after its promulgation when no Islamic state was in existence.

51. This alludes to the fact that True Faith alone is compatible with man's inherent nature as stated earlier (see v. 30 above). Contrary to the speculation of those who have imaginatively weaved a whole philosophy of religion, the fact is that True Faith did not originate with polytheism and, thereafter, gradually evolve into monotheism. On the contrary, the

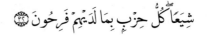

(33) (Such are human beings) that when any misfortune befalls them, they cry to their Lord, penitently turning to Him.[52] But no sooner that He lets them have a taste of His Mercy than some of them begin associating others with their Lord in His Divinity[53] (34) so that they may show ingratitude to Us for the favours We had bestowed upon them. So, enjoy yourselves a while; but then you shall soon

وَإِذَا مَسَّ ٱلنَّاسَ ضُرٌّ دَعَوْا۟ رَبَّهُم مُّنِيبِينَ
إِلَيْهِ ثُمَّ إِذَآ أَذَاقَهُم مِّنْهُ رَحْمَةً إِذَا فَرِيقٌ مِّنْهُم
بِرَبِّهِمْ يُشْرِكُونَ ﴿٣٣﴾ لِيَكْفُرُوا۟ بِمَآ ءَاتَيْنَٰهُمْ ۚ
فَتَمَتَّعُوا۟ فَسَوْفَ

---

polytheistic religions found in the world today are merely distorted versions of the true original faith centred on monotheism. Distortions crept into the religious domain because people added their innovations to the natural truths embodied in the original faith. Rather than adhere to the true original faith, they became enamoured of these innovations. Thanks to this, religious divisions emerged among mankind and every group turned into a new, distinct sect or community. The only way that now remains for those who care for true guidance is to return to that core truth, which was the foundation of the original True Faith, and to abjure all subsequent religious innovations. Any affinity with those who are responsible for distorting the True Faith will have a corrupting influence on one's own religious faith and practice.

52. This amply proves that in the depths of their hearts all testify to the truth of monotheism. Whenever faced with utter despair, their own inner voice tells them that the sovereignty of the One True God embraces the whole Universe and it is His help alone that can deliver them from distress.

53. However, once they are rescued from their distress by dint of God's mercy, they soon begin to make offerings to their false gods, claiming

come to know. (35) Have We sent down any sanction which provides support to their associating others with Allah in His Divinity?[54]

(36) When We make people have a taste of Our Mercy, they exult in it; and when any misfortune befalls them in consequence of their deeds, then lo and behold, they despair.[55] (37) Do they not see that Allah enlarges and straitens the sustenance of those

تَعْلَمُونَ ﴿٣٤﴾ أَمْ أَنزَلْنَا عَلَيْهِمْ سُلْطَٰنًا فَهُوَ
يَتَكَلَّمُ بِمَا كَانُوا۟ بِهِۦ يُشْرِكُونَ ﴿٣٥﴾ وَإِذَآ أَذَقْنَا
ٱلنَّاسَ رَحْمَةً فَرِحُوا۟ بِهَا ۖ وَإِن تُصِبْهُمْ سَيِّئَةٌۢ
بِمَا قَدَّمَتْ أَيْدِيهِمْ إِذَا هُمْ يَقْنَطُونَ ﴿٣٦﴾
أَوَلَمْ يَرَوْا۟ أَنَّ ٱللَّهَ يَبْسُطُ ٱلرِّزْقَ

---

that it is because of the intercession or blessing of such and such a saint or of such and such a saint's resting place that they have been rescued from their distress.

54. The polytheists are asked to reveal the source of their information that aught other than God can rescue mankind from their suffering and distress. Is such a claim supported by reason? Or, does any Scripture indicate that God has delegated His powers to some other beings who can use them to benefit mankind?

55. The preceding verse reproaches man for his ignorance and ingratitude, whereas the present verse takes him to task for his meanness and puerility. When he acquires wealth, power and esteem and everything seems to be going well, he forgets that he owes all this to God. He tends to think of himself as one inherently possessed of extraordinary qualities, which make him worthy of whatever he has come to possess and of which others remain deprived. Such delusions intoxicate him with arrogance and hauteur with the result that he neither pays any heed to God nor to God's creatures. However, no sooner than his success begins to fade, does he feel totally shattered and despondent. Driven by frustration, he feels no qualms in committing the most degrading acts, including suicide.

whom He pleases? There are Signs in this for those who believe.[56] (38) So give his due to the near of kin, and to the needy, and to the wayfarer.[57] That is better for

لِمَن يَشَآءُ وَيَقۡدِرُۚ إِنَّ فِى ذَٰلِكَ لَأٓيَـٰتٍ
لِّقَوۡمٍ يُؤۡمِنُونَ ٣٧ فَـَٔاتِ ذَا ٱلۡقُرۡبَىٰ
حَقَّهُۥ وَٱلۡمِسۡكِينَ وَٱبۡنَ ٱلسَّبِيلِۚ ذَٰلِكَ

56. That is, the believers are capable of drawing the right lesson from noting the impact of unbelief and polytheism on the one hand, and of belief in God on man's conduct, on the other. Those who truly believe in God and regard Him alone as the sole Master of all resources of sustenance cannot stoop to the pettiness which often characterises the attitude of those who are oblivious of Him. When such people are granted plentiful sustenance, rather than becoming haughty and arrogant they are thankful to God. Acquisition of wealth generates in them an attitude of humility and generosity towards their fellow-beings and they do not flinch from spending their wealth – which in fact belongs to God – to please God. When such people are faced with straitened circumstances, even with starvation, they still remain patient, honest, trustworthy and dignified and always look forward to God's grace and bounty. Such moral loftiness cannot be displayed either by atheists or polytheists.

57. It is significant that here man is not being asked to give charity to near of kin, the needy and the wayfarer; instead, he is being asked to give them what is their due, to render them the right that he owes them. While giving charity the thought that he is doing a favour to someone should not even cross his mind. Nor should he entertain the illusion that his wealth has made him a superior being who is lavishing benefactions on the lowly and the contemptible. Instead, he should be fully cognisant of the fact that if God, the True Owner of all wealth, has granted him a little more wealth than others then these others who have been granted less have a right over his additional wealth. This additional wealth has, in fact, been entrusted to him so that His Lord might test him and see whether he is cognisant of the rights of others or not.

Anyone who reflects on this Divine directive, and on the spirit underlying it, cannot fail to note that the course of man's moral and spiritual growth prescribed here assumes the existence of a free society and a free economy. The moral and spiritual growth envisaged here is simply inconceivable in a milieu wherein the right of individuals to own property has been abolished and the state has assumed proprietary rights

those who desire to please Allah. It is they who will prosper.[58] (39) Whatever you pay as interest so that

خَيْرٌ لِّلَّذِينَ يُرِيدُونَ وَجْهَ ٱللَّهِ ۖ وَأُو۟لَـٰٓئِكَ هُمُ ٱلْمُفْلِحُونَ ﴿٣٨﴾ وَمَآ ءَاتَيْتُم مِّن رِّبًا

---

over all resources, and the governmental machinery has taken over the responsibility of distributing income among people. Under such a system no one will be in a position to give anything to anyone as the latter's "due", nor will there be an occasion for anyone to have good-will for others on account of receiving any assistance from them.

The state of affairs we are talking about represents a patently communist economic system, which some people in our country are presently trying to promote under the deceptive euphemism of the Qur'ānic system of Divine Providence (*Qur'ānī niẓām-i rubūbīyat*). These people arbitrarily claim that this system is based on the Qur'ān although, in fact, it is diametrically opposed to the scheme of things envisaged by the Qur'ān. This, because under such a system there remains no scope for the growth of the individual's morality or the refinement of human conduct.

The Qur'ānic scheme of life can only come fully into force in a society where individuals have the right to own property and also have the freedom to use it, and yet they are willing to spend it of their own volition so as to sincerely discharge their obligations to God and to His creatures. It is only in such a social setting that it is possible for individuals to develop in themselves traits of sympathy and compassion, of altruism and sacrifice, of recognising the rights of others and having the will to render these to them. Again, it is only in such a social setting that those to whom any good is done will develop feelings of good-will and gratitude and a readiness to do similar good to those who have done good for them. In fact, it is possible that such a society might some day be able to achieve that ideal condition in which the prevention of evil and the promotion of good might not necessarily be contingent on the action of any coercive power. Instead, this might be realised by the members of that society by dint of their inner purity and good intention.

58. This does not mean that prosperity will be attained merely by fulfilling one's obligations to the poor, the wayfarer and near of kin and that nothing else needs to be done in that regard. In fact, what the verse stresses is that those who do not recognise these rights cannot prosper. Prosperity will be attained only by those who are cognisant of the rights of others and fulfil them, doing so solely in order to please God.

it may increase the wealth of people does not increase in the sight of Allah.[59] As	لِّيَرْبُوَا۟ فِىٓ أَمْوَٰلِ ٱلنَّاسِ فَلَا يَرْبُوا۟ عِندَ ٱللَّهِ ۖ

59. This is the first Qur'ānic verse expressing disapproval of interest. The verse confines itself to stressing only one point – that those who pay interest do so under the impression that the excess they pay to the lender over and above the principal will increase the latter's wealth. Contrary to this, in God's sight, it is *zakāh* rather than interest that causes increase in wealth. Subsequently, when an injunction prohibiting interest was revealed during the Madīnan period of the Prophet's life, the following addition was made: "Allah deprives interest of all blessing, whereas He blesses charity with growth", (*al-Baqarah* 2:276). (For subsequent injunctions on interest see *Āl ʿImrān* 3:130 and *al-Baqarah* 2:275-281.)

Qur'ānic commentators offer the following two interpretations of the verse under discussion. According to one group, the word *ribā* here does not refer to the kind of interest that the *Sharīʿah* has declared to be unlawful. Rather, here, the word *ribā* signifies the gift or present or donation given with the intention that its recipient give a greater amount in return, or render the benefactor some useful service; or it signifies the amount given in expectation that the recipient's prosperity will ultimately be of profit to the benefactor. This is the opinion of ʿAbd Allāh ibn ʿAbbās, Mujāhid, Ḍaḥḥāk, Qatādah, ʿIkrimah, Muḥammad ibn Kaʿb al-Qurāẓī and Shaʿbī. Their interpretation presumably rests on the assumption that the verse simply states that this action will not register any increase of wealth in God's sight. Had the forbidden variety of interest been under discussion, the Qur'ān would have specified that such an act would incur God's punishment. (See Ṭabarī, *Tafsīr*, comments on *al-Rūm* 30:39 – Ed.)

The other group, however, considers this to be the very same interest that is expressly forbidden in the *Sharīʿah*. This is the opinion of Ḥasan al-Baṣrī and al-Suddī. Ālūsī, too, subscribes to the same view and points out that the Arabic word *ribā* is used specifically for this purpose. Nīsābūrī, another Qur'ānic commentator, endorses this view.

In our own opinion, too, the latter interpretation is the correct one. This, because the argument put forward by the first group is not sufficiently convincing to prove the point that here the word *ribā* should not be understood in its well-known sense. It is pertinent to note that *Sūrah al-Rūm* was revealed at a time when the Qur'ān had not declared interest as prohibited. That declaration was made a few years later. We notice that the Qur'ān, before declaring anything unlawful, prepares the ground for this, and takes some time in doing so. With regard to wine, for instance, it

for the *Zakāh* that you give, seeking with it Allah's good pleasure, that is multiplied manifold.[60]

(40) It is Allah[61] Who created you, then bestowed upon you your sustenance,[62] and He will cause you to die and then will bring you back to life. Can any of those whom you associate

وَمَآ ءَاتَيْتُم مِّن زَكَوٰةٍ تُرِيدُونَ وَجْهَ ٱللَّهِ
فَأُوْلَـٰٓئِكَ هُمُ ٱلْمُضْعِفُونَ ۝٣٩ ٱللَّهُ ٱلَّذِى
خَلَقَكُمْ ثُمَّ رَزَقَكُمْ ثُمَّ يُمِيتُكُمْ ثُمَّ يُحْيِيكُمْ ۖ
هَلْ مِن شُرَكَآئِكُم

---

was first indicated in the Qur'ān that it is not a "wholesome sustenance", (see *al-Naḥl* 16:67). After a period of time, the Qur'ān asserted that its evil is greater than its benefit (*al-Baqarah* 2:219). This was followed by the command that people may not draw near to Prayer when intoxicated (*al-Nisā'* 4:43). It was after all this preparatory work had been completed that wine was finally and categorically declared unlawful. As for the present verse, it confines itself to declaring that interest does not bring about any increase in wealth; rather, it is through *zakāh* that wealth increases manifold. Subsequently, compound interest was forbidden, (see *Āl 'Imrān* 3:130). Thereafter, interest as such was finally outlawed in categorical terms (see *al-Baqarah* 2:275).

60. There is no upper limit to this multiplication of wealth. The greater a person's sincerity, spirit of sacrifice, and desire to seek God's good pleasure when he spends his wealth in God's cause, the greater will be his reward. Thus we find a tradition according to which the Prophet (peace be on him) said that if a person gives a single date in charity for God's sake, God can increase its reward to him manifold, so much so that it will become equal to Mount Uḥud.

61. Once again, the themes of monotheism and the Hereafter are resumed in order to elucidate them to unbelievers and polytheists.

62. God has provided man with all varieties of sustenance on earth. Furthermore, He has devised a system whereby everyone receives some portion of this sustenance.

with Allah in His Divinity do any such thing?[63] Glory be to Him and exalted be He above whatever they associate with Allah in His Divinity! (41) Evil has become rife on the land and at sea because of men's deeds; this in order that He may cause them to have a taste of some of their deeds; perhaps they will turn back (from evil).[64] (42) (O Prophet), say: "Traverse in the earth and see what was

مَّن يَفْعَلُ مِن ذَٰلِكُم مِّن شَيْءٍ ۚ سُبْحَٰنَهُۥ
وَتَعَٰلَىٰ عَمَّا يُشْرِكُونَ ﴿٤٠﴾ ظَهَرَ ٱلْفَسَادُ
فِى ٱلْبَرِّ وَٱلْبَحْرِ بِمَا كَسَبَتْ أَيْدِى
ٱلنَّاسِ لِيُذِيقَهُم بَعْضَ ٱلَّذِى عَمِلُوا۟ لَعَلَّهُمْ
يَرْجِعُونَ ﴿٤١﴾ قُلْ سِيرُوا۟ فِى ٱلْأَرْضِ
فَٱنظُرُوا۟ كَيْفَ

63. Those whom the unbelievers and polytheists associate with God in His Divinity have not created anything. Nor do they have any role in providing people with their sustenance nor do they have any control over their life and death, nor do they possess the power to resurrect the dead. One wonders, then, why they should have been set up as deities when they are so absolutely powerless.

64. This again refers to the war then raging between the Romans and the Persians which had enveloped the whole of the Middle East region.

The word "deeds" in this verse signifies the wickedness and profligacy, and the injustice and tyranny which necessarily characterise the conduct of those who succumb to polytheism or atheism and who disregard the Hereafter. The verse says that "perhaps they will turn back (from evil)". The reason for so saying is that God makes people see the evil consequences of some, though not of all their deeds before they are face to face with the chastisement of the Hereafter. God does so in order that they might perceive the Truth, realise the falsity of their erroneous notions, and turn to true beliefs. It is to these beliefs that God's Prophets have always summoned mankind and they alone provide the right foundation for human character and conduct. This theme occurs in the Qur'ān at several places. See, for instance, *al-Tawbah* 9:126; *al-Ra'd* 13:21; *al-Sajdah* 32:21 and *al-Ṭūr* 52:47.

the end of those who went before you: most of them associated others with Allah in His Divinity."[65] (43) So turn your face exclusively towards the True Faith before there comes the Day whose coming from Allah cannot be averted,[66] the Day when people will split into groups. (44) He who disbelieves will suffer the consequence of it[67] and he who acts righteously, they will pave the way for their own good (45) so that Allah may, out of His Bounty, reward those who believe and act righteously. Verily He does not love the unbelievers.

كَانَ عَـٰقِبَةُ ٱلَّذِينَ مِن قَبْلُ ۚ كَانَ أَكْثَرُهُم
مُّشْرِكِينَ ﴿٤٢﴾ فَأَقِمْ وَجْهَكَ لِلدِّينِ ٱلْقَيِّمِ مِن
قَبْلِ أَن يَأْتِىَ يَوْمٌ لَّا مَرَدَّ لَهُۥ مِنَ ٱللَّهِ ۖ يَوْمَئِذٍ
يَصَّدَّعُونَ ﴿٤٣﴾ مَن كَفَرَ فَعَلَيْهِ كُفْرُهُۥ ۖ وَمَنْ
عَمِلَ صَـٰلِحًا فَلِأَنفُسِهِمْ يَمْهَدُونَ ﴿٤٤﴾
لِيَجْزِىَ ٱلَّذِينَ ءَامَنُوا۟ وَعَمِلُوا۟
ٱلصَّـٰلِحَـٰتِ مِن فَضْلِهِۦٓ ۚ إِنَّهُۥ لَا يُحِبُّ
ٱلْكَـٰفِرِينَ ﴿٤٥﴾

---

65. There was nothing unusual about the devastating war that was then raging between the Romans and the Persians. The history of ancient nations is replete with wars that left behind a tragic trail of devastation. The root of the evils that destroyed these earlier nations was polytheism and it is precisely this evil that people were being asked to abandon.

66. There is no way to avert the Day of Judgement: neither God Himself will avert it nor has He left any possibility for anyone else to do so.

67. This pithy observation encompasses all the harms that the unbelievers incur owing to their unbelief. No list of such harms, howsoever elaborate, can be as comprehensive as that embodied here in these few words.

(46) And of His Signs is that He sends winds to herald good tidings[68] and that He may give you a taste of His Mercy, and that ships may sail at His bidding,[69] and you may seek His Bounty[70] and give thanks to Him. (47) We sent Messengers before you to their respective nations, and they brought Clear Signs to them.[71] Then We

وَمِنْ ءَايَٰتِهِۦٓ أَن يُرْسِلَ ٱلرِّيَاحَ مُبَشِّرَٰتٍ
وَلِيُذِيقَكُم مِّن رَّحْمَتِهِۦ وَلِتَجْرِىَ ٱلْفُلْكُ
بِأَمْرِهِۦ وَلِتَبْتَغُوا۟ مِن فَضْلِهِۦ وَلَعَلَّكُمْ
تَشْكُرُونَ ﴿٤٦﴾ وَلَقَدْ أَرْسَلْنَا مِن قَبْلِكَ
رُسُلًا إِلَىٰ قَوْمِهِمْ فَجَآءُوهُم بِٱلْبَيِّنَٰتِ

---

68. That is, to herald the good tidings of rainfall.

69. Mention is made here of other kinds of winds, those that make it possible for vessels to sail on water. In the past, the sailing of boats and ships depended largely on favourable winds. As for unfavourable winds, they could be precursors of doom. After mentioning God's bounty of rainfall, reference is made here to the winds that help vessels to sail on water as a special favour from God.

70. To "seek His Bounty" here signifies undertaking trade voyages.

71. There is a wide variety of God's Signs. One of these Signs is that which is interspersed throughout the Universe and which man witnesses during his life; namely the movement of winds mentioned in the preceding verse. There are also other kinds of Signs that pertain to the Prophets: the miracles they performed, the Scriptures they brought, the excellence which characterised their character and conduct, and the wholesome, life-giving impact that they had on human life and society.

Signs of both kinds emphasise the truth of monotheism which the Prophets taught mankind. Each of the two kinds of Signs reinforces the other. The Signs visible in the Universe testify, on the one hand, to the truth of the teachings of the Prophets. On the other hand, the Signs brought along by the Prophets further elucidate the truth indicated by God's Signs in the Universe.

took vengeance upon those who acted wickedly.[72] It was incumbent on Us to come to the aid of the believers.

(48) Allah sends the winds that stir up clouds and then He spreads them in the sky as He pleases and splits them into different fragments, whereafter you see drops of rain pouring down from them. He then causes the rain to fall on whomsoever of His servants He pleases, and lo, they rejoice at it, (49) although before that they were given to despair. (50) See, then, the tokens of Allah's Mercy: how He revives the earth after it is dead.[73] Verily He is the One Who will revive

فَٱنتَقَمۡنَا مِنَ ٱلَّذِينَ أَجۡرَمُواْۖ وَكَانَ حَقًّا
عَلَيۡنَا نَصۡرُ ٱلۡمُؤۡمِنِينَ ﴿٤٧﴾ ٱللَّهُ ٱلَّذِي يُرۡسِلُ
ٱلرِّيَٰحَ فَتُثِيرُ سَحَابٗا فَيَبۡسُطُهُۥ فِي ٱلسَّمَآءِ
كَيۡفَ يَشَآءُ وَيَجۡعَلُهُۥ كِسَفٗا فَتَرَى ٱلۡوَدۡقَ
يَخۡرُجُ مِنۡ خِلَٰلِهِۦۖ فَإِذَآ أَصَابَ بِهِۦ مَن
يَشَآءُ مِنۡ عِبَادِهِۦٓ إِذَا هُمۡ يَسۡتَبۡشِرُونَ ﴿٤٨﴾
وَإِن كَانُواْ مِن قَبۡلِ أَن يُنَزَّلَ عَلَيۡهِم مِّن
قَبۡلِهِۦ لَمُبۡلِسِينَ ﴿٤٩﴾ فَٱنظُرۡ إِلَىٰٓ ءَاثَٰرِ
رَحۡمَتِ ٱللَّهِ كَيۡفَ يُحۡيِ ٱلۡأَرۡضَ بَعۡدَ
مَوۡتِهَآۚ إِنَّ ذَٰلِكَ لَمُحۡيِ

72. The unbelievers are blind to both sets of Signs. They adamantly persist in rejecting monotheism and continue their insurgence against God.

73. Significantly, Prophets and rainfall are mentioned here together. This subtly alludes to the fact that the advent of Prophets is a blessing for man's moral life in much the same way that rainfall is a blessing for his material life. Rainfall instantly revives dead land, causing luxuriant vegetation. In like manner, the revelation sent down from on high revives man's moral and spiritual life as a result of which new life begins to blossom. This manifests itself in the new heights of moral and spiritual excellence that human beings achieve. It is unfortunate that the unbelievers do not give thanks to God for this great favour of His. Rather than look upon revelation as a blessing, they consider it a message of doom.

the dead. He has power over everything. (51) But if We were to send a wind and then their tilth has become yellow,[74] they would never cease to disbelieve.[75] (52) (O Prophet), you cannot make the dead hear,[76] nor can you make the deaf hear your call when they turn back in retreat,[77] (53) nor can

ٱلْمَوْتَىٰ ۖ وَهُوَ عَلَىٰ كُلِّ شَىْءٍ قَدِيرٌ ﴿٥٠﴾ وَلَئِنْ
أَرْسَلْنَا رِيحًا فَرَأَوْهُ مُصْفَرًّا لَّظَلُّوا۟ مِنۢ
بَعْدِهِۦ يَكْفُرُونَ ﴿٥١﴾ فَإِنَّكَ لَا تُسْمِعُ ٱلْمَوْتَىٰ
وَلَا تُسْمِعُ ٱلصُّمَّ ٱلدُّعَآءَ إِذَا وَلَّوْا۟ مُدْبِرِينَ ﴿٥٢﴾
وَمَآ أَنتَ

74. That is, after the cultivated fields become green in the wake of rainfall, it is possible that fiery or frosty winds might begin to blow, devastating the entire harvest.

75. When faced with adversity, the unbelievers tend to curse God, blaming Him for inflicting a host of sufferings upon them. This, despite the fact that when God lavished His favours upon them, they scarcely appreciated those favours and failed to give thanks to Him. Here again there is a subtle allusion to the fact that when God's Messengers bring His message of mercy, people tend to spurn it. Thereupon God punishes these ungrateful people for their unbelief by imposing tyrants and oppressors upon them who crush and violate their dignity. Strangely, those people react to this by blasphemously reviling God for creating a world so full of wrong and injustice.

76. The word "dead" in this context signifies those whose conscience and moral sense have become totally extinct. These are the ones whose all-out immersion in carnal desires and whose adamance and obstinacy have altogether deprived them of the capacity to comprehend and accept the Truth.

77. The word "deaf" here signifies those who have sealed their hearts as a result of which they are deaf to the call of the Truth even though their physical faculty of hearing might be fully intact. No sooner do such people hear the Truth than they clog their ears, and no sooner do they spot any exponent of the Truth than they flee. How can anyone make such people heed the Truth?

you guide the blind out of their error.[78] You can make none hear (your call) except those who believe in Our Signs and have surrendered themselves (to Him).

(54) It is Allah Who created you in a state of weakness; then after weakness He gave you strength, then after strength He made you weak and old. He creates what He pleases.[79] He is All-Knowing, All-Powerful. (55) On that Day when the Hour will come to pass[80] the wicked shall swear that they had stayed (in

بِهَـٰدِ ٱلْعُمْىِ عَن ضَلَـٰلَتِهِمْ ۖ إِن تُسْمِعُ
إِلَّا مَن يُؤْمِنُ بِـَٔايَـٰتِنَا فَهُم مُّسْلِمُونَ ﴿٥٣﴾
۞ ٱللَّهُ ٱلَّذِى خَلَقَكُم مِّن ضَعْفٍ ثُمَّ جَعَلَ
مِنۢ بَعْدِ ضَعْفٍ قُوَّةً ثُمَّ جَعَلَ مِنۢ بَعْدِ قُوَّةٍ
ضَعْفًا وَشَيْبَةً ۚ يَخْلُقُ مَا يَشَآءُ ۖ وَهُوَ ٱلْعَلِيمُ
ٱلْقَدِيرُ ﴿٥٤﴾ وَيَوْمَ تَقُومُ ٱلسَّاعَةُ يُقْسِمُ
ٱلْمُجْرِمُونَ مَا لَبِثُوا۟

---

78. It is none of a Prophet's responsibility to take hold of the blind by their hands and guide them throughout their life along the right way. All he can do is to direct such people to the right way. But how can they be of any help to those who have become altogether blind to the way that the Prophets seek to direct them to?

79. It is God Who has divided man's life into the different stages of childhood, youth and old age. It depends entirely on His will to create some who are weak and others who are strong. It also depends entirely on His will to cause someone to die before he reaches his youth, or to die in his youth, or to grant someone a long life and still keep him healthy and strong. In like manner, God can grant someone a glorious youth and then cause him to suffer a miserable old age. Man can cherish any illusions about himself that he wants to but the fact remains that he is entirely in God's control and is absolutely helpless to alter the state in which God decides to place him.

80. The "Hour" here refers to the Hour of Judgement.

the world) no more than an hour.[81] Thus they used to be deceived in the life of the world.[82] (56) But those who had been endowed with knowledge and faith shall say: "According to Allah's Record you have stayed till the Day of Resurrection. Now, this is the Day of Resurrection. But you did not know." (57) So that will be the Day when the excuses of the wrong-doers will not avail them, nor will they be asked to make amends.[83]

(58) In the Qur'ān We have explained things to

غَيْرَ سَاعَةٍ ۚ كَذَٰلِكَ كَانُوا۟ يُؤْفَكُونَ ﴿٥٥﴾
وَقَالَ ٱلَّذِينَ أُوتُوا۟ ٱلْعِلْمَ وَٱلْإِيمَـٰنَ لَقَدْ
لَبِثْتُمْ فِى كِتَـٰبِ ٱللَّهِ إِلَىٰ يَوْمِ ٱلْبَعْثِ ۖ فَهَـٰذَا
يَوْمُ ٱلْبَعْثِ وَلَـٰكِنَّكُمْ كُنتُمْ لَا تَعْلَمُونَ ﴿٥٦﴾
فَيَوْمَئِذٍ لَّا يَنفَعُ ٱلَّذِينَ ظَلَمُوا۟ مَعْذِرَتُهُمْ
وَلَا هُمْ يُسْتَعْتَبُونَ ﴿٥٧﴾ وَلَقَدْ ضَرَبْنَا لِلنَّاسِ
فِى هَـٰذَا ٱلْقُرْءَانِ

---

81. That is, they had stayed no more than an hour from the time of their death until the Day of Resurrection. Even though thousands of years might have elapsed after their death they still feel as though they had been in a state of slumber for a very short while when they were suddenly woken by some accidental commotion.

82. In like manner, they used to miscalculate while they lived in the world. Not comprehending the reality, they believed that there would be no Day of Judgement, that there would be no life after death, and that they would never be called to account by God.

83. This could also be translated as follows: "...nor will they be asked to please their Lord", for by then they will have irretrievably lost all chance to turn to the True Faith and good deeds. The time prescribed for testing man will be over by then and he will be face to face with the Hour of Judgement.

مِن كُلِّ مَثَلٍۚ وَلَئِن جِئۡتَهُم بِـَٔايَةٖ لَّيَقُولَنَّ
ٱلَّذِينَ كَفَرُوٓاْ إِنۡ أَنتُمۡ إِلَّا مُبۡطِلُونَ ٥٨
كَذَٰلِكَ يَطۡبَعُ ٱللَّهُ عَلَىٰ قُلُوبِ ٱلَّذِينَ
لَا يَعۡلَمُونَ ٥٩ فَٱصۡبِرۡ إِنَّ وَعۡدَ ٱللَّهِ حَقّٞۖ
وَلَا يَسۡتَخِفَّنَّكَ ٱلَّذِينَ لَا يُوقِنُونَ ٦٠

people in myriad ways. But no matter what Sign you bring to them, those who are resolved upon denying the Truth will say: "You are given to falsehood."
(59) Thus does Allah seal the hearts of those who have no knowledge.
(60) Therefore, (O Prophet), have patience. Surely Allah's promise is true.[84] Let those who lack certainty not cause you to be unsteady.[85]

---

84. This alludes to God's promise mentioned in an earlier verse of this *sūrah:* "We sent Messengers before you to their respective nations, and they brought Clear Signs to them. Then We took vengeance upon those who acted wickedly. It was incumbent on Us to come to the aid of the believers." (See v. 47 above.)

85. The believers should be so firmly anchored in their conviction that there should be no reason whatsoever for enemies to consider them so feeble hearted that they can be overpowered by the latters' hue and cry, cowed down by their campaigns of calumny and slander, demoralised by their taunts and ridicules, intimidated by their threats, overawed by their display of strength and by their persecution, or be tempted by their allurements. Nor should the believers feel persuaded to make any compromise with enemies under the spell of pleas in the name of national interest. On the contrary, such enemies should find the believers so vigilant as regards their objectives, so mature and deeply entrenched in their beliefs, so determined in their resolve, and so firm in their character that no threat can frighten them, nor can any price howsoever high cajole them, nor can any danger, loss or suffering deflect them from their chosen path and nor can their religious faith ever be a matter of bargain and haggle. All these ideas are encompassed, thanks to the Qur'ān's consummate eloquence, in these few words: "Let those who lack certainty not cause you to be unsteady."

History bears out that the Prophet (peace be on him) proved himself to be as firm and solid as God had wanted His last Messenger to be. If anyone challenged him, regardless of the arena of the challenger, he was unfailingly brow-beaten by the Prophet (peace be on him). In the course of time, his powerful personality brought about a revolution that could not be thwarted by the combined forces of unbelief and polytheism across the Arabian Peninsula, and this despite the fact that his opponents spared no weapons available to them.

Sūrah 31

Luqmān

(Makkan Period)

Title

Verses 13-19 of this *sūrah* contain the sage Luqmān's advice to his son. Accordingly, the *sūrah* was named after him.

Period of Revelation

A careful study of the *sūrah*'s contents indicates that it was revealed at a time when Islam's opponents had begun to adopt a variety of oppressive measures to arrest the spread of its message. At the time, however, this storm of hostility had not yet reached its peak. This seems to be indicated by verses 14-15, whereby those youths, who had freshly converted to Islam, were told that they ought to be dutiful to their parents, this being next only to their duty to God. At the same time, they were also directed to pay no heed to them if they prevented them from embracing Islam or compelled them to revert to their original polytheistic faith. The same directive is also found in *Sūrah al-ʿAnkabūt* (see verse 8). This shows that both *sūrahs* – *Luqmān* and *al-ʿAnkabūt* – were revealed around the same time. However, the content and overall stylistic features of these *sūrahs* suggest that of the two, *Sūrah Luqmān* was revealed prior to *al-ʿAnkabūt*. This because the former does not betray that it was revealed in the context of the unbelievers' vehement opposition to Islam. Conversely, anyone who reads *Sūrah al-ʿAnkabūt* cannot fail to notice that it was revealed when the Muslims were being subjected to severe persecution.

Subject Matter and Themes

The *sūrah* impresses on people the utter falsehood and absurdity of polythesism. Conversely, it stresses how absolutely sound and reasonable monotheism is. It also invites people to abandon blindly following the ways of their forefathers and to consider, with unbiased minds, what the Prophet Muḥammad (peace be on him) was teaching them on God's behalf. They were also asked to look around and observe the innumerable Signs in the Universe and within their own beings that bore witness to the truth of the Prophet's teachings.

In this regard, it also emphasises that the Islamic call to acknowledge God as the only Lord is not new at all. It had not just risen for the first time in the world nor was it new to the Arabian Peninsula. Monotheism was, therefore, neither bizarre nor alien to the Arabs. People known in the past for their knowledge, reason and wisdom had said much the same that the Prophet Muḥammad (peace be on him) was saying. It was also significant that in Arabia itself there had lived some time previously a sage called Luqmān whose wisdom and insight were proverbial among the Arabs. Thanks to this legendary fame, Luqmān's maxims had become commonplace and were often quoted in day-to-day conversation and had also found their way into oratory and poetry.

People are being asked in this *sūrah* to consider the beliefs Luqmān expounded and the morals he sought to promote. The implicit suggestion is that they should examine whether or not the beliefs and morals expounded by him conform with what the Prophet Muḥammad (peace be on him) was teaching them.

In the name of Allah, the Most Merciful, the Most Compassionate.

(1) *Alif. Lām. Mīm.* (2) These are the verses of the Wise Book,[1] (3) a guidance and mercy for the doers of good,[2] (4) who establish Prayer and pay *Zakāh*, and have firm faith in the Hereafter.[3] (5) It is they

بِسْمِ ٱللَّهِ ٱلرَّحْمَٰنِ ٱلرَّحِيمِ

الٓمٓ ﴿١﴾ تِلْكَ ءَايَٰتُ ٱلْكِتَٰبِ
ٱلْحَكِيمِ ﴿٢﴾ هُدًى وَرَحْمَةً لِّلْمُحْسِنِينَ ﴿٣﴾
ٱلَّذِينَ يُقِيمُونَ ٱلصَّلَوٰةَ وَيُؤْتُونَ ٱلزَّكَوٰةَ
وَهُم بِٱلْـَٔاخِرَةِ هُمْ يُوقِنُونَ ﴿٤﴾ أُو۟لَٰٓئِكَ

---

1. That is, this is the Book whose verses are permeated with wisdom, the Book whose every part is full of beneficial insights.

2. The Qur'ānic verses guide people to the Straight Way and represent God's mercy to mankind. However, it is only those who adopt good conduct and who seek righteousness and virtue that can benefit from God's guidance and mercy. The distinguishing characteristic of such people is that when they are warned against evil, they desist from it. Likewise, when they are informed what the ways of goodness are, they follow them. As for the wicked who relish evil, they will neither benefit from Qur'ānic guidance nor receive any portion of God's mercy.

3. This does not mean that those described here as "doers of good" have none other than these three qualities – that they establish Prayer, pay *zakāh* and firmly believe in the Hereafter. Here, some people are first characterised as "doers of good" so as to allude to the fact that they are the ones who desist from all the evils the Qur'ān forbids and perform all good works it enjoins. This is followed by identifying the following three chief qualities of these "doers of good", the reason being that all good works proceed from them: (i) They establish Prayer as a result of which they develop God-consciousness, and their sense of being God-fearing becomes second nature. (ii) They pay *zakāh*, which strengthens in them the spirit of sacrifice and selfless concern for others. It also helps them suppress excessive love of worldly objects and prompts them to earnestly seek to please God. (iii) They also have firm belief in the Hereafter which

who are on true guidance from their Lord, and it is they who shall prosper.[4]

(6) There are some human beings[5] who purchase an

عَلَىٰ هُدًى مِّن رَّبِّهِمْ وَأُولَٰٓئِكَ هُمُ ٱلْمُفْلِحُونَ ۝٥ وَمِنَ ٱلنَّاسِ مَن يَشْتَرِى

---

imbues them with a sense of accountability so that they do not behave like unbridled animals left free to graze in green pastures. Instead, their conduct reflects a responsible attitude worthy of a human being, whereby they are acutely aware that they should act with full consciousness of being their Lord's servants to Whom they are accountable for all their deeds.

Viewed in this context, these "doers of good" are not those who would do good works accidentally and who would feel equally free to commit evil. On the contrary, the three qualities mentioned above institute in them a system of belief and morality from which good works flow as a matter of course. Whenever they lapse and commit some evil, it is by way of accident. They are not then impelled towards evil because of any driving factor inherently rooted in their belief system.

4. At the time of the revelation of these verses, the unbelieving Makkans thought and publicly stated that the Prophet Muḥammad (peace be on him) and his followers were set on a course of self-destruction. The Qur'ān refutes this contention and asserts that, contrary to their supposition, the believers were not doomed to suffer loss or destruction; rather, they would succeed and prosper. It is also those who refuse to believe that will fail to achieve success and prosperity.

Were one to interpret the Qur'ānic concept of *falāḥ* (prosperity) purely in material and mundane terms, one would be committing a serious error. In order to correctly understand this term, readers should peruse the following Qur'ānic verses along with the relevant explanatory notes in this work: *al-Baqarah* 2:2-5; *Āl ʿImrān* 3:102, 130 and 200; *al-Māʾidah* 5:35 and 90; *al-Anʿām* 6:21; *al-Aʿrāf* 7:7-8 and 157; *al-Tawbah* 9:88; *Yūnus* 10:17; *al-Naḥl* 16:116; *al-Ḥajj* 22:77; *al-Muʾminūn* 23:1 and 117; *al-Nūr* 24:51 and *al-Rūm* 30:38.

5. Some people are fortunate enough to draw upon God's guidance and mercy. By contradistinction are the wicked who not only fail to do so, but who even contrive to lure people away from the Straight Way.

enchanting diversion[6] in order to lead people away from the way of Allah without having any	لَهْوَ ٱلْحَدِيثِ لِيُضِلَّ عَن سَبِيلِ ٱللَّهِ بِغَيْرِ

6. The words in the text are *"lahw al-ḥadīth"* which suggest an amusement or diversion that completely absorbs people, making them oblivious to everything around them. This expression is used to denote those things that are worthless, perverse or vile such as gossip, jest, vain tales, bootless fiction, dissolute singing and dancing, and other similar forms of amusement.

The expression "purchasing an enchanting diversion" can also be considered to mean opting for falsehood at the cost of truth or God's Guidance and embracing things that neither bring any good in the present life nor in the Next.

This, however, is the figurative sense of the expression. Literally speaking, it simply means to spend one's money on things that are vile and perverse. Several traditions corroborate this meaning of the verse. Ibn Hishām, for instance, narrated a tradition on Muḥammad ibn Isḥāq's authority that when the Prophet's message began to spread despite the efforts of the Quraysh, al-Naḍr ibn al-Ḥārith told the Quraysh how to counter it. He said that the manner in which they were trying to oppose the Prophet's call would prove of no avail. After all, he had lived all his life and had reached middle-age in their midst and was known to be the best of them as regards moral conduct. He was also the most truthful and trustworthy of them. It was only after Muḥammad had declared himself to be God's Messenger that the same people who had held him in the highest esteem began to variously dub him as a soothsayer, a sorcerer, a poet and one devoid of sanity. Yet he could not be called a sorcerer for there was no trace of the sorcerer's hocus pocus in him. Nor was there any resemblance between him and soothsayers who are known for their mumbo jumbo and rhymed exclamations. Nor could he be identified as a poet for people knew only too well what poetry was like. Nor did he seem to betray insanity or any of the states associated with it. Hence, no one would believe such statements about Muḥammad and none would desert him on account of descriptions of him as a soothsayer, sorcerer, poet or madman. Al-Naḍr ibn al-Ḥārith therefore volunteered to do something he considered effective in preventing the spread of

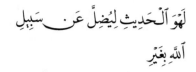

Islam's message. For this purpose he went to Iraq and brought back interesting tales about the Persian royalty and such fabulous personalities as Rustam and Asfandyār. After his return, he held sessions in which these tales were narrated to wean people away from the Qur'ān and absorb them in amusing stories. (See Ibn Hishām, *Sīrah*, Vol. I, pp. 320-321.)

Al-Wāḥidī narrated substantially the same on the authority of al-Kalbī and Muqātil in his *Asbāb al-Nuzūl*. In addition to this Ibn 'Abbās says that Naḍr ibn Ḥārith also purchased slave girls adept at singing and dancing to turn people's attention away from the Qur'ān. Whenever he learned that someone was attracted by the Prophet's message, he would ask one of these slave girls to take care of him. In this respect, she was directed to feed him sumptuously, enchant him with melodious songs and so distract his attention from the Prophet's message. (See Jalāl al-Dīn al-Suyūṭī, *Lubāb al-Naqūl fī Asbāb al-Nuzūl*, II edn., Cairo: Muṣṭafā al-Bābī al-Ḥalabī, n.d., p. 172 – Ed.)

Proponents of evil have resorted to similar devices throughout history. They have always tried to engross people in play and amusement, music and dance, euphemistically calling them "cultural" activities. They do so in order to prevent people from paying heed to the serious problems of life. Thanks to the inebriation caused by these amusements, the victims lose all awareness that they are being driven towards destruction.

Many Companions and Successors have also given the same explanation of *lahw al-ḥadīth*. On being asked to explain what the actual expression meant, 'Abd Allāh ibn Mas'ūd emphatically stated on three occasions: "By God, it means singing." (See al-Bayhaqī, *al-Sunan al-Kubrā, Bāb: Mā jā' min al-Ma'āṣī min al-Ma'āzif wa al-Mazāmīr*; al-Ḥākim al-Nīsābūrī, *al-Mustadrak, K. al-Tafsīr, Bāb: Tafsīr Sūrah Luqmān*, comments on *Luqmān* 31:6; Ṭabarī, *Tafsīr*, comments on *Luqmān* 31:6; Ibn Abī Shaybah, *Muṣannaf, K. al-Buyū', Bāb: Li hādhihi al-Āyah wa min al-Nās ...*; Ṭabarī, *Tafsīr*, comments on *Luqmān* 31:6 – Ed.) Similar views have also been reported from 'Abd Allāh ibn 'Abbās, Jābir ibn 'Abd Allāh, Mujāhid, 'Ikrimah, Sa'īd ibn Jubayr, al-Ḥasan al-Baṣrī and Makḥūl. Ibn Jarīr al-Ṭabarī, Ibn Abī Ḥātim and al-Tirmidhī have reported on the authority of Abū Umāmah al-Bāhilī that the Prophet (peace be on him) said: "It is not lawful to buy and sell singing girls, or to trade in them, or to subsist on their [i.e., singing girls'] earnings." In another version, the last part of the tradition has the following words: "It is not lawful to subsist on their earnings." Abū Umāmah also narrated another tradition according to which the Prophet (peace be on him) said: "It is not lawful to instruct slave girls in singing and dancing, or to trade in them, and it is prohibited to accept their earnings". These three traditions also specify that the verse, "There are some human beings who purchase an enchanting diversion ...."

knowledge,[7] who hold the call to the Way of Allah to ridicule.[8] A humiliating	عِلْمٍ وَيَتَّخِذَهَا هُزُوًا أُولَٰئِكَ

was revealed with regard to these damsels whose occupation was to sing and dance. Abū Bakr ibn al-ʿArabī records the following *ḥadīth* narrated by ʿAbd Allāh ibn al-Mubārak and Imām Mālik on the authority of Anas ibn Mālik: "The Prophet (peace be on him) said: Anyone who sits in the concert of a singing girl will have molten lead poured into his ears on the Day of Judgement." (Ibn al-ʿArabī, *Aḥkām al-Qur'ān,* comments on *Luqmān* 31:6 – Ed.)

It is pertinent to add in this regard that the whole culture of singing and dancing in those days was wholly dependent on slave girls. Free women had not yet assumed the role of "artists". It is for this reason that the Prophet (peace be on him) made a pointed reference to the sale and purchase of singing damsels, using the term *thaman* (price) to denote the fee they charged. Significantly, he also used the word *qaynah,* meaning "slave girl" for them.

7. That the unbelievers' action is "without having any knowledge" either qualifies the phrase "purchasing an enchanting diversion" or the phrase "in order to lead people away from the way of Allah". If the words "without having any knowledge" are taken to qualify "purchasing an enchanting diversion", the verse would mean that because of ignorance a person is so lured to this enchanting diversion without realising that they are losing something as precious as faith.

The irony of the situation was that on the one hand people had access to the Qur'ānic verses permeated with wisdom and true guidance just for the asking. Yet, they still turned away from them. On the other hand the same people sought perverse diversions, which they acquired at hefty prices, even though they were bound to vitiate their thinking and ruin their morality.

Alternatively, the expression "without having any knowledge" might be taken to qualify the phrase: "to lead people away from the way of Allah". In this case, the verse would mean that a person had taken it upon himself to guide others even though he himself lacked knowledge and was unaware that he had incurred a heavy and sinful burden by trying to mislead God's creatures from His way.

8. This unbeliever sought to engross people in various entertaining stories, dance and music. He had a contemptuous attitude towards the

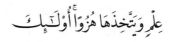

chastisement awaits them.[9] (7) When Our verses are recited to such a person, he arrogantly turns away, as though he had not heard them, or as though there was a deafness in his ears. So announce to him the tidings of a grievous chastisement. (8) Surely those who believe and do good deeds shall have Gardens of Bliss.[10]

لَهُمْ عَذَابٌ مُّهِينٌ ﴿٦﴾ وَإِذَا تُتْلَىٰ عَلَيْهِ ءَايَٰتُنَا
وَلَّىٰ مُسْتَكْبِرًا كَأَن لَّمْ يَسْمَعْهَا كَأَنَّ فِىٓ
أُذُنَيْهِ وَقْرًا ۖ فَبَشِّرْهُ بِعَذَابٍ أَلِيمٍ ﴿٧﴾ إِنَّ
ٱلَّذِينَ ءَامَنُوا۟ وَعَمِلُوا۟ ٱلصَّٰلِحَٰتِ لَهُمْ
جَنَّٰتُ ٱلنَّعِيمِ ﴿٨﴾

---

verses revealed by God and sought to drown the Qur'ān's message in a sea of laughter and mirth. No sooner had the Prophet Muḥammad (peace be on him) recited a Qur'ānic verse than he would arrange for concerts of beautiful damsels to enchant people with their melodies. Such was this unbeliever's strategy to immerse people in amusements, so that they were no longer in the mood to attend to anything serious – be it God, the Hereafter or morality.

9. That is, the unbelievers will be recompensed with humiliating chastisements in keeping with the gravity of their crimes. This, because they brazenly blasphemed the faith God prescribed, reviled the verses He revealed, and heaped insults on the Messenger He raised.

10. Here, the believers are not simply being promised the "bliss of Paradise"; rather, they are being promised "Gardens of Bliss". Had the former expression been used, it would have meant that they would enjoy the delights of the Gardens of Paradise. However, this falls short of saying that the Gardens of Paradise would be theirs. Hence why the present verse goes even beyond this. It says that they shall have "Gardens of Bliss". The message conveyed here is quite unmistakable. They are being told that whole Gardens full of bliss will be bestowed upon them and that they will enjoy the delights of these Gardens as their owners rather than as those simply entitled to enjoy their delights while the Gardens belonged to someone else.

(9) They shall abide in them forever. This is Allah's promise that shall come true. He is the Most Powerful, the Most Wise.[11]

(10) He[12] created the heavens without any pillars visible to you[13] and He placed mountains in the earth as pegs lest it should

خَـٰلِدِينَ فِيهَا ۖ وَعْدَ ٱللَّهِ حَقًّا ۚ وَهُوَ ٱلْعَزِيزُ
ٱلْحَكِيمُ ﴿٩﴾ خَلَقَ ٱلسَّمَـٰوَٰتِ بِغَيْرِ عَمَدٍ
تَرَوْنَهَا ۖ وَأَلْقَىٰ فِى ٱلْأَرْضِ رَوَٰسِىَ أَن

11. Nothing can deter God from fulfilling His promise. Moreover, whatever He does is fully in accord with the requirements of justice and wisdom. The Qur'ānic assertion that "This is Allah's promise that shall come true", is followed by specifically mentioning two attributes of God: His being the Most Powerful and the Most Wise. This underscores the fact that God neither goes back on His promise of His own accord nor can any power deter Him from fulfilling it. Therefore, there is no reason for anyone to entertain any fear that he will be denied the reward promised to those who believe and do good works. Moreover, God's proclamation of this reward is anchored in His wisdom and justice. Hence, He will not reward any who does not deserve it. Furthermore, those who believe and do good works are bound to be rewarded because they deserve to be so recompensed.

12. These preliminary observations are followed by stating the real purpose of the discourse – refutation of polytheism and invitation to monotheism.

13. That God has "created the heavens without any pillars visible to you" is open to two interpretations. First, that man himself can observe that the heavens are without any pillars to support them. Second, that although the heavens are supported by pillars, these are not visible to man. The latter interpretation is preferred by ʿAbd Allāh ibn ʿAbbās and Mujāhid. Quite a few other Qur'ānic commentators, however, subscribe to the former interpretation.

Were one to explain this Qur'ānic statement in the light of modern scientific knowledge, it would be said that countless stars and planets of colossal magnitude have been placed in their respective orbits in the

turn topsy turvy with you,[14] and He dispersed all kinds of animals over the earth, and sent down water from the sky causing all kinds of excellent plants to grow on it. (11) Such is Allah's creation. Show me, then, what any others, apart from Allah, have created.[15] Nay, the fact is that the wrong-doers are in manifest error.[16]

تَمِيدَ بِكُمْ وَبَثَّ فِيهَا مِن كُلِّ دَآبَّةٍ ۚ وَأَنزَلْنَا
مِنَ ٱلسَّمَآءِ مَآءً فَأَنۢبَتْنَا فِيهَا مِن كُلِّ زَوْجٍ
كَرِيمٍ ﴿١٠﴾ هَٰذَا خَلْقُ ٱللَّهِ فَأَرُونِى مَاذَا
خَلَقَ ٱلَّذِينَ مِن دُونِهِۦ ۚ بَلِ ٱلظَّٰلِمُونَ فِى
ضَلَٰلٍ مُّبِينٍ ﴿١١﴾

---

heavens without any visible props. These heavenly bodies are not bound by any cable, nor are there any visible barriers preventing them from falling on one another. It is only the law of gravity that keeps the entire system in its place.

This interpretation reflects the extent of our present knowledge. With the passage of time as our knowledge advances, perhaps it will be possible to offer an even more plausible explanation of the reality under discussion.

14. For details see *Towards Understanding the Qur'ān*, Vol. IV, *al-Naḥl* 16: n. 12, p. 317.

15. The unbelievers are challenged to identify what their deities had created. Those same deities which, according to their fancy, had the power to make or mar their destiny and which they insisted on worshipping.

16. The unbelievers were unable to point to anything that their deities had created. Therefore, nothing other than sheer irrationality explained their ascribing Divinity to such deities, their subservient prostrations before them, or their invocations of them to fulfil their needs. Only those who are totally devoid of common sense would accept in one breath that their deities lack the power to create anything and that God alone is the Creator of everything, and still insist in the other, that those same powerless deities ought to be worshipped. Any person with even an iota of understanding is bound to ask: why worship an object that is altogether

(12) We[17] bestowed wisdom upon Luqmān, (enjoining): "Give thanks | وَلَقَدْ ءَاتَيْنَا لُقْمَـٰنَ ٱلْحِكْمَةَ أَنِ ٱشْكُرْ

devoid of creative power and that does not have even a minimal part in creating a single thing in the heavens and the earth? Why prostrate before such a thing, making it the object of reverential devotion? Why treat it as a deity when it does not have the power to hear its devotees' petitions and is in any case powerless to fulfil any needs? Being absolutely powerless, it can obviously neither make nor mar anyone's destiny.

17. After advancing a weighty and rational argument to repudiate polytheism, the people of Arabia are being told that this reasonable doctrine of monotheism was not being expounded to them for the first time in history by the Prophet Muḥammad (peace be on him). Sages of the past had also expounded much the same truth. Luqmān, who was well known to them, was an illustrious instance in point. The people of Arabia, therefore, had no truly valid reason to reject the Prophet Muḥammad's summons to monotheism on the grounds that even if it was a reasonable proposition, nobody had articulated it before.

As for Luqmān, he was widely acclaimed as a paragon of wisdom throughout Arabia. Pre-Islamic poets such as Imra' al-Qays, Labīd, al-A'shā and Ṭarafah all refer to him in their poetry. Some well-read Arabs even possessed a copy of his collection of wise sayings. According to some traditions, the first Madīnan who was impressed by the Prophet (peace be on him) about three years before the *Hijrah* was Suwayd ibn Ṣāmit. He had gone to Makkah in connection with *Ḥajj*. The Prophet (peace be on him) used to visit the camps of pilgrims who came from different parts of the Peninsula and preached Islam to them. When Suwayd heard the Prophet's discourse, he said to him: "Perhaps you have something like that which I have." "And what is that?" the Prophet (peace be on him) asked. "Luqmān's scroll", he replied. At the Prophet's request Suwayd recited from his scroll. The Prophet (peace be on him) remarked: "This discourse is fine, but what I have is still better", and then he recited some verses from the Qur'ān. Thereupon Suwayd acknowledged it to be decidedly better than Luqmān's wisdom. (Ibn Hishām, *Sīrah*, Vol. 2, pp. 67-68 and *Usd al-Ghābah*, Vol. 2, p. 378.)

Historians of the time state that in view of his talents, bravery, poetic skills and social prestige, Suwayd was popularly known in Madīnah as *al-kāmil*, "the perfect one". Suwayd returned to Madīnah after meeting the Prophet (peace be on him). Thereafter he was slain in the Battle of

Bu'āth. His tribesmen generally thought that after meeting the Prophet (peace be on him) he had embraced Islam.

There is wide divergence of opinion regarding the historical Luqmān. During the dark centuries of *Jāhilīyah,* history was not committed to writing. Historical information was based on an accumulation of oral reports which had been in circulation for centuries. In light of these reports, some scholars tend to regard Luqmān as a member of the 'Ād and one of the kings of Yemen. In his *Arḍ al-Qur'ān* Sayyid Sulaymān Nadwī considers him, on the basis of these reports, to be a descendant of the believers who, along with the Prophet Hūd (peace be on him), had survived God's scourge that struck Hūd's nation. Reportedly, Luqmān's people had established a kingdom in Yemen and he was one of that nation's kings. However, other reports narrated on the authority of some leading Companions and Successors sharply conflict with this report and depict him quite differently. 'Abd Allāh ibn 'Abbās, for instance, was of the opinion that Luqmān was an Abyssinian slave. Abū Hurayrah, Mujāhid, 'Ikrimah and Khālid al-Ruba'ī also held the same opinion. According to Jābir ibn 'Abd Allāh al-Anṣārī, he hailed from Nubia. Sa'īd ibn al-Musayyib considered Luqmān to be a person of black complexion who belonged to Egypt. (See Ṭabarī, *Tafsīr*, comments on *Luqmān* 31:12 and Shawkānī, *Fatḥ al-Qadīr*, comments on *Luqmān* 31:19 – Ed.) All of these opinions are more or less alike. This because the Arabs of the time referred to persons belonging to Egypt, Abyssinia or Nubia as blacks. Nubia lay to the south of Egypt and to the north of the Sudan. Hence, there is no substantial difference in calling Luqmān Egyptian, Nubian or Abyssinian. Suhaylī, in his *Rawḍ al-Unuf* and Mus'ūdī in his *Murūj al-Dhahab* explain how the sayings of this black slave gained currency in Arabia. It appears from Suhaylī's and Mas'ūdī's statements that Luqmān was originally a Nubian. However, he lived in the region of Madyan and Aylah (present-day 'Aqabah). His mother tongue was Arabic and therefore his sayings first gained currency in Arabia. However, Suhaylī has also expressed the view that Luqmān, the wise, and Luqmān of the 'Ād were two different historical figures and that it would be wrong to consider the two as the same (See *Rawḍ al-Unuf*), Vol. 1, p. 266 and *Murūj al-Dhahab*, Vol. 1, p. 57.)

Another point worth clarifying is that the Orientalist scholar Derenbourg's *Fables de Loqman le Sage*, published from the Library of Paris, is a fictitious work which has nothing to do with the collection of Luqmān's sayings. These *Fables* were rather compiled by someone during the thirteenth century. Furthermore, the compiler displays a pitiably poor knowledge of Arabic. After reading this work it appears that it is undoubtedly a translated version of some other work which the compiler ascribes to Luqmān. Orientalists are quite adept at producing

to Allah."[18] Whoso gives thanks to Allah, does so to his own good. And whoso disbelieves (let him know that) Allah is All-Sufficient, Immensely Praiseworthy.[19]

(13) And call to mind when Luqmān said to his son while exhorting him: "My son, do not associate others

لِلَّهِ ۚ وَمَن يَشْكُرْ فَإِنَّمَا يَشْكُرُ لِنَفْسِهِۦ ۖ وَمَن
كَفَرَ فَإِنَّ ٱللَّهَ غَنِىٌّ حَمِيدٌ ﴿١٢﴾ وَإِذْ قَالَ
لُقْمَـٰنُ لِٱبْنِهِۦ وَهُوَ يَعِظُهُۥ يَـٰبُنَىَّ لَا تُشْرِكْ

---

such fabricated materials. By so doing, they merely seek to discredit the Qur'ānic narratives, showing them to be legends devoid of all historical value. All this is well illustrated by B. Heller's article on Luqmān in *The Encyclopaedia of Islam*. (See B. Heller [N.A. Stillman], art. "Luḳmān", EI^2, vol. V, pp. 811-813 – Ed.)

18. God has endowed man with intelligence, wisdom, reason and perspicacity. All these necessitate that he be grateful to God instead of thankless. In fact thankfulness to God should embrace every aspect of man's life. He should be cognizant in the deepest recesses of his being that he owes all that he has to God. He should also express his thankfulness verbally. This thankfulness should also manifest itself in behaviour by his abstaining from sin. It should also be manifest in his sparing no effort to please God, by sharing with God's creatures whatever God has bestowed upon him, and by striving against God's rebels. All such actions testify that he is truly grateful to God.

19. Whoever disbelieves in God incurs his own loss. As for God, man's disbelief causes Him no harm because He is self-sufficient and does not stand in need of anyone's thanks. Man's expression of gratitude to God adds nothing to His dominion. Nor does anyone's denial of God's Divinity detract from the fact that He is the only source of all the bounties that human beings enjoy. God is Innately Praiseworthy regardless of whether others praise Him or not. Every particle of the Universe testifies to His perfection and magnificence, to His infinite power of creation and to His all-embracing Providence. In actuality, every living being, by the mere fact of its existence, celebrates God's glory.

with Allah in His Divinity.[20] Surely, associating others with Allah in His Divinity is a mighty wrong."[21]	بِٱللَّهِ إِنَّ ٱلشِّرْكَ لَظُلْمٌ عَظِيمٌ ﴿١٣﴾

20. Out of all of Luqmān's wise counsels, this particular one is brought into sharp relief for two reasons. First, that this was what he had counselled his own son. It goes without saying that one acts with utmost sincerity towards one's own children. One might deceive others or be hypocritical towards them. But not even the most wicked person will ever wilfully mislead his own children. Hence, the advice that Luqmān tendered to his son clearly demonstrates that he truly believed polytheism to be the worst kind of monstrosity. It was precisely because he sincerely believed that he counselled his son, the very apple of his eyes, to shun polytheism. Second, that the advice was especially relevant because many unbelieving Makkan parents were guilty of compelling their children to revert to polytheism and abandon the Prophet Muḥammad's call to monotheism. This is indicated by the verses that follow.

The ignorant, unbelieving Makkans are being told that Luqmān, the illustrious sage of their land, had admonished his son – and obviously for no other reason than sincere concern for his son's well-being – to give up polytheism. Is it not strange then that the Prophet's contemporaries in Arabia were forcing their offspring to embrace the very same polytheism? After all, one should consider whether compelling children to adopt polytheism is conducive to their well-being or whether it spells their doom.

21. Injustice consists in denying a person his due, in acting in contravention of the dictates of right and equitableness. Polytheism is a "mighty wrong" precisely because a polytheist elevates to the status of the Creator and the Provider of all bounties those who have neither any share in creation, nor in the provision of sustenance or of the bounties that man enjoys.

This is the worst kind of wrong that one can conceive of. Being one of His creatures, it is God's right that His creatures exclusively serve and worship Him. By serving others besides God, one denies God His due. Worse, whenever one embraces polytheism one uses one's faculties, both mental and physical, as well as myriad objects of the heavens and the earth that have been created by the One True God. For this reason, a person has no right to use these in serving anyone other than Him. Moreover, a

(14) We enjoined upon man[22] to be dutiful to his parents. His mother bore him in weakness upon weakness, and his weaning lasted two years.[23] (We, therefore, enjoined upon him): "Give thanks to Me and to your parents. To Me is your ultimate return.

وَوَصَّيْنَا ٱلْإِنسَـٰنَ بِوَٰلِدَيْهِ حَمَلَتْهُ أُمُّهُۥ وَهْنًا عَلَىٰ وَهْنٍ وَفِصَـٰلُهُۥ فِى عَامَيْنِ أَنِ ٱشْكُرْ لِى وَلِوَٰلِدَيْكَ إِلَىَّ ٱلْمَصِيرُ ﴿١٤﴾

person's own being has the right that it should not court degradation or incur God's wrath. However, when someone worships a created being in disregard of the One True God, he degrades himself as well as invites punishment upon himself. In sum, a polytheist's entire life becomes a constant series of wrongs and injustices. There is not even a moment when he is not engaged in committing this "mighty wrong".

22. The statement beginning with "We enjoined upon man" till "two years", is a parenthetical one. The words are from God and are intended to further elucidate and elaborate upon Luqmān's statement.

23. Imām Shāfiʿī, Imām Aḥmad ibn Ḥanbal, Imām Abū Yūsuf and Imām Muḥammad ibn al-Ḥasan infer from these words that a child's suckling period comes to an end at the expiry of two years. Hence, if a woman suckles a child within this period, this gives rise to the prohibition of marriage on the grounds of suckling. However, if a woman continues to suckle a child after it has attained more than two years of age, this does not give rise to the usual matrimonial prohibitions on the grounds of suckling. A statement by Imām Mālik has also been reported in support of this doctrine. By way of precaution, however, Imām Abū Ḥanīfah proposes that this period be of two and a half years. Furthermore, he made the additional observation that if a child was weaned within two or less years and if it did not subsist just on the breast milk of the suckling woman, the mere fact of suckling the child does not give rise to matrimonial prohibitions on that account. However, if the milk of the foster-mother's breast was the child's staple diet, the suckling of the child would entail matrimonial prohibitions even though occasionally the child might have been fed other things as well. (Jaṣṣāṣ, *Aḥkām al-Qur'ān*,

(15) But if they press you to associate others with Me in My Divinity, (to associate) those regarding whom you have no knowledge (that they are My associates),[24] do not obey them. And yet treat them well in this world, and follow the way of him who turns to Me in devotion. Eventually it is to Me that all of you shall return,[25] and I shall then tell you all that you did."[26]

وَإِن جَٰهَدَاكَ عَلَىٰٓ أَن تُشْرِكَ بِى
مَا لَيْسَ لَكَ بِهِۦ عِلْمٌ فَلَا تُطِعْهُمَا ۖ وَصَاحِبْهُمَا
فِى ٱلدُّنْيَا مَعْرُوفًا ۖ وَٱتَّبِعْ سَبِيلَ مَنْ أَنَابَ
إِلَىَّ ۚ ثُمَّ إِلَىَّ مَرْجِعُكُمْ فَأُنَبِّئُكُم بِمَا كُنتُمْ
تَعْمَلُونَ ﴿١٥﴾

comments on *al-Baqarah* 2:233 – Ed.) This, because the verse does not require, in a mandatory sense, that the child must necessarily be breast fed until two years of age. In this regard, another related Qur'ānic command seems pertinent: "If they (fathers) wish that the period of suckling for their children be completed, mothers may suckle their children for two whole years" (*al-Baqarah* 2:233).

'Abd Allāh ibn 'Abbās's inference, which has been endorsed by other scholars, is that the minimum period of conception is six months. (See Jaṣṣāṣ, *Aḥkām al-Qur'ān*, comments on *Luqmān* 31:14 – Ed.) It is for this reason that it has been laid down elsewhere in the Qur'ān: "The carrying of the child to his weaning is a period of thirty months", (*al-Aḥqāf* 46:15). This is an important legal injunction which settles the issue about whether a child's birth was legitimate or not.

24. "... [T]hose regarding whom you have no knowledge", that is, those regarding whom you have no categorical knowledge that they are God's associates in His Divinity.

25. That is, their parents, their children, and, in fact, everybody will return to God.

26. For details see *al-'Ankabūt* 29: nn. 11-12.

(16) (Luqmān said):[27] "Son, Allah will bring forth everything even if it be as small as the grain of a mustard seed even though it be hidden inside a rock or (anywhere) in the heavens or earth.[28] Allah is Most Subtle, All-Aware. (17) Son, establish Prayer, enjoin all that is good and forbid all that is evil, and endure with patience whatever affliction befalls you.[29] Surely these have been emphatically

يَٰبُنَيَّ إِنَّهَآ إِن تَكُ مِثْقَالَ حَبَّةٍ مِّنْ خَرْدَلٍ
فَتَكُن فِى صَخْرَةٍ أَوْ فِى ٱلسَّمَٰوَٰتِ أَوْ فِى
ٱلْأَرْضِ يَأْتِ بِهَا ٱللَّهُ ۚ إِنَّ ٱللَّهَ لَطِيفٌ
خَبِيرٌ ﴿١٦﴾ يَٰبُنَيَّ أَقِمِ ٱلصَّلَوٰةَ وَأْمُرْ بِٱلْمَعْرُوفِ
وَٱنْهَ عَنِ ٱلْمُنكَرِ وَٱصْبِرْ عَلَىٰ مَآ أَصَابَكَ ۖ
إِنَّ ذَٰلِكَ مِنْ

---

27. Other pieces of Luqmān's advice are recounted here in order to stress that his views regarding morality, as also his views regarding matters of belief, were no different from the Prophet's. People should, therefore, not be astonished at the Prophet's teachings for these were not at all outlandish for the people of Arabia.

28. Nothing escapes God's knowledge and nothing is beyond His grasp. A grain hidden in a rock might be beyond man's ken, but God knows it. Again, for man, a particle in the heavens might be too distant, but for God it is very close. Anything buried deep under the soil might be invisible to man, but to God it is clearly visible. In sum, whatever man does, be it good or bad, publicly or secretly, is not hidden from Him. God is not only aware of all man's deeds but He will also present him with a record of all these deeds on the Day of Reckoning.

29. What is subtly implicit here is the message that anyone who embarks on enjoining good and forbidding evil is bound to encounter hardship. This, because others become upset with such a person and obstinately try to hurt him. The result being that he has to face a host of hardships on their account.

enjoined.[30] (18) Do not (contemptuously) turn your face away from people,[31] nor tread haughtily upon earth.[32] Allah does not love the arrogant and the vainglorious. (19) Be moderate in your stride[33] and lower your voice. Verily the most disgusting of all

عَزۡمِ ٱلۡأُمُورِ ۝١٧ وَلَا تُصَعِّرۡ خَدَّكَ لِلنَّاسِ
وَلَا تَمۡشِ فِي ٱلۡأَرۡضِ مَرَحًاۖ إِنَّ ٱللَّهَ
لَا يُحِبُّ كُلَّ مُخۡتَالٖ فَخُورٖ ۝١٨ وَٱقۡصِدۡ فِي
مَشۡيِكَ وَٱغۡضُضۡ مِن صَوۡتِكَۚ إِنَّ أَنكَرَ

---

30. This can also be translated as follows: "Surely this is a thing requiring great resolve." Those who undertake to reform their fellow beings when they themselves are lacking firm resolve will find the task daunting, for the accomplishment of the task calls for enormous courage and determination.

31. The Qur'ān's words are: *"lā tuṣa‘‘ir khaddaka li al-nās"*. *Ṣa‘r* is a disease that afflicts a camel's neck as a result of which its head is always turned in the same direction. An Arabic idiom states, *"fulān ṣa‘‘ara khaddahū"* (so and so turned his cheek away [like a camel]), meaning that he behaved arrogantly with people, talking to them but keeping his face turned away from them. The same idiom figures in a couplet of the Taghlibite poet ‘Amr ibn Ḥuyayy: "Whenever we found a tyrant who arrogantly turned his face away, we fully removed his crookedness and he became straight." (See Ṭabarī, *Tafsīr*, comments on *Luqmān* 31:18 – Ed.)

32. The Qur'ān here employs the words *mukhtāl* and *fakhūr*. The former denotes an arrogant person who thinks too highly of himself. The latter denotes someone who boasts about his greatness before others. A person's gait manifests arrogance, overweening and haughtiness when he is puffed up with pride and superciliousness. Hence why he deliberately walks in a manner that impresses his greatness upon others.

33. Some Qur'ānic scholars interpret this to mean that one's walk should be neither too brisk nor too slow; rather, it should be at a moderate pace. It is clear from the context, however, that what is meant here is not walking in the physical sense of the term. The fact is that moral judgements regarding good and bad are not applicable to the pace at which one walks, be it fast or slow. Whenever a person has to finish some

task quickly he is bound to walk fast. On the other hand, anyone who is on a stroll might well be inclined to walk slowly. There is nothing morally wrong about one or the other and it is difficult to lay down any universal rule as to what constitutes a "moderate" pace of walking.

The real objective of this directive is to bring about reform in man's inner state. As long as this state remains vitiated, man's external behaviour reflects it, even in the way he walks. If someone is arrogant, this inevitably manifests from his gait. Furthermore, a person's gait precisely betrays the kind of arrogance he suffers from. Wealth, power, beauty, knowledge, authority and such other things make man arrogant and each kind of arrogance gives rise to a particular kind of gait. On the other hand, manifestations of excessive humbleness and self-abasement in one's gait also stem from a debased psychological state. At times, it is a person's suppressed feeling of pride that prompts him to make a show of utter austerity and devotion to God and this is displayed in his gait. In other cases, a person is so overpowered by adverse circumstances in this worldly life that he feels utterly frustrated and loses self-esteem. As a result, his gait becomes devoid of all zest and energy. Luqmān's advice is that man should mend his mental and psychological state and walk in a dignified way, neither strutting with overweening nor parading an artificial display of meekness.

The way the Companions of the Prophet (peace be on him) felt about this issue is illustrated by the following incident. Once ʿUmar saw someone walking with his head downcast. He said to him: "Come on! Walk with your head upright. Islam is not sick."* Likewise, he censured someone who was walking languidly: "O miscreant! Why are you deadening our faith."** In ʿUmar's view, religiosity did not consist in walking listlessly as though one were sick. He resented anyone who wore a cloak of artificial humility. Indeed, he considered that this made-up meekness depicted a distorted image of Islam before others and further that it gave rise to an inert and sluggish attitude among the Muslims.

A similar incident is also related with regard to ʿĀ'ishah. Once she spotted someone walking in a manner that suggested he was utterly debilitated. She asked what had happened to him and was told that he was one of the *qurrā'*. Thereupon she exclaimed: "ʿUmar was the most prominent of the *qurrā'*, and yet when he walked, he walked swiftly: when he spoke, he was heard; and when he thrashed, he caused pain." (See Ālūsī, *Rūḥ al-Maʿānī*, comments on *Luqmān* 31:19 – Ed.) (For further

* and ** We were unable to trace the source of these statements. However, a statement close in spirit to these statements is found in Ibn Kathīr, *Tafsīr*, comments on *al-Furqān* 25:63: It is narrated about ʿUmar that he saw a young man walking sluggishly. He said: 'What's the matter with you? Are you sick?' The man said: 'No'. Thereupon he straightened him up with the whip and ordered him to walk with vigour – Ed.

voices is the braying of the donkey."[34]

ٱلۡأَصۡوَٰتِ لَصَوۡتُ ٱلۡحَمِيرِ ١٩ أَلَمۡ تَرَوۡاْ

(20) Have you not seen that Allah has subjected to your service all that is in the heavens and on the earth[35] and has abundantly bestowed upon you all His bounties, both visible

أَنَّ ٱللَّهَ سَخَّرَ لَكُم مَّا فِي ٱلسَّمَٰوَٰتِ وَمَا فِي ٱلۡأَرۡضِ وَأَسۡبَغَ عَلَيۡكُمۡ نِعَمَهُۥ ظَٰهِرَةً

---

details see *Towards Understanding the Qur'ān*, Vol. V, *Banī Isrā'īl* 17: n. 43, p. 44; and Vol. VII, *al-Furqān* 25: n. 79, pp. 37-38.)

34. The injunction to "lower your voice" does not mean that one must invariably speak in a low pitch and never speak loudly. The example of the donkey's braying in the verse is meant simply to emphasise the point about speaking in a moderate voice. One is, of course, free to raise or lower one's voice, depending on the situation. While talking to those around one and in close proximity, one is naturally expected to speak in a soft voice. On the other hand, one has to raise one's pitch when addressing those at a distance, or when speaking in public.

Tonal variations are naturally made in consonance with the context. A word of praise is delivered differently from a word of a censure, and good-will is expressed in a different way from disapproval. There is obviously nothing wrong in this variation. Luqmān did not counsel his son to altogether disregard the need for tonal variation and invariably speak in a low voice. What is reprehensible, however, is to cry at the top of one's voice in order to humiliate others or to impress others with one's superiority. This is what has been likened to a donkey's braying.

35. A thing can be subjected to someone's service in two ways. First, that the thing be made subservient to him, and he be enabled to use it as he wills. Second, that the thing be made part of a system in such a way that it is endowed with utility and made conducive to serve his interests.

Now, while it is true that everything in the heavens and the earth has been subjected to man's service, not everything has been subjected to that service in a uniform manner. To illustrate, God has subjected air, water, earth, fire, vegetation, minerals, cattle and many other objects to man's service in the sense that he has been given the power to use them

and invisible?[36] Yet some persons dispute regarding Allah[37] without having any knowledge or guidance or any illuminating Book.[38] (21) When they are told: "Follow what Allah has revealed," they say: "We will rather follow that which we have found our forefathers following." (Will they follow that) even though Satan might invite

وَبَاطِنَةً وَمِنَ ٱلنَّاسِ مَن يُجَـٰدِلُ فِى ٱللَّهِ
بِغَيْرِ عِلْمٍ وَلَا هُدًى وَلَا كِتَـٰبٍ مُّنِيرٍ ﴿٢٠﴾
وَإِذَا قِيلَ لَهُمُ ٱتَّبِعُوا۟ مَآ أَنزَلَ ٱللَّهُ قَالُوا۟ بَلْ
نَتَّبِعُ مَا وَجَدْنَا عَلَيْهِ ءَابَآءَنَآ أَوَلَوْ كَانَ
ٱلشَّيْطَـٰنُ يَدْعُوهُمْ

as he wishes. On the other hand, although the sun, the moon, etc., have also been subjected to man's service, this subjection means that they have been invested with utility and have been rendered useable in a manner that is conducive to man's interests.

36. "Visible bounties" denote bounties that are palpable or lie within the range of man's knowledge. "Invisible bounties", on the other hand, are those that are beyond the ken of man's sense perception. Numerous things are at work in man's own body and in the world around him which are conducive to his best interests even though he does not even have the faintest idea as regards the extent of God's arrangements for his protection, sustenance, growth and well-being. As man's research in different fields of science advances, an increasing number of God's hitherto unknown bounties are being unravelled. It is obvious that the bounties that are known so far will appear to be utterly insignificant were we to compare them with those that will become known in the future.

37. They wrangle over questions such as the following: is there a God or not? Is He the only God or is there a multiplicity of gods? What are God's attributes and what is their nature? What is the nature of the relationship between God and His creatures?

38. The unbelievers do not have any source of knowledge that would enable them to observe or experience the reality at first hand. Nor do they have any guide who has informed them of the reality on the basis

them to the chastisement of the Blazing Fire?[39]

(22) Whoever surrenders himself to Allah[40] and lives righteously[41] grasps the most firm handle.[42] The ultimate decision of all matters rests with Allah. (23) So let the unbelief of the unbeliever not grieve you.[43] To Us is their return

إِلَىٰ عَذَابِ ٱلسَّعِيرِ ﴿٢١﴾ ۞ وَمَن يُسۡلِمۡ وَجۡهَهُۥٓ
إِلَى ٱللَّهِ وَهُوَ مُحۡسِنٞ فَقَدِ ٱسۡتَمۡسَكَ
بِٱلۡعُرۡوَةِ ٱلۡوُثۡقَىٰۗ وَإِلَى ٱللَّهِ عَٰقِبَةُ ٱلۡأُمُورِ ﴿٢٢﴾
وَمَن كَفَرَ فَلَا يَحۡزُنكَ كُفۡرُهُۥٓۚ إِلَيۡنَا مَرۡجِعُهُمۡ

---

of direct observation and knowledge. Indeed, they do not possess any Scripture on which they might anchor their beliefs.

39. It is not at all necessary that the ancestors of a person, family or nation were on the right way. The mere fact that some belief or practice can be traced back to the times of someone's forefathers does not necessarily mean that it is also sound. No intelligent person can blindly follow the ways of their forefathers disregarding the possibility that they might have been misguided. Nor should anyone be averse to finding out for themselves what the consequences would be of adhering to those ways.

40. A person should surrender themselves wholly to God and refer all their affairs to Him, treating God's directives as the law for the whole of their lives.

41. That is, one's practical life should conform to righteousness. Submission to God should not be merely a verbal claim while one's actual life is far from being one of obedience and servitude to Him.

42. After one learns how to hold this handle, one is immune to misguidance. Furthermore, one need not entertain any fear of self-destruction providing one truly serves God.

43. This is addressed to the Prophet (peace be on him). He is being told that the unbelievers suffer from the delusion that by rejecting Islam and persisting in unbelief they only cause harm to the Prophet (peace be on him).

and then We shall inform them of all that they did. Surely Allah knows well even the secrets that are hidden in the breasts (of people). (24) We allow them to enjoy themselves a while in the world and then We shall drive them in utter helplessness to a harsh chastisement.

(25) If you were to ask them: "Who created the heavens and the earth?" they will certainly reply: "Allah." Say: "All praise and thanks be to Allah."[44] Yet most of them do not know.[45] (26) All that is in the heavens and the

فَنُنَبِّئُهُم بِمَا عَمِلُوٓاْۚ إِنَّ ٱللَّهَ عَلِيمُۢ بِذَاتِ
ٱلصُّدُورِ ٢٣ نُمَتِّعُهُمۡ قَلِيلٗا ثُمَّ نَضۡطَرُّهُمۡ إِلَىٰ
عَذَابٍ غَلِيظٖ ٢٤ وَلَئِن سَأَلۡتَهُم مَّنۡ خَلَقَ
ٱلسَّمَٰوَٰتِ وَٱلۡأَرۡضَ لَيَقُولُنَّ ٱللَّهُۚ قُلِ
ٱلۡحَمۡدُ لِلَّهِۚ بَلۡ أَكۡثَرُهُمۡ لَا يَعۡلَمُونَ ٢٥
لِلَّهِ مَا فِي ٱلسَّمَٰوَٰتِ

The fact is that by so doing they only hurt themselves. Far from being able to cause any harm to the Prophet (peace be on him), they courted their own destruction. The Prophet (peace be on him) naturally felt grieved by the unbelievers' attitude. Here God apprises him that if the unbelievers persist in disbelieving, he need not torment himself on their account.

44. Even the unbelievers conceded that God alone created the heavens and the earth. Hence why all praise should be exclusively for God because none else has any share in the creation of the universe.

45. Most people do not realise the implications and requirements of belief in God as the sole Creator of the Universe. Nor do they know what is inconsistent with this belief. Once a person recognises that God alone is the Creator of the heavens and the earth, he must also recognize that He is the only Lord, and the Deity Who is exclusively entitled to every kind of worship, obedience and service. Hence why one should not celebrate

earth belongs to Allah.[46] Verily He is All-Sufficient, Immensely Praiseworthy.[47] (27) If all the trees on earth become pens, and the sea replenished by seven more seas were to supply them with ink, the Words of Allah would not be exhausted.[48]

وَٱلْأَرْضِ ۚ إِنَّ ٱللَّهَ هُوَ ٱلْغَنِىُّ ٱلْحَمِيدُ ﴿٢٦﴾
وَلَوْ أَنَّمَا فِى ٱلْأَرْضِ مِن شَجَرَةٍ أَقْلَٰمٌ
وَٱلْبَحْرُ يَمُدُّهُۥ مِنۢ بَعْدِهِۦ سَبْعَةُ أَبْحُرٍ
مَّا نَفِدَتْ كَلِمَٰتُ ٱللَّهِ ۗ

---

the glory or sing the praises of any other than the One True God. All invocations and supplications are also to be addressed only to Him. None but God can be regarded as the Sovereign or Law-Giver of His creatures. It is illogical to recognise someone as the Creator and accept others as objects of worship and service. To do so amounts to rank irrationality, and is as preposterous as simultaneously affirming two mutually contradictory propositions. Such a notion can only be entertained by those who are steeped in ignorance. No sane person is prepared to recognise someone as the Almighty Creator in one breath and regard others, in the next, as having the power to fulfil needs and remove distresses. Nor would such a person prostrate himself in veneration of others than the Creator, nor would they hold anyone other than the One True God as their Sovereign and as One worthy of absolute obedience. To do so would be like being in constant and blatant conflict, all of which is unacceptable to a person of knowledge and understanding.

46. The fact of the matter is not simply that God is the Creator of the heavens and earth, but rather that He is also the Owner of all that exists in the heavens and on earth. It would be idle to fancy that God, after having created the Universe, simply abandoned it, leaving others to claim its ownership, whether wholly or partially, if they so wished. In point of fact it is God alone Who is the Sole Owner of all that He has created. All that exists in the Universe is solely His, and He alone is invested with Divine authority.

47. For its explanation see n. 19 above.

48. "Words of Allah" here stand for the wonders of God's creation and the marvels of His power and wisdom. The same idea is expressed in *Sūrah al-Kahf* 18:109. At the first instance, one might feel that this statement – that were all the trees on earth to become pens and the seas

Verily Allah is Most Mighty, Most Wise. (28) To create all of you or to resurrect all of you is to Him like (creating or resurrecting) a single person. Verily Allah is All-Hearing, All-Seeing.[49]

إِنَّ ٱللَّهَ عَزِيزٌ حَكِيمٌ ﴿٢٧﴾ مَّا خَلْقُكُمْ
وَلَا بَعْثُكُمْ إِلَّا كَنَفْسٍ وَٰحِدَةٍ ۗ إِنَّ ٱللَّهَ
سَمِيعٌۢ بَصِيرٌ ﴿٢٨﴾

---

replenished by seven more seas were to supply them with ink, the Words of Allah would not be exhausted – is an exaggeration. However, on further reflection one realises that there is not the least exaggeration in this statement. For quite literally, if all the trees on earth were to become pens, and the seas, replenished by seven more seas so as to supply them with ink, even this would be insufficient to make a bare catalogue of all that exists in the world, let alone suffice to describe God's power and wisdom. When it is impossible to simply record all that exists on earth, how can we even conceive that man will ever be able to record all that exists in the vast Universe?

This statement drives home the fact that, when compared with Almighty God Who brought this enormous Universe into existence and Who constantly controls it, the puny beings whom people set up as their deities pale into utter insignificance. It is not only that they have no part in the governance of this Universe, but they lack even partial knowledge, let alone have full knowledge of even a small part of God's dominion. Hence, how can it be conceived that they will ever be invested with even a limited share of Divine powers that would enable them to answer prayers and make or mar the destinies of others?

49. God hears all voices and all sounds quite distinctly at one and the same time. He does so in such a way that none of the sounds or voices make Him oblivious of others. In like manner, He simultaneously observes the entire Universe and all objects and events in it in the minutest detail. Yet the observation of these objects does not absorb Him totally so as to prevent Him from observing other objects and events. The same holds true about His causing the birth of human beings and raising them to life after they die. God has the power to resurrect all those who were ever born, right from the beginning of human life until the Last Day. His creating some does not prevent Him from simultaneously creating others. For Him, it is all the same whether He creates a single person or billions of them.

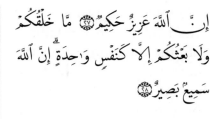

(29) Do you not see that Allah makes the night phase into the day and makes the day phase into the night and has subjected the sun and the moon to His will[50] so that each of them is pursuing its course till an appointed time?[51] (Do you not know that) Allah is well aware of all that you do? (30) All this is because Allah, He alone, is the Truth[52] and all that which they call upon beside Him is false.[53] Surely

أَلَمْ تَرَ أَنَّ ٱللَّهَ يُولِجُ ٱلَّيْلَ فِى ٱلنَّهَارِ وَيُولِجُ
ٱلنَّهَارَ فِى ٱلَّيْلِ وَسَخَّرَ ٱلشَّمْسَ وَٱلْقَمَرَ كُلٌّ
يَجْرِىٓ إِلَىٰٓ أَجَلٍ مُّسَمًّى وَأَنَّ ٱللَّهَ
بِمَا تَعْمَلُونَ خَبِيرٌ ﴿٢٩﴾ ذَٰلِكَ بِأَنَّ ٱللَّهَ
هُوَ ٱلْحَقُّ وَأَنَّ مَا يَدْعُونَ مِن دُونِهِ
ٱلْبَٰطِلُ وَأَنَّ

---

50. The constant alternation of night and day underscores the fact that the sun and the moon are bound in a meticulously regulated system of laws. The sun and the moon are specifically mentioned because from ancient times people have held these two prominent heavenly bodies as objects of worship. In fact, even today many regard them as deities. The truth, however, is that God has subjected all the stars and planets, including the sun and the moon, to an inexorable law from which they cannot deviate even in the slightest.

51. Everything in the Universe pursues its course till its appointed time. Nothing in it is eternal and everlasting, be it the sun, the moon or any other star or planet. Everything came into existence at an appointed time before which it did not exist. Likewise, everything will cease to exist after an appointed time. This truth is highlighted so as to stress that helpless objects, which have had a beginning in time and will have an end at a certain time, can never rightfully become deities.

52. That is, God is the only powerful actor. He is the One Who alone has the power to create things and to manage them.

53. It is only the unbelievers' imagination that had contrived these false deities. They had assumed that such deities had a share in Divinity

Allah, He alone, is All-High, Incomparably Great.[54]

(31) Do you not see that ships sail in the sea by Allah's Grace that He may show you some of His Signs?[55] Surely there are Signs in this for everyone who is steadfast, thankful.[56] (32) When waves engulf them (in the sea) like

ٱللَّهَ هُوَ ٱلۡعَلِيُّ ٱلۡكَبِيرُ ۝٣٠ أَلَمۡ تَرَ أَنَّ ٱلۡفُلۡكَ
تَجۡرِي فِي ٱلۡبَحۡرِ بِنِعۡمَتِ ٱللَّهِ لِيُرِيَكُم مِّنۡ
ءَايَٰتِهِۦٓۚ إِنَّ فِي ذَٰلِكَ لَأٓيَٰتٖ لِّكُلِّ
صَبَّارٖ شَكُورٖ ۝٣١ وَإِذَا غَشِيَهُم مَّوۡجٞ

---

or the power to remove man's distresses and fulfil his needs. In truth, no one and nothing has the power to accomplish any of these, even to the slightest degree.

54. God is All-High and Incomparably Great; when compared to Him, all are lowly and inferior.

55. There are distinct Signs which affirm that all power and authority belong wholly to God. The ships that man builds might be very solid and the extent of his navigational experience might also be immense. Yet, at sea, ships are exposed to such horrendous forces of nature that man's skill and experience alone cannot enable a voyage to be accomplished safely. It is only by dint of God's grace and mercy that man is able to reach the shores of safety. As soon as someone is denied God's gracious protection, he comes to recognise the inadequacy and inefficiency of his own tools and skills. One might be a staunch atheist or a diehard polytheist, but no sooner does one encounter a truly tempestuous storm while at sea than one comes to know that God indeed exists and that He is the only God.

56. People who are steadfast and thankful to God are more likely to perceive the truth of monotheism. Once this truth dawns upon them, they hold fast to it. Steadfastness is their first and foremost trait. They stand out for being constant rather than for having a wavering and vacillating disposition. They adhere to their faith through thick and thin. They are not capricious so that they forget God when they enjoy prosperity and turn to Him in utter humility only when a calamity befalls them. Nor are they

canopies, they call upon Allah, consecrating their faith solely to Him. But when He delivers them safely to the land, some of them become lukewarm.[57] None denies Our Signs except the perfidious, the ungrateful.[58]

كَٱلظُّلَلِ دَعَوُاْ ٱللَّهَ مُخۡلِصِينَ لَهُ ٱلدِّينَ فَلَمَّا
نَجَّىٰهُمۡ إِلَى ٱلۡبَرِّ فَمِنۡهُم مُّقۡتَصِدٞۚ وَمَا يَجۡحَدُ
بِـَٔايَٰتِنَآ إِلَّا كُلُّ خَتَّارٖ كَفُورٖ ٣٢

---

such who revile God when they are struck with affliction. Their second significant attribute is that they are ever thankful to God. They value the bounties He has granted them and they are consistent in expressing gratitude to their Benefactor.

57. The word used here is *muqtaṣid* which is open to more than one meaning. Were we to take *iqtiṣād* to mean rectitude and uprightness, the phrase would mean that even after the crisis is over and the person facing it lands on the shores of safety, he still adheres to *tawḥīd,* something to which he committed himself during his state of crisis. Experiencing such a crisis gave these righteous people constancy in adhering to *tawḥīd*. Alternatively, if the word is taken to signify a medial, moderate attitude, the verse would mean that the crisis they experienced had a moderating effect on some ardent devotees of atheism and polytheism. It may also mean that once the worst is over, people lose a part of their fervour and enthusiasm for God, which had been aroused as a result of the threatening circumstances that had come to surround them.

It is likely that the present verse embraces all these shades of meaning. The point stressed is that people perceive the truth when they are exposed to a severe storm during a sea voyage. In that hour of crisis they abjure both polytheism and atheism and invoke the One True God to help them out of the crisis. However, once God delivers them safely to land, only a few appear to have learnt any lasting lesson from the experience. Even those few can be divided into the following categories: (i) some truly mend their ways; (ii) the disbelief of some becomes somewhat diluted, and (iii) some retain a part of the sincerity engendered by the crisis.

58. These two attributes are sharply opposed to the two attributes mentioned in the verse just above (i.e. verse 31). A perfidious person is one who is prone to treachery and disposed to break his word. As for

(33) O people, fear (the wrath) of your Lord, and dread the Day when no father will stand for his child, nor any child stand for his father.[59] Surely

يَـٰٓأَيُّهَا ٱلنَّاسُ ٱتَّقُوا۟ رَبَّكُمْ وَٱخْشَوْا۟ يَوْمًا لَّا يَجْزِى وَالِدٌ عَن وَلَدِهِۦ وَلَا مَوْلُودٌ هُوَ جَازٍ عَن وَالِدِهِۦ شَيْـًٔا ۚ

an ungrateful person, he is one who never acknowledges the favours done him by his Benefactor, howso numerous they might be. Worse still, he even has the temerity to be rebellious towards his Benefactor. Those tainted with such traits brazenly revert to atheism or polytheism after they have been rescued from the crisis. In this changed state, they deny the Signs of God which they had observed in their own selves and around them at the time they were caught in the storm. They allow themselves to forget that when they had prayed in distress to the One True God, it was because of an intuition deeply ingrained in their very own nature. Atheists might try to explain away their instinctive response to such crises by saying that they were momentarily overcome with weakness. For in their view, it was not God Who rescued them; rather, they were saved because of the different means and devices to which they had resorted. As for polytheists, they attribute their return to safety to the blessings they owe to holy personages whom they revere or to gods and goddesses to whom they are devoted. Accordingly, on reaching the shore they soon take to thanking their false gods by making offerings at their altars. They are totally unable to recall that in their hour of utter despair when they had no one else to turn to, they had called upon The One True God with utmost sincerity and devotion.

59. One's relations with one's friends, leaders, spiritual guides and other such people are not always very close. The closest mutual relation in the world is that found between parents and their offspring. But so horrendous will the Day of Reckoning be that no father will step forward and offer to redeem his son. Nor will any son come to his father's rescue and suffer chastisement on his father's behalf. In such a situation, how can it even be conceived that anyone will volunteer to ruin the everlasting life of the Hereafter for someone else's sake? It would be utterly silly for anyone to destroy his prospects in the Everlasting Life so as to provide worldly benefit to others. It would also be stupid if anyone were to follow the course of sin and error under the illusion that someone else will come to his aid in the Next Life.

Allah's promise is true.[60] So let the life of this world not beguile you,[61] nor let the	إِنَّ وَعْدَ ٱللَّهِ حَقٌّ ۖ فَلَا تَغُرَّنَّكُمُ ٱلْحَيَوٰةُ ٱلدُّنْيَا

At this point one should take into consideration the content of verse 15 above wherein children have been told that while they ought to serve their parents as far as worldly matters are concerned, they should not obey them if they direct them to error in matters pertaining to faith and religion.

60. "Allah's promise" here signifies the promise that resurrection will necessarily occur, that the Day of Resurrection is bound to come, that some day God's Court of Justice will inevitably come to order and everyone will be called to account.

61. The life of this world beguiles the superficially-minded, filling their minds with a variety of misconceptions. Some fall prey to the mistaken notion that everything is confined just to this world, and that there will be no Afterlife. Those who think along these lines believe that there is nothing beyond the grave and, hence, they concentrate on making the most of whatever there is in this world. Intoxicated with wealth, affluence and power, such people completely forget the inevitability of death, victims as they are of the delusion that luxuriant living, power or authority will endure. Consigning spiritual and moral objectives to oblivion, these people become wholly engrossed in the pursuit of material gain and pleasure, exalting them as ends in themselves. Such people constantly hanker after ever-higher standards of living, relegating everything else to insignificance. They do so disregarding the fact that this wild goose chase for higher standards of living might lead to a lowering in the standard of their humanity. In such an atmosphere, some people even begin to believe that worldly prosperity is the right standard by which to judge what is true and what is false, what is right and what is wrong. Hence they tend to conclude that whatever leads to material prosperity is good and whatever does not lead to it is evil. Some even begin to consider material prosperity an indicator of being blessed with God's approval. They even generalise that he who is successful in this world, regardless of how he has achieved that success, is *ipso facto*, one loved by God. On the contrary, anyone who is ill-off in the world, even if his lack of success might be due to his veraciousness and his being morally scrupulous, is doomed to failure even in the Next World.

According to this Qur'ānic verse, these and all such misconceptions are the guiles of this world.

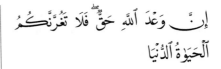

Deluder delude you about Allah.[62]

(34) Surely Allah alone has the knowledge of the Hour. It is He Who sends down the rain and knows what is in the wombs, although no person knows what he will earn tomorrow, nor does he know in which land he will die. Indeed,

وَلَا يَغُرَّنَّكُم بِٱللَّهِ ٱلْغَرُورُ ﴿٣٣﴾ إِنَّ ٱللَّهَ
عِندَهُۥ عِلْمُ ٱلسَّاعَةِ وَيُنَزِّلُ ٱلْغَيْثَ وَيَعْلَمُ
مَا فِى ٱلْأَرْحَامِ ۖ وَمَا تَدْرِى نَفْسٌ مَّاذَا
تَكْسِبُ غَدًا ۖ وَمَا تَدْرِى نَفْسٌۢ بِأَىِّ
أَرْضٍ تَمُوتُ ۚ

62. "The Deluder" could be Satan himself, a single person, a group of people, one's own base self, or any other object that deludes man. The reason for using the word "deluder" here in its generality, without specifying any particular person or thing, is that the basic cause of each person's delusion is different. Every person's deluder is that which leads him astray, that which causes his life to take a turn in the wrong direction.

The Qur'ānic command not to "let the Deluder delude you about Allah" embraces a whole range of deception and befooling. Some are befooled by a deluder who encourages them to believe that God does not exist. Some are led to believe that after having created the world, God retired into isolation, leaving the world to the tender mercy of His creatures. The deluder of others makes them fancy that some people are so dear to God that anyone who curries favour with them might act similarly and feel assured that God will necessarily forgive him. Others are deluded into believing that since God is Forgiving and Merciful, they can go about sinning to their heart's fill for God will continue to pardon them. The deluder also makes some subscribe to determinism. This makes them convinced that if they commit evil they are helpless for it is God Who makes them do so. Furthermore, if they shun good works, this too is because God does not enable them to do good works.

There are innumerable delusions of this kind to which humans fall prey. Yet the basic cause behind all man's intellectual waywardness, for all his sins and crimes is that he is a victim of delusion, of one kind or the other. It is only when he falls prey to such delusions that he becomes enmeshed in erroneous beliefs.

Allah is All-Knowing, All-Aware.[63]	إِنَّ ٱللَّهَ عَلِيمٌ خَبِيرٌ ﴿٣٤﴾

63. This verse is, in fact, a response to the question the unbelieving Makkans used to ask the Prophet (peace be on him) about when the Last Day would occur. They raised this question whenever he tried to explain to them the doctrines about the Last Day and the Hereafter. At times the Qur'ān responds to this by specifically mentioning the question, while at other times, it responds without mentioning it. The present verse is of the latter kind.

"Surely Allah alone has the knowledge of the Hour" is the core reply to the question. The statements in this verse that follow provide evidentiary support to this reply. It is clearly stated that man does not even have knowledge of some of the matters that are of the utmost interest to him. This being so, how can he know for sure when this whole Universe will come to an end?

Let us consider some of the obvious limitations of man's knowledge. For instance, man's material prosperity and adversity depend mainly on rainfall, yet rainfall is totally under God's control. God causes rain to fall as and when and in the quantity that He wills. He stops it, again at His will. Man does not know where and when it will rain and in what quantity. Nor does man know which part of the earth will remain deprived of rainfall; nor yet, for which part of the earth rainfall would be harmful. Consider another case: a woman becomes pregnant with her husband's seed. This is the process that perpetuates man's progeny. Yet neither the husband nor the wife is aware as regards the foetus being nurtured in the womb and what its shape and its good and bad qualities will be at the time it is born. In fact, man does not even know what his next day will be like. A sudden accident can change the entire course of his life. Yet he cannot anticipate that accident even by just a minute before it occurs. Man does not even know where he will breathe his last. All these crucial bits of knowledge rest only with God, man being denied the least bit of such knowledge. Man would, of course, love to have such knowledge to hand so that he can prepare himself to deal with the resultant situations. Yet he has no other option but to be content with the fact that it is God's will that prevails in his as in all other cases. In like manner, there is no other course for man but to have faith in God's Will as the sole determinant of the Last Hour. No precise knowledge of that Hour has been divulged to anyone nor will it be so divulged in the future.

It is pertinent to note that the present verse does not provide an exhaustive list of the matters that belong to the realm of the Unseen, of matters that are known to God alone. This verse mentions only a few examples for illustrative purposes. It states certain matters that are of vital concern to man but about which he is still in the dark. It would be wrong to assume that only these five matters mentioned here are in God's exclusive knowledge. *Ghayb* (the Unseen) comprises all things that lie beyond the range of man's knowledge and which are exclusively known to God. The range of *ghayb* in this sense is vast; it is veritably limitless. (For further elaboration see *Towards Understanding the Qur'ān,* Vol. IV, *Sūrah al-Naḥl* 16: n. 83, p. 354.)

Sūrah 32

Al-Sajdah

(Prostration)

(Makkan Period)

Title

The word *sajdah* (prostration) occurs in verse 15 of this *sūrah*. The *sūrah*'s title is, thus, derived from that reference.

Period of Revelation

The stylistic features of the *sūrah* seem to indicate that it must have been revealed in the early part of the middle Makkan period. This, because the discourse does not seem to be set against the backdrop of the Muslims' severe persecution which underlies the later Makkan *sūrahs*.

Subject Matter and Themes

The *sūrah* aims to dispel people's doubts about the Islamic doctrines of monotheism, the Hereafter and Prophethood and invites them to believe in them. The Makkan unbelievers used to say, among themselves, that the Prophet (peace be on him) made up and then propagated strange things. He announced, for example, what would happen after death: that people will be resurrected after they had been absorbed into the earth, that they will have to face a reckoning and that there is a Paradise and Hell. He also stressed that their gods and goddesses and their holy men were of no consequence. Instead, the One True God should be the sole object of their worship and devotion. He also claimed that he was God's Messenger who received revelation from on high and that what he expounded was the Word of God rather than his own. Strange indeed were the things, they said, he sought to instruct them in. The *sūrah* thus focuses on responding to the unbelievers' contentions.

The unbelievers were asked in the *sūrah* to reflect on the truths propounded by the Qur'ān. They were also asked to consider the working of the heavens and the earth and to ponder over their births, their structures and constitutions. Do these not bear out the veracity of the Prophet's message given to them through the Qur'ān? Does the working of the Universe provide any rational basis to affirm the existence of One God or is it of a multiplicity of gods? Is reflection on the Universal system as a whole not sufficient to persuade one to believe that He Who created human beings in the first instance certainly has the power to create them again?

The *sūrah* graphically portrays what will happen in the Hereafter. After giving people tidings of the rewards they will receive if they choose to believe and warning them of the dire consequences they will face if they choose to disbelieve, the Qur'ān exhorts them to give up unbelief before they are overtaken by its evil consequences. They are also urged to embrace the teachings of the Qur'ān, which are conducive to their own well-being in the World-to-Come.

They are then told that God, out of His Mercy, does not seize the wrong-doers instantly after they commit wrongs, inflicting grievous punishment on them. Rather, He subjects them only to minor losses, sufferings and adversities. These are intended to alert them and arouse them from their state of negligence and heedlessness. If a person wakes up as a result of these minor sufferings and injuries it is all the better for him.

The unbelievers are then told that the Scripture was not being sent to the Prophet Muḥammad (peace be on him) for the first time in history. After all, the Arabs knew that in the past the Prophet Moses (peace be on him) had received the Scripture. Thus, there was no justification for them making a big fuss about the Qur'ān's revelation. They are, however, emphatically told that the Qur'ān is certainly the Word of God; that what had happened in Moses' time as far as revelation from God is concerned had been repeated with the Prophet Muḥammad (peace be on him). Leadership from now on would be entrusted only to those who believed in the Scripture revealed to the Prophet Muḥammad (peace be on him). As for those who rejected it, their fate was sealed.

The unbelievers' attention is then drawn to the ruins of those earlier nations that they encountered when traversing their trade routes. They are asked to ponder the tragic end of those evil-doing nations and to consider whether they would like to follow in their footsteps, meeting the same fate. They are also asked not to be swayed by the glittering appearance of things. True, at the time none but a few youths, slaves and poor people paid heed to the Prophet's message and a torrent of taunts and ridicule was showered upon such believers from all directions. All this had led many people to believe that Islam would not endure; that in a short while it would flop. But all this was sheer misperception. For we find over and over again that highly unexpected changes occur in the annals of history. Could the unbelievers not observe that a patch of land that had lain dead up until a moment ago was suddenly revived by a little rainfall whereby the earth began to pour out its treasure of luxuriant vegetation?

At the end of the *sūrah*, the Prophet (peace be on him) is told that the unbelievers mock his teachings. Furthermore, they derisively ask him when he will achieve the decisive victory he has been predicting. In response, the unbelievers are told that when the Day to judge between the believers and unbelievers comes, the time for acceptance of the Prophet's teaching will already have passed. So now is the right time to accept his teaching. However, if they are keen to see God's final decision, they should bide their time.

In the name of Allah, the Most Merciful, the Most Compassionate.

بِسْمِ ٱللَّهِ ٱلرَّحْمَٰنِ ٱلرَّحِيمِ

(1) *Alif. Lām. Mīm.* (2) This Book, beyond all doubt, was revealed by the Lord of the Universe.[1]

الٓمٓ ﴿١﴾ تَنزِيلُ ٱلْكِتَٰبِ لَا رَيْبَ فِيهِ
مِن رَّبِّ ٱلْعَٰلَمِينَ ﴿٢﴾

1. Several Qur'ānic *sūrahs* open with an introductory statement of the kind we find here, the purpose of it being to identify the true source of the Qur'ān. This introductory statement seems to be similar to the announcement made before the commencement of a radio station's broadcast, whereby its specifics are identified. Notwithstanding this apparent similarity, the Qur'ānic declaration about its provenance is much more significant. For when it is proclaimed at the very outset of a Qur'ānic *sūrah* that the message comes from the Lord of the Universe, this not only indicates the origin and true source of the Qur'ān, but also amounts to making a colossal claim, to hurling a stupendous challenge and to issuing a grim warning to the audience.

It is declared right away that the Qur'ān is not a product of the human mind; rather, it is the Word of God. This declaration instantly places a grave question before man: should he believe this claim as true, or should he reject it as false? If one affirms its Divine origin, one has to surrender oneself to it in obedience. In this case, one no longer enjoys the freedom to act as one pleases. On the other hand, if one rejects it, one exposes oneself to serious hazard. For, if the Qur'ān indeed is the Word of God, one's wilful rejection of it will lead to eternal perdition. In this respect, this opening declaration puts one on high alert, impels one to pay full heed to the discourse, and, thereafter, prompts one to decide whether it is the Word of God or not.

Here, however, it has not simply been stated that the Qur'ān was revealed by the Lord of the Universe. Instead, the assertion is couched in highly emphatic terms: "This Book, beyond all doubt, was revealed by the Lord of the Universe", a statement that leaves no room for uncertainty about its Divine provenance. Were one to consider this assertion in the circumstantial setting of the Qur'ān's revelation and in the overall context of the Qur'ān's teaching, it is evident that the claim contains within itself its own supporting evidence.

This was not hidden from the Qur'ān's immediate audience – the Makkans. This because they were thoroughly familiar with the life and conduct of its recipient, the Prophet Muḥammad (peace be on him) – both

(3) Or do they say:[2] "He has fabricated it?"[3] Nay, it is	أَمْ يَقُولُونَ ٱفْتَرَىٰهُ ۚ بَلْ هُوَ

before and after this Book was revealed to him. They knew him to be the most honest, trustworthy, earnest and sincere member of their community, one who possessed an absolutely unblemished character. It was also well-known to them that before expounding the Qur'ān and claiming to be God's Messenger, he had never uttered anything similar to what he suddenly began to expound after his designation as God's Messenger. They were also cognizant of the unmistakable difference between the Prophet's own utterances and the Qur'ān. They knew that stylistically the two were poles apart. They also realised that it was impossible for someone to adopt and master both these distinct styles, one that characterised his own utterances and the other that characterised the Qur'ān.

The miraculous features of the Qur'ān as a literary text were also not lost on them. Being well-versed in their own language, Arabic, they could clearly perceive that the Qur'ān was beyond the ability of their best poets and litterateurs to compose. The vast difference between the Qur'ān and the compositions of their poets, soothsayers and orators was also quite apparent to them. They could fully appreciate how noble and sublime the contents of the Qur'ān were. It was also beyond them to identify any selfish motive in the Book or in its recipient of the kind that is noticeable in the works and claims of imposters. Even after a microscopic scrutiny of the Prophet's life it was impossible for them to say that the Prophet's mission was motivated by any desire to acquire benefit for himself, his family, his clan, or his tribe. It was perfectly obvious that he had no personal axe to grind and no material benefit in mind. Moreover, his audience also witnessed the wholesome changes that were manifest in the lives of those who were attracted towards and accepted the Prophet's message.

Taken together, these facts constituted a strong argument to confirm the veracity of the Prophet's claim as God's Messenger. Seen against this backdrop, it becomes clear how perfectly appropriate it was to assert that the Qur'ān was, *beyond all doubt*, revealed by the Lord of the Universe. The reasons for the assertion were so evident that explicitly adducing any further argument to support the assertion was unnecessary.

2. After making this introductory statement, the very first objection that the Makkan polytheists put forward against the Prophet Muḥammad's claim to be God's Messenger is taken up for examination.

3. This is not merely an interrogative statement, it also expresses a strong sense of astonishment at the unbelievers' implied charge that the Prophet (peace be on him) himself had fabricated the Qur'ān. The purpose

the Truth from your Lord[4] so that you may warn a	ٱلْحَقُّ مِن رَّبِّكَ لِتُنذِرَ

of the statement was to emphasise that the unbelievers were making an audacious claim, one that completely disregarded the myriad facts that established the Qur'ān as God's Word beyond all doubt, for it was simply out of the question that the Prophet (peace be on him) had made it up and then falsely attributed it to God. How come they felt no shame in making such absurd and baseless claims? Why were they not even deterred by what opinions others who thoroughly knew the Prophet (peace be on him) would think of them? After all, these people well knew the task in which he was engaged, the message he was giving to his people, and the Book he had brought.

4. In the previous verse (v. 2) it was deemed enough to say merely that this Book had, "beyond all doubt, been revealed by the Lord of the Universe". The truth of the statement that the Qur'ān had been revealed by God was so obvious that no further evidence was needed to reinforce it. Likewise, in the present verse we find that in order to refute the allegation that it had been fabricated it was considered sufficient to simply say the Qur'ān, that is the "Truth from your Lord".

The reason for this is the same as has been explained in note 1 above. People knew all there was to know about the great person who had brought the Book, the milieu and the dignified manner in which he expounded it. Moreover, the Makkans were also witnesses to the high literary quality of the Qur'ān, to the sublimity of its content, and to its wholesome impact on the lives of the people who accepted the Prophet's teachings. In view of all this, the Qur'ān's being the "Truth from your Lord" was so patently evident that it only needed to be so stated in order to repudiate the unbelievers' allegations regarding its fabrication. Were one to proffer arguments to establish its Divine provenance, instead of strengthening that might in fact weaken the claim. This can be illustrated by the following example. Suppose the sun is shining and someone contends that it is both dark and night. Here, one does not need to adduce specious arguments to establish the manifest truth that the sun is shining. It is enough to respond to such a brazenly absurd contention by simply saying: "Do you claim this to be night, when a radiant, sunny day is right in front of you?" When something is so evident, any attempt to put forward logical and rational arguments to prove it, in fact fail to lend any support to it. If anything, the arguments might weaken the force of a simple statement expressing a very evident fact.

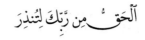

people to whom no warner came before you; perhaps they will be guided to the Right Way.[5]

قَوْمًا مَّآ أَتَـٰهُم مِّن نَّذِيرٍ مِّن قَبْلِكَ لَعَلَّهُمْ يَهْتَدُونَ ﴿٣﴾

5. Apart from being the Truth and being from God, the other evidently distinct features of the Qur'ān are its being based on wisdom and its being a blessing for those to whom it was addressed. The people of Arabia knew that no Messenger had come to them for centuries. They were also well aware that their nation had been subjected to ignorance, moral degeneration and backwardness for a long time. There was, then, no reason for them to be astonished at the advent of a Messenger in their midst for the purpose of directing them to the Right Way. In fact the raising of a Messenger among them was what they sorely needed. God had fulfilled this need by sending the Prophet Muḥammad (peace be on him) and this was for their own good.

It is pertinent to note that the true faith preached earlier in Arabia was by the Prophets Hūd and Ṣāliḥ (peace be on them). Both of them belonged to pre-historical times. However, around 2,500 years before the Prophet Muḥammad's advent, the Prophets Abraham and Ishmael (peace be on them) were sent to the people of Arabia. They were followed by the Prophet Shu'ayb (peace be on him), who was the last Messenger raised among them before the advent of the Prophet Muḥammad (peace be on him). However, two thousand years had already elapsed since the time of Shu'ayb (peace be on him).

It was, therefore, quite justifiable to say that no warner had come to the people of Arabia. The present verse, however, does not mean quite literally that no warner had ever come to them; rather, the purpose of the statement is to stress that this had been the case for a very long time and so the people of Arabia were in need of a warner.

Here, another question arises and this ought to be resolved before proceeding further. While studying this verse one is likely to countenance the question: on what basis will the Arabs, who had lived during the centuries of *Jāhilīyah*, a period during which no Messenger came to them, be called to account by God in the Hereafter? This because they did not know True Guidance from error. Hence, if they fell into error, how can they be held accountable for it?

This problem is resolved when we bear in mind that while the people of Arabia of the *Jāhilīyah* period might not have had an extensive knowledge of the true faith, they knew well enough that monotheism represents the truth and that the earlier Prophets never endorsed idolatry.

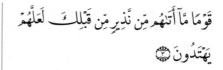

This was part of the Arab tradition, one that had come down to them from the Prophets of yore and in their own land. They also knew that monotheism was taught by the Prophets Moses, David, Solomon and Jesus (peace be on them) who were raised in lands adjacent to Arabia. It was also well-known that the Arabs of the past had followed the Abrahamic faith, and that idolatry had been introduced among them at a much later date by ʿAmr ibn Luḥayy.

Notwithstanding the prevalence of polytheism and idolatry in the Arabian Peninsula on the eve of the Prophet's advent, there were still many noble souls in different parts of Arabia who proclaimed their adherence to monotheism. Such people publicly condemned sacrificial offerings made to idols. A little before the Prophet's advent, one comes across a large number of people of this orientation known as Ḥunafā' such as Quss ibn Sāʿidah al-Iyādī, Umayyah ibn Abī al-Ṣalt, Suwayd ibn ʿAmr al-Muṣṭaliqī, Wakīʿ ibn Salamah ibn Zuhayr al-Iyādī, ʿAmr ibn Jundub al-Juhanī, Abū Qays Ṣarmah ibn Abī Anas, Zayd ibn ʿAmr ibn Nufayl, Waraqah ibn Nawfal, ʿUthmān ibn al-Ḥuwayrith ibn Jaḥsh, ʿĀmir ibn al-Ẓarb al-ʿAdwānī, ʿAllāf ibn Shihāb al-Tamīmī, al-Mutalammis ibn Umayyah al-Kinānī, Zuhayr ibn Abī Sulmā, Khālid ibn Sinān ibn Ghayth al-ʿAbsī, ʿAbd Allāh al-Quḍāʿī and others.

The *ḥunafā'* openly proclaimed monotheism to be the true faith and strongly dissociated themselves from the creed of the Arab polytheists. This, thus, indicates the impact of the vestiges of earlier Prophets' teachings. Furthermore, the inscriptions discovered in the course of modern archaeological research in Yemen of the fourth and fifth centuries, confirm that a monotheistic creed had currency in South Arabia. Adherents of this monotheistic faith recognised *al-Raḥmān* and the "Lord of the heavens and the earth" as the only True God. An inscription of 378 C.E., excavated from the ruins of a place of worship, reads as follows: "This place of worship has been built for the worship of God, the Lord of the heavens." In another inscription of 465 C.E., we find the words of similar import: ((بنصر وردأ الهن بعل سمين وأرضين (بنصر وبعون الإله ربّ السمّاء والأرض)).

All this points to the vogue of monotheism and is an indication of belief in the Most Compassionate God. Another inscription of 512 C.E. was discovered at Zabad, which is located between the River Euphrates and Qinnaṣrīn in northern Arabia. It reads as follows: "In the name of God. There is no power except His and no thanks are due to any except to Him." All this conclusively establishes that prior to the Prophet Muḥammad's advent the teachings of the earlier Prophets had not been altogether reduced to oblivion. Not all traces of the past had been erased. There was still much in Arabia to remind people that their God was One. (For further details see *Towards Understanding the Qur'ān*, Vol. VII, *al-Furqān* 25: n. 84, pp. 40-41.)

(4) It is Allah[6] Who created the heavens and the earth and all that is between the two, in six days, and then He established Himself on the Throne.[7] You have no guardian or intercessor other than He. Will you, then, not take heed?[8] (5) He governs from the heaven to the earth and then the record (of this governance) goes up to Him in a day whose measure is

ٱللَّهُ ٱلَّذِى خَلَقَ ٱلسَّمَٰوَٰتِ وَٱلْأَرْضَ
وَمَا بَيْنَهُمَا فِى سِتَّةِ أَيَّامٍ ثُمَّ ٱسْتَوَىٰ عَلَى
ٱلْعَرْشِ ۖ مَا لَكُم مِّن دُونِهِۦ مِن وَلِىٍّ
وَلَا شَفِيعٍ ۚ أَفَلَا تَتَذَكَّرُونَ ﴿٤﴾ يُدَبِّرُ
ٱلْأَمْرَ مِنَ ٱلسَّمَآءِ إِلَى ٱلْأَرْضِ ثُمَّ يَعْرُجُ
إِلَيْهِ فِى يَوْمٍ كَانَ مِقْدَارُهُۥٓ

---

6. Here, another objection put forward by the Makkan polytheists against the Prophet's call to monotheism is taken up for examination. The Makkans were incensed by the Prophet's denial of the Divinity of their idols and holy men and by his pronouncement that none besides the One True God was their deity. They were further incensed that he said no one other than He could dispose of their needs, heed their prayers, and remove their distresses, and that there was no Lord other than He Who had absolute power and authority.

7. For further elaboration see *al-Aʿrāf* 7:54; *Yūnus* 10:3 and *al-Raʿd* 13:2.

8. Their true God is He Who created the heavens and the earth. The unbelievers are grossly mistaken in believing that anyone other than He has any share in the authority of God, the Creator of the Universe and of all that is in it. Everything and everyone other than God is necessarily a created being. Moreover, God has not retired from the scene after having created the Universe. He fully remains the Lord and Master, the Sovereign and Ruler of His Universe. How foolish it is, then, on the unbelievers' part to consider created beings to be in control of their destiny! If God does not come to their rescue in their hour of distress, who has the power to rescue them? By the same token, if God seizes them with punishment, who has the power to secure their release? If God decides not to entertain someone's intercession, who has the power to thrust that intercession on Him?

a thousand years in your reckoning.[9] (6) He knows all that is beyond as well as all that is within a creature's sense-perception.[10] He is

أَلْفَ سَنَةٍ مِّمَّا تَعُدُّونَ ۝ ذَٰلِكَ عَـٰلِمُ
ٱلْغَيْبِ وَٱلشَّهَـٰدَةِ

9. This means that a thousand years of man's history are no more than a day in God's reckoning. The tasks God entrusts His angels with on a particular day are completed by them before they are given further tasks for the following day. Such a day, however, is equal to a thousand years according to human computation.

This idea is also expressed in two other places in the Qur'ān. One can better comprehend what is being said here by considering the relevant verses. The unbelieving Arabs used to say that the Prophet (peace be on him) had been warning them for years that their rejection of his call would bring about God's scourge on them. Despite repeated statements to this effect over the course of several years, no scourge struck them. This even though they had repeatedly rejected the Prophet's message in quite categorical terms. Had the Prophet's warnings been true, they contented, they should have been annihilated long ago. The Qur'ān responded to this by saying: "They ask you to hasten the punishment. Allah shall most certainly not fail His promise; but a Day with your Lord is a thousand years of your reckoning", (*al-Ḥajj* 22:47). At another place, the Qur'ān says: "A beseecher besought the visitation of chastisement, (a chastisement meant) for the unbelievers, one which none can avert; a chastisement from Allah, the Lord of the ascending steps, by which the angels and the spirit ascend to Him in one Day, the duration of which is fifty thousand years. So, (O Prophet), persevere with gracious perseverance. Verily they think that the chastisement is far off, while We think that it is near at hand." (*Al-Maʿārij* 70:1-7.)

These statements drive home the point that God's decisions do not necessarily conform to human computations of time. If a nation is warned of disastrous consequences because of following a particular course of action, it would be altogether puerile to interpret this warning to mean that the evil consequence of its misconduct will invite a scourge upon it the very next day. The evil consequences of its misconduct might come to the surface not just after some months or some years, but possibly after centuries.

10. Creatures know only a little. Numerous things are beyond the ken of their knowledge. Of these creatures – be they angels, *jinn*, prophets, saints or pious people – none is All-Knowing. Omniscience is

the Most Mighty,[11] the Most Compassionate,[12] (7) He Who excelled in the creation of all that He created.[13] He originated the creation of man from clay, (8) then made his progeny from the extract of a mean fluid,[14] (9) then He	ٱلْعَزِيزُ ٱلرَّحِيمُ ۝٦ ٱلَّذِىٓ أَحْسَنَ كُلَّ شَىْءٍ خَلَقَهُۥ ۖ وَبَدَأَ خَلْقَ ٱلْإِنسَـٰنِ مِن طِينٍ ۝٧ ثُمَّ جَعَلَ نَسْلَهُۥ مِن سُلَـٰلَةٍ مِّن مَّآءٍ مَّهِينٍ ۝٨ ثُمَّ

an attribute that is exclusively God's. Everything is known to Him, be it something that happened in the past, or occurs today, or will take place in the future.

11. He is the One Who prevails over all else. There is no power to resist His will or to prevent the fulfilment of His command. Everything is subservient to God and none has the power to oppose Him.

12. Despite being Most Mighty and having overwhelming power, God does not wrong anyone; rather, He is Most Merciful and Most Clement towards His creatures.

13. God's creations in the Universe are innumerable. Of them, none is flawed or blemished, or out of tune with the overall scheme of things. On the contrary, each object has an elegance and grace of its own; each is well proportioned and in its proper place. God has created everything in the best shape and has invested it with the most suitable features. For instance, one cannot even imagine a better shape than that of eyes and ears for seeing and hearing. Air and water are also there for the purpose for which they have been created. Water is possessed of all the features required of it. Man cannot identify any flaw in God's grand design. Nor is it possible for him to suggest any improvement in His scheme of things.

14. God first brought man into being by an act of direct creation and then equipped him with procreative powers, thereby ensuring the continuity of the human race. God's creative power was manifest first in investing the elements drawn from the earth with life, consciousness and reason as a result of which a species as wonderful as man came into being. God's next wondrous act was that He installed an amazing reproductive machinery within man's own body. The structure and function of this machinery are simply mind-boggling.

duly proportioned him,[15] and breathed into him of His spirit,[16] and bestowed upon you ears and eyes	سَوَّىٰهُ وَنَفَخَ فِيهِ مِن رُّوحِهِۦۖ وَجَعَلَ لَكُمُ ٱلسَّمْعَ وَٱلْأَبْصَـٰرَ

This Qur'ānic verse clearly affirms the direct creation of the first man. Scientists under the spell of Darwin's theory raise their eyebrows at the very notion of man's direct creation. Yet they cannot deny the direct creation of the first living cell, if not of man then of other species of living beings. For in the absence of the direct creation of the first living cell, one would have to accept that life began by sheer accident. Even a single cell creature, notwithstanding its simple appearance, is so complex, delicate and replete with such wisdom that it would be patently foolish to consider it to have come into being accidentally rather than by God's command. Such a notion is much more unscientific and illogical than the concept of direct creation which the adherents of the theory of evolution find hard to digest. Furthermore, once it is affirmed that the first living cell came into existence by an act of direct creation, there is no difficulty in believing that the first member of every living species owes its existence to God's direct creation, followed by varying forms of procreative arrangements.

This idea resolves all the vexing problems that emanate from the well-known missing links and other gaps that riddle the Darwinian theory of evolution. (For further discussion of the issue, see *Towards Understanding the Qur'ān*, Vol. I, *Āl ʿImrān* 3: n. 54, p.260; Vol. II, *al-Nisā'* 4: n. 1, p. 5 and *al-Anʿām* 6: n. 63, p. 258; Vol. III, *al-Aʿrāf* 7: nn. 10 and 145, pp. 7-10 and 107; Vol. IV, *al-Ḥijr* 15: n. 17, pp. 288-289; Vol. VI, *al-Ḥajj* 22: n. 5, p. 7, and *al-Mu'minūn* 23: nn. 12-13, pp. 87-88.)

15. God causes the sperm – microscopic though its volume is – to grow into a full-fledged human being along with his various limbs and internal organs.

16. The word "spirit" here does not merely denote the life owing to which the body of a living being is activated; rather, it signifies a specific essence comprised of intellect, consciousness, reason, discernment, choice and free-will. It is by dint of these that man is distinguished from all other species of earthly creatures and is invested with a specific personality, individuality, and God's vicegerency.

God has identified that this "spirit" is His. This could be either in the sense in which any other thing is mentioned as belonging to its owner.

and hearts.[17] And yet, little thanks do you give.[18] | وَٱلْأَفْـِٔدَةَ قَلِيلًا مَّا تَشْكُرُونَ ۝٩

Alternatively, it might mean that the qualities of knowledge, reflection, cognition, volition, judgement and authority which characterise man are reflections of God's qualities. These qualities are not derived from matter; rather, they are attributable to God Himself. Man's knowledge is derived from God's knowledge. Likewise, man's wisdom and authority are also derived from God's wisdom and authority. In other words, these qualities have no other source but God Himself. (For further explanation see *Towards Understanding the Qur'ān*, Vol. IV, *al-Ḥijr* 15: nn. 17-19, pp. 288-290.)

17. There is great subtlety in this statement. Before mentioning God's breathing of His spirit into man, all references to him are in the third person – that God originally created man from clay, that He then made man's progeny from the extract of a mean fluid, and that He duly proportioned him. Even after all this was accomplished, man was still not worthy of being addressed by God. However, as soon as man was infused with God's spirit, he assumed a distinct identity making him worthy of direct address from God. He is then told that God has "bestowed *upon you* ears and eyes and hearts". This transition from the use of the third to the second person pronoun is significant.

The words "ears" and "eyes" here represent the means through which man obtains knowledge. Doubtlessly, man has also been endowed with the senses of taste, touch, and smell. Still, sight and hearing are more important than the other means of sense perception. Accordingly, the Qur'ān speaks of these two as God's great bounties. This is followed by mentioning that man has been granted *qalb* (heart), which indeed signifies "mind". In Qur'ānic parlance *qalb* signifies the faculty that sifts and arranges the information acquired through the senses, draws conclusions from it, chooses one of various possible courses of action, and then decides to follow it.

18. Man is told that he was not granted something so immensely valuable as spirit and other highly noble characteristics merely to enable him to live in the world like animals, pursuing a scheme of life that befits brutes. Instead, man was granted eyes so that he might have insight into the truth, rather than being blind to it. He was granted ears to pay heed to the call of the truth rather than being deaf to it. He was also granted a "heart" in order to comprehend the truth and choose the right course of thought and action rather than to pander to his animal instincts, or to use them to weave perfidious philosophies and chalk out programmes

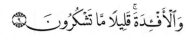

(10) They say:[19] "Shall we be created afresh after we have become lost in the earth?" Nay, the fact is that they deny that they will meet their Lord.[20] (11) Tell them: "The angel of death who has been charged with

وَقَالُوٓا۟ أَءِذَا ضَلَلْنَا فِى ٱلْأَرْضِ أَءِنَّا لَفِى خَلْقٍ
جَدِيدٍۭ ۚ بَلْ هُم بِلِقَآءِ رَبِّهِمْ كَـٰفِرُونَ ﴿١٠﴾
۞ قُلْ يَتَوَفَّىٰكُم مَّلَكُ ٱلْمَوْتِ ٱلَّذِى وُكِّلَ

of rebellion against his Creator. It is possible that after receiving all these enormous bounties from God, man might succumb to polytheism or atheism, or fall prey to deifying himself or any of God's other creatures, or he may idolize his carnal desires and immerse himself in sensual pleasures. If he does any of these, this amounts to his declaring that he is altogether unworthy of the wonderful bounties he received from God, and further that instead of having been created as a human being he might as well have been created as a monkey, a wolf, a crocodile or a crow.

19. After having responded to the unbelievers' objections to the doctrines of monotheism and Prophethood, the discourse is now directed at demolishing their misconceptions about the third major doctrine of Islam – the Hereafter. Verse 10 opens with the phrase "[And] they say", which connects the present paragraph with the previous one. This implies that those who deny that human beings will be raised after death are the very same people who deny that Muḥammad (peace be on him) is God's Messenger and that God is the only deity.

20. There is a subtle gap between the earlier sentence and the present one. Readers are expected to fill this gap, which in fact comprises a great wealth of ideas. The earlier sentence records the unbelievers' objection. The objection is so absurd and preposterous that it is not even worthy of refutation. It is simply stated because its very mention is enough to establish its utter absurdity.

Objections to the doctrine of the Hereafter rest on two contentions and both are flawed, irrational. The unbelievers rejected the concept of resurrection, saying: "Shall we be created afresh after we have become lost in the earth?" But do the beings called "we" here really "become lost in the earth?" Let us consider this. As long as we are alive, several of our bodily limbs may be amputated. Nevertheless, the entity called "we" remains fully intact. No part of that entity is removed alongside

your souls shall gather you, and then you shall be brought back to your Lord."[21]	بِكُمْ ثُمَّ إِلَىٰ رَبِّكُمْ تُرْجَعُونَ ۝١١

the amputated bits. But once the essence of what "we" are comprised of is extracted from our body, then although we still see the body, the entity called "we" ceases to exist. Hence, once this happens, even the most ardent lover carries his beloved's body and buries it. This because after death, the beloved has ceased to be. The lover, therefore, consigns the body, which had once housed his beloved, to the grave. So the very first premise of the unbelievers' contention is baseless.

The unbelievers also posed the question: "Shall we be created afresh?" So doing, they expressed both astonishment and denial. Had they reflected even a little on what is meant by "we", the very question would not have arisen. For how did "we" come into being? Did it not happen that earthly elements such as coal, iron and calcium carbonate were brought together to create that physical skeleton, which then became the locus of "our" existence? Then, what happens after death? Once "we" leave this skeleton, the material constituents of the body, which had been drawn from the earth, are returned to it. The question then is: cannot He Who originally provided a locus for "us", by bringing together a few earthly elements, not provide "us" with the same kind of locus again by bringing together the same material constituents? If something happened once, what can prevent its recurrence? All this is pretty evident and one only has to use one's common sense to easily grasp it. But why do the unbelievers not allow their minds to move in this direction? Why do they constantly invent baseless objections against the concept of Life after Death and the possible occurrence of the Hereafter?

Disregarding all secondary matters, God indicates the basic reason for their flawed thinking by saying: "... they deny that they will meet their Lord". The pith of the matter is not that they find resurrection too weird to fathom or something they really feel deeply convinced to be beyond the range of the possible. What really prevents them from comprehending this concept is their overwhelming desire to lead an unbridled life, their inclination to commit as many sins as they wish, and to still leave the world without being called to account. Denial of resurrection comes in handy for all those who cherish such a licentious way of life.

21. The Qur'ān tells the unbelievers that the true essence of their existence will not be lost in the earth. When the appointed time comes,

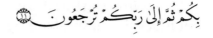

(12) Would that[22] you could see the guilty standing before their Lord with their	وَلَوْ تَرَىٰٓ إِذِ ٱلْمُجْرِمُونَ نَاكِسُواْ

the angel of death will seize a person's essence in its fullness, allowing no part of it to be lost. The whole of it will be taken by the angel of death and he will subsequently place it before his Lord.

This verse throws light on a number of truths that merit serious consideration:

i. The verse clarifies that death is not a mechanical process; it is not like a watch that automatically comes to a standstill because its machine needs rewinding. On the contrary, God has appointed a special angel who seizes every person's soul at an appointed time in the manner an official takes something into his custody on behalf of the state.

 We learn from other Qur'ānic verses that the angel of death is assisted in his task by his staff who perform a variety of functions pertaining to bringing about death, extracting souls from people's bodies and keeping them in their custody. We are also told that they treat the souls of righteous believers in one way and those of criminals in quite a different way. (For detailed information see *al-Nisā'* 4:97; *al-Anʿām* 6:93; *al-Naḥl* 16:28 and *al-Wāqiʿah* 56:83-94.)

ii. It also clarifies that death does not lead to man's extinction. After being extracted from a person's body, the soul continues to exist. The Qur'ān says: "The angel of death who has been charged with your souls shall gather you and then you shall be brought back to your Lord." This clearly indicates that people's souls will continue to exist, for obviously a non-existent thing cannot be placed in someone's charge. The statement also implies that what has been taken charge of will remain intact with its custodian, the angel of death.

iii. It also indicates that what the angel of death seizes at the time of a man's death is his "ego" rather than his biological being. Man's ego lies at the core of his being. His ego is extracted intact, without subjecting it to any addition or diminution in respect of its essential features. Thereafter, it is this ego that is brought back to the Lord. It will be restored to a new body when man is resurrected on the Day of Judgement and will face God's reckoning and receive reward or punishment.

22. The reference here is to the spectacle of the Hereafter when the human ego, after returning to the Lord, will stand before Him to face reckoning.

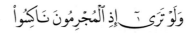

heads downcast, (saying to Him): "Our Lord, we have now seen and heard, so send us back (to the world) that we might act righteously. For now we have come to have firm faith." (13) (They will be told): "If We had so willed, We could have bestowed guidance on every person.[23] But the Word from Me that I will fill Hell with men and *jinn*, all together,

رُءُوسِهِمْ عِندَ رَبِّهِمْ رَبَّنَآ أَبْصَرْنَا وَسَمِعْنَا
فَٱرْجِعْنَا نَعْمَلْ صَـٰلِحًا إِنَّا مُوقِنُونَ ﴿١٢﴾
وَلَوْ شِئْنَا لَأَتَيْنَا كُلَّ نَفْسٍ هُدَىٰهَا وَلَـٰكِنْ
حَقَّ ٱلْقَوْلُ مِنِّى لَأَمْلَأَنَّ جَهَنَّمَ مِنَ
ٱلْجِنَّةِ وَٱلنَّاسِ

---

23. Had it been in God's scheme of things to direct man to the Right Way after making him directly observe and experience the reality of the Hereafter, it would not have been necessary to put him through a long series of trials and tribulations in this world. In God's scheme of things, however, it was necessary that man should be tested while the ultimate reality is hidden from him, and remains beyond the ken of his perception. The reason being that man is expected to recognise the truth as a result of reflecting on God's Signs in his own being and in the Universe around him. God assists him in this regard by sending Messengers and Scriptures so that he is tested as to whether he avails himself of the guidance so sent him.

He is also tested on another count: this being whether, after knowing the truth, he is able to exercise due control over his baser self and remain free from the bondage of desires and worldly interests so as to accept the truth and mould his conduct accordingly. If he fails in these tests there would be no point in putting him to the same tests again. If he were sent back to the world after having witnessed the Day of Judgement and the Reckoning at first hand, he would in fact not be put to any test at all. Likewise, if his mind is purged of all that he had observed and he is returned to the world while the larger reality is still hidden from him, he will perform exactly as he did before, and the result is bound to be the same. (For further elaboration see *Towards Understanding the Qur'ān*, Vol. I, *al-Baqarah* 2: n. 228, pp. 163-164; Vol. II, *al-An'ām* 6: nn. 6 and 141, pp. 217-218 and 297-298; Vol. IV, *al-Ra'd* 13, p. 218 and *al-Ḥijr* 15: n. 39, pp. 297-298; Vol. IV, *Yūnus* 10: n. 26, pp. 24-25, and Vol. VI, *al-Mu'minūn* 23: n. 91, p. 125.

has been fulfilled.[24] (14) So taste the chastisement on account of your forgetting the encounter of this Day.[25] We, too, have forgotten you. Taste the eternal chastisement as a requital for your misdeeds."

(15) None believes in Our Signs except those who, when they are given good counsel through Our verses, fall down prostrate and celebrate the praise of their Lord and do not wax proud.[26] (16) Their sides forsake their beds,

أَجۡمَعِينَ ١٣ فَذُوقُواْ بِمَا نَسِيتُمۡ لِقَآءَ
يَوۡمِكُمۡ هَٰذَآ إِنَّا نَسِينَٰكُمۡۖ وَذُوقُواْ
عَذَابَ ٱلۡخُلۡدِ بِمَا كُنتُمۡ تَعۡمَلُونَ ١٤ إِنَّمَا
يُؤۡمِنُ بِـَٔايَٰتِنَا ٱلَّذِينَ إِذَا ذُكِّرُواْ بِهَا
خَرُّواْ سُجَّدٗا وَسَبَّحُواْ بِحَمۡدِ رَبِّهِمۡ وَهُمۡ
لَا يَسۡتَكۡبِرُونَ۩ ١٥ تَتَجَافَىٰ جُنُوبُهُمۡ عَنِ
ٱلۡمَضَاجِعِ

24. The allusion here is to God's address to *Iblīs* at the time of Adam's creation. The account in *Sūrah Ṣād* 38: vv. 65 ff. which narrates the whole story of Adam's creation mentions that *Iblīs* refused to prostrate himself before Adam and sought respite till the Last Day during which time he would try to mislead Adam's progeny. In response, God told him: "This is the truth – and I only speak the truth – I will certainly fill Hell with you and with all those among them who follow you", (*Ṣād* 38:84-85).

Here the word *ajmaʿīn* (all) is used. This does not mean, however, that all men and *jinn* will be hurled into Hell. What is rather stated is that devils and those human beings who follow them will all be consigned to Hell.

25. Engrossed in worldly pleasures as the unbelievers are, they completely forget that a day will come when they will have to return to their Lord.

26. The believers stand out for abjuring erroneous ideas and readily accepting God's directives and humbly serving Him.

and they call upon their Lord in fear and hope,[27] and expend (in charity) out of the sustenance We have granted them.[28] (17) No one knows what delights of the eyes are kept hidden for them as a reward for their deeds.[29] (18) Would a true believer be like him who

يَدْعُونَ رَبَّهُمْ خَوْفًا وَطَمَعًا وَمِمَّا رَزَقْنَـٰهُمْ
يُنفِقُونَ ﴿١٦﴾ فَلَا تَعْلَمُ نَفْسٌ مَّآ أُخْفِىَ لَهُم مِّن
قُرَّةِ أَعْيُنٍ جَزَآءًۢ بِمَا كَانُوا۟ يَعْمَلُونَ ﴿١٧﴾ أَفَمَن
كَانَ مُؤْمِنًا

27. Rather than immerse themselves in an orgy of pleasures in the watches of the night, the believers devote themselves to worshipping their Lord. They are unlike those who need long nocturnal sessions of singing, dancing and entertainment of different kinds to get over the strains of their working days. By contrast, after they have worked hard to perform their duties during the day, they spend their nights in remembering and worshipping their Lord; they quiver for fear of Him, concentrate all their hopes in Him. The words "their sides forsake their beds" does not mean that they never go to sleep at night. The point is rather that they devote a good portion of the night to worshipping God.

28. The word "sustenance" in this context obviously means lawful, wholesome sustenance. Unlawfully earned sustenance is not reckoned in the Qur'ān as sustenance granted by God.

Another distinguishing feature of believers is that they expend in charity out of the lawful sustenance bestowed on them by God, be it large or small. The believers never spend beyond what they have lawfully earned and refrain from having recourse to unlawful earnings to meet their needs.

29. The following *ḥadīth* was narrated by Abū Hurayrah from the Prophet (peace be on him) and can be found in the *Ḥadīth* collections of Bukhārī, Muslim, Tirmidhī and in the *Musnad* of Aḥmad ibn Ḥanbal through several different chains of narration. "The Messenger of God said: God says: 'I have prepared for My pious servants what no eye has ever seen, nor any ear ever heard, nor any man ever imagined'." (See Bukhārī, *K. al-Tawḥīd, Bāb: Yurīdūna an yubaddilū Kalām Allāh;* Muslim, *K. al-Jannah ..., Bāb*: *Ṣifat al-Jannah*; Tirmidī, *K. (Abwāb) Tafsīr al-Qur'ān, Bāb*:

was an evil-doer?[30] Surely they are not equal.[31] (19) As for those who believe and act righteously, theirs shall be Gardens to dwell in,[32] a hospitality to reward them for their deeds. (20) As for the evil-doers, their refuge shall be the Fire. Every time they want to escape from it they shall be driven back and shall be told: "Taste the chastisement of the Fire which you used to reject as a lie."

كَمَن كَانَ فَاسِقًا ۚ لَّا يَسْتَوُۥنَ ﴿١٨﴾ أَمَّا ٱلَّذِينَ
ءَامَنُوا۟ وَعَمِلُوا۟ ٱلصَّـٰلِحَـٰتِ فَلَهُمْ
جَنَّـٰتُ ٱلْمَأْوَىٰ نُزُلًۢا بِمَا كَانُوا۟ يَعْمَلُونَ ﴿١٩﴾
وَأَمَّا ٱلَّذِينَ فَسَقُوا۟ فَمَأْوَىٰهُمُ ٱلنَّارُ ۖ كُلَّمَآ
أَرَادُوٓا۟ أَن يَخْرُجُوا۟ مِنْهَآ أُعِيدُوا۟ فِيهَا
وَقِيلَ لَهُمْ ذُوقُوا۟ عَذَابَ ٱلنَّارِ ٱلَّذِى كُنتُم
بِهِۦ تُكَذِّبُونَ ﴿٢٠﴾

Wa min Sūrat al-Sajdah; Aḥmad ibn Ḥanbal, *Musnad*, vol. 2, p. 313 – Ed.) A tradition embodying the same content but with slight verbal variations was narrated by Abū Saʿīd al-Khudrī, Mughīrah ibn Shuʿbah and Sahl ibn Saʿd al-Saʿīd, and is recorded by Muslim, Aḥmad ibn Ḥanbal, Ibn Jarīr al-Ṭabarī and Tirmidhī. (See Muslim, *K. al-Jannah, Bāb: Ṣifat al-Jannah*; Aḥmad ibn Ḥanbal, *Musnad*, vol. 5, p. 334; Ṭabarī, *Tafsīr*, *K. al-Tafsīr*, *Bāb: Wa min Sūrat al-Sajdah*. – Ed.)

30. In this verse, the Qur'ān employs two mutually opposed expressions: "those who believe and act righteously" and "the evil-doers". The people of the first group accept God as their Lord and sole deity and obey the law transmitted through His Messengers. By contrast, the evil-doers follow the path of rebellion, arrogate to themselves the right to behave as they please, and are prone to obey others than God.

31. The thought patterns and ways of living of the two groups are markedly different in this world. In like manner, the treatment that will be meted out to each of them by God in the Hereafter will be different.

32. For the believers, the Gardens of Paradise will not serve the purpose of occasional promenade; they will rather be the places where they will dwell forever.

(21) We shall certainly have them taste some chastisement in this world in addition to the greater chastisement (of the Hereafter); perhaps they will retract (from their transgression).[33]

وَلَنُذِيقَنَّهُم مِّنَ ٱلْعَذَابِ ٱلْأَدْنَىٰ دُونَ
ٱلْعَذَابِ ٱلْأَكْبَرِ لَعَلَّهُمْ يَرْجِعُونَ ﴿٢١﴾

---

33. "The greater chastisement" here refers to the chastisement to which the unbelievers and evil-doers will be subjected in the World-to-Come. The verse, however, also speaks of "some chastisement" in this world, which refers to things like serious diseases, death of kith and kin, tragic accidents, and losses and failures of various types which people face in the course of their worldly lives. There are also storms, earthquakes, floods, epidemics, famines, riots, warfares and other calamities which befall a people collectively, sometimes affecting the lives of millions.

These calamities afflict people in order that they may take heed before the greater chastisement overtakes them. They should give up those patterns of thought and action that lead them to the immense chastisement of the Hereafter. In other words, God has not made man's life in the world to be spent without care and concern. Man has not been granted an altogether smooth sail in this life. Calamities visit him so that he may purge his mind of the delusion that there is no power above him capable of causing harm.

God has so arranged the order of things in the world that individuals, nations and countries are periodically afflicted with devastating calamities in order to remind them of their utter helplessness and to impress upon them that there exists a pervasive supreme power.

They are thus made to realise that their destiny is controlled by someone else other than themselves. This real power and authority rests with God, not with man. Whenever any calamity from God strikes man it becomes evident that he can neither avert it himself nor by invoking any *jinn*, spirit, or god. Far from being simply natural disasters, these calamities serve as warnings from God to dispel man's misperceptions and prompt him to recognise the reality of things. By deriving lessons from these, man can mend his ways during his existence by embracing right beliefs and reforming his conduct. This alone will save him from the greater chastisement of the Hereafter.

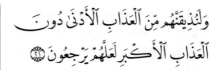

(22) And who is more unjust than he who is given good counsel through the Signs of his Lord and yet he turns away from them?[34] Surely We will exact full retribution from such criminals.

وَمَنْ أَظْلَمُ مِمَّن ذُكِّرَ بِـَٔايَـٰتِ رَبِّهِۦ
ثُمَّ أَعْرَضَ عَنْهَآ ۚ إِنَّا مِنَ ٱلْمُجْرِمِينَ
مُنتَقِمُونَ ﴿٢٢﴾

---

34. "The Signs of the Lord" are quite pervasive and cover a pretty wide range. If one bears in mind the Qur'ānic descriptions of these Signs, one will find they fall under the following six categories:

i. The Signs found in the wide expanses of the heavens and the earth and in the overall system underlying the workings of the Universe;
ii. The Signs manifest in man's procreation, his structure, and his existence as a whole;
iii. The Signs found in man's intuition, in his unconscious and subconscious, and in his moral conceptions;
iv. The Signs in the human experience of history;
v. The Signs manifest in the earthly and heavenly calamities that befall man, and
vi. Finally, the Signs that God has sent down through the agency of His Messengers in order to apprise man, in a reasonable and persuasive manner, of the truths that are corroborated by these Signs.

Taken together, these Signs consistently and emphatically impress upon man that he is neither without any God nor is he the servant of a multiplicity of gods. Rather, the only right course for him is to serve and worship the One True God. Furthermore, man has not been sent to this world as one who is absolutely free and unaccountable, as one endowed with the right to act as one pleases, nor as an irresponsible being accountable to no one. On the contrary, after man completes the term of his worldly life, he will return to his Lord with the record of his deeds to face God's reckoning. Thereafter he will be rewarded or punished in light of his performance. Hence, it is in man's own interest to follow the guidance sent to him by his Lord through His Prophets and as embodied in the Scriptures and to give up acting as though he were endowed with the right to act as he pleases.

Thus, all possible measures have been taken by God to direct man to the Right Way. The truth has been explained to him in a myriad of ways. A whole range of Signs provide for his admonition. He has also been

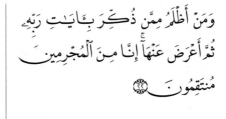

(23) Verily We bestowed the Book upon Moses. So entertain no doubt if (the Prophet Muḥammad) received the same.[35] We had made that Book a guidance for the Children of Israel,[36]

وَلَقَدْ ءَاتَيْنَا مُوسَى ٱلْكِتَـٰبَ فَلَا تَكُن
فِى مِرْيَةٍ مِّن لِّقَآئِهِۦ ۖ وَجَعَلْنَـٰهُ هُدًى لِّبَنِىٓ
إِسْرَـٰٓءِيلَ ﴿٢٣﴾

---

granted the faculties of sight, hearing and rational thinking. So if man then turns a blind eye to all these Signs, closes his ears to every instruction and admonition, and uses his head and heart to weave together warped philosophies of life, it would be no exaggeration to say that none is more criminal than man himself. Hence, when such a man returns to his Lord after completing his term of life, he certainly deserves a severe punishment for his rebellion.

35. This message, although apparently addressed to the Prophet (peace be on him), is meant to be directed to those who had doubts about his being God's Messenger and the recipient of His Book.

From here on the discourse turns to the theme broached in the opening verses (vv. 2-3) of this *sūrah*. The Makkan unbelievers flatly denied that any Scripture had been granted by God to the Prophet (peace be on him). Rather, they accused him of having forged something which he subsequently ascribed to God. This is clearly refuted in the opening verses of the *sūrah*.

Here, a further answer to this objection is provided. The unbelievers had expressed astonishment at the very idea that God revealed any Book to the Prophet (peace be on him), dismissing such a notion as patently impossible. They wanted that all others should either deny this or at least consider it a doubtful proposition. However, the fact is that there was nothing unusual about God's revelation of a heavenly Book to His Prophets. This was, after all, not the first instance of a Book being revealed. Many Prophets had received Scriptures in the past, the best known example being the grant of the Torah to Moses (peace be on him). Hence, if a Scripture of the same kind was made available to the people of Arabia through the Prophet Muḥammad (peace be on him), what was there that was so novel or weird about this to give rise to doubt and skepticism?

36. In the same way that the Torah was meant to guide the Children of Israel – a point already made in verse 3 of this *sūrah* – a Scripture has now been sent to guide the people of Arabia.

(24) and when they remained steadfast and firmly believed in Our Signs, We created among them leaders who guided people by Our command.[37]

وَجَعَلْنَا مِنْهُمْ أَئِمَّةً يَهْدُونَ بِأَمْرِنَا
لَمَّا صَبَرُوا۟ وَكَانُوا۟ بِـَٔايَـٰتِنَا يُوقِنُونَ ﴿٢٤﴾

This statement can be better appreciated if it is viewed in its proper historical context. It is a fact of history – a fact with which the Makkan unbelievers were well acquainted – that the Children of Israel had been subjected to a life of great hardship and indignity for several centuries during their existence in Egypt. Then, God raised among them the Prophet Moses (peace be on him) and through him they were emancipated from the yoke of slavery. God also revealed His Book to Moses (peace be on him) and thanks to its blessings the Children of Israel rose, under its guidance, to become an illustrious nation. By alluding to this historical fact, the people of Arabia are being told that the Qur'ān was their Book of guidance in the same way that the Torah had been revealed to provide guidance to the Children of Israel.

37. True, the Torah changed the course of the Israelites' history. All this was not because a Heavenly Book was sent to them for the Book was not some kind of amulet that the Israelites wore around their necks and no sooner than they did so did they begin to scale the heights of greatness and glory. Instead, the fact is that the Israelites owed their historical achievements to the fact that they chose to believe in the teachings of God's Book that had come to them and because they followed its teaching with patience and perseverance. Furthermore, the leadership of the Israelites was entrusted to those who truly believed in the Scripture and who were not obsessed with the pursuit of worldly gain and pleasure. On the contrary, they resolutely braved every danger and endured every loss and suffering which came their way because of their devotion to the Truth. They vigorously resisted the promptings of carnal desires within themselves and valiantly fought against the enemies of the true faith without. It is only after they had done so that they were granted world leadership.

The purpose of highlighting all this is to warn the Arabian unbelievers that in the same way that the revelation of God's Book to the Israelites determined their destiny, so too the destiny of the Arabian unbelievers would be determined by the revelation of God's Book to them. Leadership would henceforth go to those who believed in God's Book and who followed the Truth with patience and perseverance. As for those who turned away from it, their future was doomed.

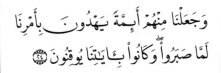

(25) Surely your Lord will judge among them on the Day of Resurrection concerning the matters about which the Children of Israel used to differ.[38]

(26) Did (these historical events) not make them realise that We destroyed many nations before them amidst whose dwellings they now move about?[39] Surely there are many Signs in this. Are they unable to hear? (27) Have they not seen that We drive water to the parched land, thereby bringing forth crops which

إِنَّ رَبَّكَ هُوَ يَفۡصِلُ بَيۡنَهُمۡ يَوۡمَ ٱلۡقِيَٰمَةِ
فِيمَا كَانُواْ فِيهِ يَخۡتَلِفُونَ ٢٥ أَوَلَمۡ يَهۡدِ لَهُمۡ
كَمۡ أَهۡلَكۡنَا مِن قَبۡلِهِم مِّنَ ٱلۡقُرُونِ يَمۡشُونَ
فِي مَسَٰكِنِهِمۡۚ إِنَّ فِي ذَٰلِكَ لَأٓيَٰتٍۚ أَفَلَا
يَسۡمَعُونَ ٢٦ أَوَلَمۡ يَرَوۡاْ أَنَّا نَسُوقُ ٱلۡمَآءَ إِلَى
ٱلۡأَرۡضِ ٱلۡجُرُزِ فَنُخۡرِجُ بِهِۦ زَرۡعٗا

38. This alludes to the rise of schisms, sectarian dissensions and bickerings among the Children of Israel. This characterised their collective existence after they had lost firm religious faith, abandoned following their pious leaders, and immersed themselves in crass worldliness. One of the changes that came about among the Israelites is evident to the whole world – the ignominy and humiliation to which they were subjected in their long history. There is also another consequence of their back-sliding of which the world is not so much aware; this will only come to light on the Day of Judgement.

39. The unbelieving Arabs are exhorted to learn from the long historical record of the Israelites. It should have been abundantly clear to them that the fate of every nation among whom a Messenger is raised is contingent on the attitude it adopts towards him. Never was a nation that rejected its Messenger and called him a liar able to escape God's scourge. It is only the believers who escape God's chastisement. As for the unbelievers, they are always reduced to the level of an example to be learned from.

they and their cattle eat? Are they unable to see?[40] (28) They say: "If you are truthful, (tell us) when will the Judgement come?"[41] (29) Tell them: "If the unbelievers were to believe on the Day of Judgement that will not avail them. For then they will be granted no respite."[42] (30) So (leave them to themselves and) turn away from them and wait; they too are waiting.

تَأْكُلُ مِنْهُ أَنْعَـٰمُهُمْ وَأَنفُسُهُمْ ۖ أَفَلَا
يُبْصِرُونَ ﴿٢٧﴾ وَيَقُولُونَ مَتَىٰ هَـٰذَا ٱلْفَتْحُ
إِن كُنتُمْ صَـٰدِقِينَ ﴿٢٨﴾ قُلْ يَوْمَ ٱلْفَتْحِ
لَا يَنفَعُ ٱلَّذِينَ كَفَرُوٓا۟ إِيمَـٰنُهُمْ وَلَا هُمْ
يُنظَرُونَ ﴿٢٩﴾ فَأَعْرِضْ عَنْهُمْ وَٱنتَظِرْ إِنَّهُم
مُّنتَظِرُونَ ﴿٣٠﴾

40. The context indicates that this was not put forward by way of an argument to confirm the Hereafter, though the Qur'ān often employs it for that purpose. Instead, it was stated here to drive home the following point: a man who observes a sterile patch of land can hardly imagine that one day it will be in full bloom. Yet just one powerful downpour can change all that. In like manner, the unbelievers had dismissed Islam as a non-starter. Yet if God so wills, His power can make it flourish in the same way that a sterile patch of land flourishes, bringing forth abundant luxuriant vegetation.

41. The unbelievers persistently asked the Prophet (peace be on him) about when God's help would come to him and when they would be annihilated. In effect, they asked: when will God judge between the believers and the unbelievers?

42. The unbelievers are told that God's punishment is not something they should eagerly look forward to. Rather, they should avail themselves of the respite that they presently have, one that they can enjoy until they are confronted with God's punishment. For once this strikes them, there will be no escape. If they decide to follow faith after confronting God's punishment, this is all too late and of no avail.

Glossary of Terms

Al-Ākhirah (Afterlife, Hereafter, Next World). The term embraces the following ideas:

1. That man is answerable to God;
2. that on a pre-determined day the present order of existence will come to an end;
3. that thereafter God will bring another order into being in which He will resurrect all human beings, gather them together and examine their conduct, and reward them with justice and mercy;
4. that those who are reckoned good will be rewarded whereas the evil-doers will be punished; and
5. that the real measure of success or failure of a person is not the extent of his prosperity in the present life, but his success in the Next.

Anṣār means 'Helpers'. In Islamic parlance the word refers to the Muslims of Madīnah who helped the Muhājirūn of Makkah in the process of the latter's settling down in the new environment.

ʿAṣr Prayer is one of the five obligatory Prayers and is performed after the time for the *Ẓuhr* Prayer (q.v.) ends and before the time for *Maghrib* Prayer begins. The time for *ʿAṣr* Prayer is reckoned to start when the shadow of an object exceeds its size (according to the Ḥanafī school, when the shadow of an object becomes double its size), and ends with sunset.

Dīn has the core meaning of obedience. As a Qur'ānic technical term, *dīn* refers to the way of life and the system of conduct based on recognizing God as one's sovereign and committing oneself to obeying Him. From the Islamic perspective, true *dīn* consists of man's living in total submission to God, and the way to do so is to accept as binding the guidance communicated through the Prophets.

Faḥshā' see ***Fawāḥish***.

Falāḥ means success and prosperity. It is used as an antonym of *khusrān* which signifies loss and failure. To say that someone has acquired *falāḥ*, therefore, amounts to saying that he has achieved his objective, that he has attained prosperity and well-being, that his efforts have borne fruit.

Fawāḥish, sing. *fāḥishah*, applies to all those acts whose abominable character is self-evident. In the Qur'ān all extra-marital sexual relationships, homo-sexuality, nudity, false accusation of unchastity, and taking as one's wife a woman who had been married in the past to one's father are specifically called *fawāḥish*. In *Ḥadīth*, theft, taking intoxicating drinks and begging have also been characterized as *fawāḥish* as have several other brazenly evil and indecent acts.

Fiqh, which literally means 'understanding of a speaker's purpose from his speech', technically refers to the branch of learning concerned with the injunctions of the *Sharī'ah* relating to human actions, derived from the detailed evidence pertaining to them.

Fī sabīl Allāh (in the way of Allah) is a frequently used expression in the Qur'ān which emphasizes that good acts ought to be done exclusively to please God. Generally the expression has been used in the Qur'ān in connection with striving or spending for charitable purposes.

Fisq transgression; consists of disobedience to the command of God.

Ghayb literally means "hidden, covered, or concealed". As a term, it means all that is unknown and is not accessible to man by the means of acquiring knowledge available to him. *Ghayb* therefore refers to the realm that lies beyond the ken of perception.

Ḥadīth literally means communication or narration. In the Islamic context it has come to denote the record of what the Prophet (peace be on him) said, did, or tacitly approved. According to some scholars, the word *ḥadīth* also covers reports about the sayings and deeds, etc. of the Companions of the Prophet in addition to those of the Prophet (peace be on him). The whole body of traditions is termed *Ḥadīth* and its science *ʿIlm al-Ḥadīth*.

Ḥajj (Major Pilgrimage) is one of the five pillars of Islam, a duty one must perform during one's life-time if one has the means to do so. It resembles *ʿUmrah* in some respects, but differs from it insofar as the former can be performed during certain specified dates of Dhū al-Ḥijjah alone. In addition to *ṭawāf* and *saʿy* (which are also required for *ʿUmrah*), there are a few other requirements but especially 'standing' (*wuqūf*) in ʿArafāt during the day-time on 9th of Dhū al-Ḥijjah. For details of the rules of *Ḥajj*, see the relevant sections of the books of *Fiqh*.

Ḥanīf, pl. *Ḥunafāʾ* was the generic appellation of those persons of Arabia prior to Islam who had given up polytheistic belief and practice, affirmed claiming to follow the Abrahamic faith. On the advent of the Prophet (peace be on him) quite a few of them embraced Islam.

Ḥashr literally means 'to gather', signifies the doctrine that with the blowing of the Second Trumpet all those who had ever been created will be resurrected and brought forth to the Plain where all will be made to stand before God for His judgement.

Ḥijābah and ***Siqāyah*** (q.v.), it was considered an important and honoured function in Makkah on the eve of Islam.

Hijrah signifies migration from a land, where a Muslim is unable to live according to the precepts of his faith to a land where it is possible to do so. The *hijrah par excellence* for Muslims is the *hijrah* of the Prophet (peace be on him) which not only provided him and his followers refuge from persecution, but also an opportunity to build a society and state according to the ideals of Islam.

ʿIbādah is used in three meanings: (1) worship and adoration; (2) obedience and submission; and (3) service and subjection. The fundamental message of Islam is that man, as God's creature, should direct his *ʿibādah* to God in all the above-mentioned meanings of the term, and in rendering it associate none with God.

Iblīs literally means 'one thoroughly disappointed; one in utter despair'. In Islamic terminology it denotes the *jinn* (q.v.) who out of arrogance and vainglory, refused the command of God to prostrate before Adam. He also asked God to allow him a term during which he might mislead and tempt mankind to error. This term was granted to *Iblīs* by God whereafter he became the chief promoter of evil and prompted Adam and Eve to disobey God's order. He is also called *al-Shayṭān* (Satan). He is possessed of a specific personality and is not just an abstract force.

ʿIddah denotes the waiting period that a woman is required to observe as a consequence for the nullification of her marriage with her husband or her husband's death. During this period she may not marry. The waiting period after a divorce is three months and after the death of her husband is four months and ten days.

Iḥrām refers to the state in which a Pilgrim is required to honour certain restrictions from the commencement of *iḥrām* until such time that the religious law releases him from the restrictions imposed by *iḥrām*. *Iḥrām* is so called in view of the numerous prohibitions that ought to be observed (e.g. abstention from all sexual acts, from the use of perfume, from hunting or killing animals, from cutting the beard or shaving the head, cutting the nails, plucking blades of grass or cutting green trees). *Iḥrām* also requires male Pilgrims to cover their body with seemless garments, rather than wear tailored clothes, and to leave the head uncovered. As for female Pilgrims, *iḥrām* requires them to dress according to ordinary rules of the *Sharīʿah* provided they keep their face uncovered.

Īlā' denotes a husband's vow to abstain from sexual relations with his wife. The maximum permissible limit for abstaining from such relations under that vow is four months, after which the marriage becomes void.

Injīl signifies the inspired orations and utterances of Jesus (peace be on him) which he delivered during the last two or three years of his earthly life in his capacity as a Prophet. The *Injīl* mentioned by the Qur'ān should, however, not be identified by the four Gospels of the New Testament which contain a great deal of material in addition to the inspired utterances of the Prophet Jesus (peace be on him). Presumably the statements explicitly attributed to Jesus (peace be on him) constitute parts of the true, original *Injīl*. It is significant that the statements explicitly attributed to Jesus in the Gospels contain substantively the same teachings as those of the Qur'ān.

Jāhilīyah on the eve of Islam all those world-views and ways of life which are based on rejection or disregard of heavenly guidance communicated to mankind through God's Prophets and Messengers of God; the attitude of treating human life, either wholly or partly, as independent of the directives of God. *Jāhilīyah* also has a temporal signification; it refers to the pre-Islamic period of Arabia when Divine Guidance was not available to people.

Jihād means 'to strive or to exert to the utmost'. The word *jihād* implies the existence of forces of resistance against whom it is necessary to engage in struggle. *Jihād* embraces all kinds of striving aimed at making the Word of God supreme in humans. It includes the effort to subdue one's carnal self and make it subservient to God's Will. The juxtaposition of the expression *fī sabīl Allāh* with *jihād* also underlines that a person's intention in making *jihād* should be to seek the good pleasure of God rather than for renown or worldly benefits.

Jinn are an independent species of creation about which little is known except that unlike man, who was created out of earth, the *jinn* were created out of fire. But like man, a Divine Message has also been addressed to them and they too have been endowed with the capacity, again like man, to choose between good and evil, between obedience or disobedience to God.

Liwā' means banner, flag, standard. In pre-Islamic Makkah, it was an honoured function assigned to one of the clans of Quraysh which signified its position of leadership on the battlefield.

Ma'rūf refers to the conduct which is instinctively regarded as good and fair by human beings in general.

Munkar signifies the conduct which is instinctively considered bad by human beings in general.

Nabī, a term for which we have used the word Prophet as an equivalent, refers to a person chosen by God to whom He entrusts the task to warn people against that which would lead to their perdition and to direct them to the way that would lead to their felicity. Prophets are enabled to perform this task because of the special power that is bestowed upon them by God (which is evident from the miracles they are enabled to perform), and because of the special ability to live a life of absolute probity. The function of a *nabī* is close to, but not necessarily identical with, that of a *rasūl*.

Nubūwah means prophethood.

Rabb has three meanings: (i) Lord and master; (ii) Sustainer, Provider, Supporter, Nourisher and Guardian; and (iii) Sovereign and Ruler, He who controls and directs everything. God is *Rabb* in all three meanings of the term. The rationale of the basic Qur'ānic message – 'serve none but God' – is that since God is man's *Rabb*, He alone should be the object of man's worship and service. See, for example, *al-Baqarah* 2:21.

Rifādah was the function of providing food to the Pilgrims. Like *ḥijābah* and *siqāyah* (q.v.), it was considered an important and honoured function in Makkah on the eve of Islam.

Sā'ah literally means "time" or "hour" of day or night. The word has been generally used in the Qur'ān with the prefix *al*, signifying the Day of Judgement or the "Hour" about which man has been forewarned.

Sajdah means prostration. It is one of the prescribed rites of prayer requiring one to put one's forehead down on the floor in humility and out of worshipful reverence for God.

Sa'y is a rite which is part of both *Ḥajj* and *'Umrah* and consists of seven laps of brisk walk (literally, 'running') between Ṣafā and Marwah, two hillocks near the Ka'bah. This commemorates Abraham's wife Hagar's search for water for her baby child.

Sharī'ah signifies the entire Islamic way of life, especially the Law of Islam.

Siqāyah signifies the function of providing water to the Pilgrims during the Pilgrimage season. *Siqāyah*, like *ḥijābah* (q.v.), was an office of great honour.

Sunnah signifies the normative life-pattern of the Prophet (peace be on him) as evident from his sayings, deeds and tacit approvals. In this regard *Sunnah* and *Ḥadīth* (q.v.) are cognate terms, but not quite the same. Stated succinctly, while *Sunnah* represents the Prophet's normative life-pattern, *Ḥadīth* is its record and repository.

Tahajjud is the Prayer offered in the last quarter of the night, at any time before the commencement of the time of *Fajr* Prayer. It is a supererogatory rather than an obligatory Prayer, but one which has been emphasised in the Qur'ān and in the *Ḥadīth* as meriting great reward from God.

Ṭawāf is a rite which is part of both *Ḥajj* and *'Umrah* and consists of circumambulating the Ka'bah seven times.

Tawḥīd, which is the quintessence of Islam, besides being the doctrinal affirmation of God's Oneness and Unity, it also represents man's commitment to render God worship, service and absolute obedience, and to consecrate them for Him alone.

Ummī means 'unlettered'. It is also used to refer to those who do not possess Divine revelation.

Wuḍū' refers to the ablution performed for acquiring the state of ritual purity which is a pre-requisite to perform Prayers. It requires washing (1) the face from the top of the forehead to the chin and as far as each ear; (2) the hands and arms up to the elbows; (3) wiping with wet hands a part of the head; and (4) washing the feet to the ankles.

Zakāh literally means purification, whence it is used to denote a portion of property bestowed in alms, which is a means of purifying the person who dispenses it and his property. It is among the five pillars of Islam and refers to the mandatory amount that a Muslim is required to pay in alms out of his property. The detailed rules of *zakāh* are laid down in books of *Fiqh*.

Zinā means illegal sexual intercourse and embraces both fornication and adultery.

Ẓuhr Prayer is one of the five obligatory Prayers which is performed after the sun has passed the meridian. It may be performed until the time for the beginning of *ʿAṣr* Prayer (q.v.).

Ẓulm literally means placing a thing where it does not belong. Technically, it refers to exceeding the limits of right and hence committing wrong or injustice. *Ẓulm*, however, does not signify any one specific act; rather it embraces all acts that are inconsistent with righteousness and justice and to which, in one sense or the other, the attribute of 'wrong-doing' can rightly be applied.

Biographical Notes

ʿĀʾishah, d. 58 A.H./678 C.E., daughter of Abū Bakr, was a wife of the Prophet (peace be on him). She has transmitted a wealth of traditions, especially those concerning the Prophet's personal life. She was also regarded very highly for her mature and sharp understanding of the teachings of Islam.

ʿAbd Allāh ibn ʿAbbās, d. 68 A.H./687 C.E., a Companion of the Prophet (peace be on him), was the most outstanding scholar of Qur'ānic exegesis in his time.

ʿAbd Allāh ibn al-Mubārak, d. 181 A.H./797 C.E., was a noted scholar of *Ḥadīth, Fiqh* and Arabic language.

ʿAbd Allāh ibn Masʿūd, d. 32 A.H./653 C.E., one of the most learned Companions of the Prophet (peace be on him), was celebrated for his juristic calibre. He is held by the Iraqi school of law as one of its main authorities.

ʿAbd al-Muṭṭalib ibn Hāshim ibn Abd Manāf, d. 45 B.H./579 C.E., the Prophet's grandfather, was a prominent chieftain of the Quraysh who was responsible for provision of water and food (*siqāyah* and *rifādah*) to the pilgrims.

ʿAbd al-Razzāq al-Ṣanʿānī, d. 211 A.H./827 C.E., was a distinguished scholar of *Ḥadīth*. His most outstanding work is *al-Muṣannaf.*

Abraham (Ibrāhīm) was one of the greatest Prophets of all times and the ancestor of a large number of Prophets including the Prophets Moses, Jesus and Muḥammad (peace be on all of them). Abraham was born and lived his early life in Iraq but later embarked on a sojourn in God's cause: from his homeland in Ur he travelled all the way northwards to Ḥarrān and then southwards to Jerusalem, journeying in between to Makkah where he erected the Sacred House for God's worship as well as to Egypt. He went about preaching that God be held as one and unique and worship and service be consecrated to Him alone. Three of the foremost religions of the world, Judaism, Christianity and Islam, revere Abraham as their Patriarch and a major source of inspiration.

Abū Bakr, ʿAbd Allāh ibn ʿUthmān, d. 13 A.H./634 C.E., was the most trusted Companion of the Prophet (peace be on him) and the first Caliph of Islam. Abū Bakr's wisdom and indomitable will ensured the survival of Islam after the Prophet's demise.

Abū al-Dardā', ʿUwaymir ibn Mālik, d. 32 A.H./652 C.E., was a famous Companion who contributed significantly to the collection of the Qur'ān on the heels of the Prophet's demise. Apart from knowledge, he was also known for his bravery, piety and religious devotion.

Abū Dāwūd Sulaymān ibn al-Ashʿath, d. 275 A.H./889 C.E., was a famous traditionist whose *Kitāb al-Sunan* is one of the six most authentic collections of *Ḥadīth*.

Abū Ḥanīfah, al-Nuʿmān ibn Thābit, d. 150 A.H./676 C.E., was a theologian and jurist who dominated the intellectual life of Iraq in the later part of his life and became the founder of a major school of law in Islam known after his name.

Abū Hurayrah, d. 59 A.H./679 C.E., was a Companion of the Prophet (peace be on him) who transmitted a very large number of traditions.

Abū Jaḥl, ʿAmr ibn Hishām ibn al-Mughīrah, d. 2 A.H./624 C.E., was an arch-enemy of Islam who was killed during the Battle of Badr in which he was the leading commander on the side of the Quraysh.

Abū Lahab, ʿAbd al-ʿUzzā ibn ʿAbd al-Muṭṭalib ibn Hāshim, d. 2 A.H./624 C.E., was an uncle of the Prophet (peace be on him). He was, however, one of Islam's fiercest enemies.

Abū Sufyān, Ṣakhr ibn Ḥarb ibn Umayyah, d. 31 A.H./652 C.E., was one of the foremost opponents of Islam and the Prophet (peace be on him) till the conquest of Makkah, when he embraced Islam. In subsequent military encounters, he valiantly fought on the Muslim side.

Abū Yūsuf, Ya'qūb ibn Ibrāhīm, d. 182 A.H./798 C.E., an outstanding jurist, was one of the most prominent disciples of Abū Ḥanīfah and is considered among the founders of the Ḥanafī school of law.

'Ād, the people among whom God raised Hūd, lived in al-Aḥqāf in the Southern part of Arabia, not far from Ḥaḍramawt. 'Ād denied God's Messengers, charging them with falsehood, and brutally oppressed others. 'Ād were totally annihilated by God for their iniquity.

Aḥmad ibn Ḥanbal, d. 243 A.H./885 C.E., was the founder of one of the four Sunnī schools of law in Islam. He patiently endured persecution for the sake of his religious convictions.

'Alī ibn Abī Ṭālib, d. 40 A.H./661 C.E., was a cousin and son-in-law of the Prophet (peace be on him) and the fourth Caliph of Islam. He was known for his many qualities, especially piety and juristic acumen.

Al-Ālūsī, Maḥmūd ibn 'Abd Allāh al-Ḥusaynī, d. 1270 A.H./1854 C.E., was a leading commentator of the Qur'ān as well as a distinguished litterateur, jurist and Sufi of the nineteenth century. His commentary, *Rūḥ al-Ma'ānī,* is an encyclopaedic work which continues to command respect.

Al-A'mash, Sulaymān ibn Mahrān, d. 148 A.H./765 C.E., was a Successor (*Tābi'ī*) who distinguished himself for his knowledge of the Qur'ān and *Ḥadīth* and his mastery of the laws of inheritance.

'Amr ibn al-'Āṣ ibn Wā'il, d. 43 A.H./664 C.E., was a noted Companion of the Prophet (peace be on him) who commanded the Muslim army that conquered Egypt. He also commanded the Muslim army in many battles during the lifetime of the Prophet (peace be on him) and the Caliphates of Abū Bakr and 'Umar ibn al-Khaṭṭāb.

Anas ibn Mālik, d. 93 A.H./712 C.E., was a distinguished Companion who had the honour of serving the Prophet (peace be on him) for many years.

Al-Aʿshā, Maymūn ibn Qays, d. 7 A.H./629 C.E., was among the foremost poets of Arabic.

Al-ʿĀṣ ibn Wā'il al-Sahmī, d. 1 A.H./622 C.E., was a fierce enemy of the Prophet (peace be on him) who expressed his hostility to him in the most bitter terms. He died at the age of 85 as a result of an accident.

ʿAwn ibn ʿAbd Allāh, d. circa 115 A.H./circa 733 C.E., was an orator, a poet as well as a narrator of poetry and a specialist in genealogy. He lived in Kūfah and was respected for his devotion and piety.

Al-Bāhilī, Abū Umāmah Ṣadā ibn ʿAjlān ibn Wahb (d. 81 A.H./701 C.E.), was a Companion who supported ʿAlī in the Battle of Ṣiffīn. He lived in Syria and died in Ḥimṣ. He was the last Companion who died in Syria.

Al-Barā' ibn ʿĀzib, d. 71 A.H./690 C.E., was a Companion who embraced Islam at a tender age, participated in several military expeditions and played significant roles in them.

Al-Bayhaqī, Aḥmad ibn al-Ḥusayn, d. 458 A.H./1066 C.E., was an authority on *Ḥadīth*. He left a vast treasure of scholarly works of which the following deserve special mention: *al-Sunan al-Kubrā, al-Sunan al-Ṣughrā, Dalā'il al-Nubūwah* and *Manāqib al-Imām al-Shāfiʿī*.

Al-Bukhārī, Muḥammad ibn Ismāʿīl, d. 256, A.H./870 C.E., is regarded as the most famous traditionist of Islam whose work is one of the six most authentic collections of *Ḥadīth*, generally considered by Muslims to be the "soundest book after the Book of Allah".

Dhū al-Ḥilm ʿĀmir ibn al-Ẓarb, d. 100 B.H./525 C.E., was a pre-Islamic chieftain, a man of wisdom, and an orator. He was well recognized as an arbitrator in the famous Fair of ʿUkāẓ. He was among those pre-Islamic Arabs who considered wine unlawful.

Hāmān was a notable aide of Pharaoh in Moses' time. He was asked by the Pharaoh to build a tower so that the latter could climb up to see the god of Moses, in whom he disbelieved. He is mentioned in several *sūrahs*, often together with Pharaoh and Qārūn.

Ḥamnah bint Sufyān ibn Umayyah ibn ʿAbd Shams who tried to put the utmost pressure on her son, Sa ʿd, to abjure Islam. She told him that she would not sit in shade, eat any food or drink anything until Sa ʿd gave up his new religious faith. This occasioned the revelation of the following verse: "... But if they press you to associate others with Me in My Divinity, (to associate those) regarding whom you have no knowledge (that they are My associates), do not obey them. And yet treat them well in this world ...." (Luqmān 31:15).

Al-Ḥasan al-Baṣrī, d. 110 A.H./728 C.E., known primarily for his piety, was a major theologian of Baṣrah around the turn of the first century of *Hijrah*.

Heraclius Augustus, r. 610-641 C.E., grew up in Roman Africa, defeated Phocas II (q.v.) and was crowned in Constantinople as Emperor. In the course of time Heraclius engaged in fierce military encounters with the Persians. After some initial setbacks, Heraclius was able to gain the upper hand against the Persians. Eventually, however, he came into conflict with the nascent power of Islam (634-641 C.E.) which cost him Syria, Palestine and Egypt.

Hūd was an Arabian Prophet of the ʿĀd, a people who lived in al-Aḥqāf in northern Ḥadramawt. Hūd has been mentioned in the Qur'ān several times. For the Qur'ānic references to Hūd see especially 7:65-72.

Ibn Abī Ḥātim, ʿAbd al-Raḥmān, d. 327 A.H./938 C.E., was a great scholar of *Ḥadīth*, especially of its branch called *Rijāl*. He also distinguished himself as a scholar of *Fiqh, Uṣūl al-Fiqh, Kalām* and *Tafsīr*.

Ibn Abī Shaybah, ʿAbd Allāh ibn Muḥammad, d. 235 A.H./849 C.E., was an outstanding scholar of *Ḥadīth*. His most noted work is *al-Muṣannaf*.

Ibn al-ʿArabī, Abū Bakr ibn Muḥammad ibn ʿAbd Allāh, d. 543 A.H./1148 C.E., was one of the foremost commentators of the Qur'ān. He was the author of a *tafsīr* work entitled *Aḥkām al-Qur'ān*. As the title indicates, it is especially oriented to highlighting the legal aspects of the Qur'ān.

Ibn Ḥazm, ʿAlī ibn Aḥmad, d. 456 A.H./1064 C.E., was an encyclopaedic scholar of Spain who was renowned for his contributions in different scholarly fields including law and jurisprudence, comparative religion, history, literature and poetry.

Ibn Hishām, ʿAbd al-Malik, d. 213 A.H./828 C.E., was an outstanding historian who is best known for his *Sīrah* (Biography) of the Prophet (peace be on him).

Ibn Isḥāq, Muḥammad, d. 151 A.H./768 C.E., was a scholar of Madīnah, and one of the earliest historians and biographers of the Prophet (peace be on him). His biography of the Prophet (peace be on him) has had a lasting influence on the works of that genre.

Ibn Kathīr, Ismāʿīl ibn ʿUmar, d. 774 A.H./1373 C.E., was a famous traditionist, historian, jurist and author of one of the best known commentaries on the Qur'ān.

Ibn Mājah, Muḥammad ibn Yazīd, d. 273 A.H./887 C.E., was a famous traditionist whose work, *Kitāb al-Sunan*, is one of the six most authentic collections of *Ḥadīth*.

Ibn Shabbah, ʿUmar, d. 262 A.H./876 C.E., was a poet and historian who was known for having committed to memory a large number of traditions. A scholar from Baṣrah, he wrote a large number of works on several subjects but especially on history and poetry.

Ibn Zayd, Jābir, d. 92 A.H./712 C.E., was a jurist who belonged to the generation of Successors (*Tābiʿī*). He was a disciple of ʿAbd Allāh ibn ʿAbbās.

ʿIkrimah ibn ʿAbd Allāh al-Barbarī al-Madanī, d. 105 A.H./723 C.E., a *mawlā* of ʿAbd Allāh ibn ʿAbbās, was a Successor (*Tābiʿī*) who was celebrated as a scholar of *Tafsīr* and *Maghāzī*.

ʿIkrimah ibn Abī Jahl, d. 13 A.H./634 C.E., was a Companion of the Prophet (peace be on him) whose father, Abū Jahl, was one of the staunchest enemies of Islam. After conversion to Islam, however, ʿIkrimah fought valiantly for the cause of Islam and was martyred in the Battle of Yarmūk.

ʿImrān ibn Ḥuṣayn ibn ʿUbayd, d. 52 A.H./672 C.E., was among the Companions known for their knowledge. He was at the head of the Khuzāʿah tribesmen on the day of the conquest of Makkah.

Imra' al-Qays ibn Ḥijr ibn al-Ḥārith al-Kindī (d. 80 B.H./545 C.E.), was a pre-Islamic poet, who ranks among the best poets of Arabic.

Isaac (Isḥāq) was a Prophet and a son of Abraham from his wife Sara (Sārah). Isaac remained with his father and is buried in Hebron.

Jābir ibn ʿAbd Allāh, d. 78 A.H./697 C.E., was a Companion who is noted for having transmitted a very large number of traditions from the Prophet (peace be on him).

Jacob (Yaʿqūb) was Isaac's son and Abraham's grandson. Jacob's Hebrew name was Israel which explains that his descendants came to be known as "Children of Israel". After Joseph assumed power in Egypt, Jacob came to Egypt at his son's invitation and settled there.

Jāʿfar al-Ṣādiq ibn Muḥammad al-Bāqir ibn ʿAlī Zayn al-ʿĀbidīn ibn al-Ḥusayn ibn ʿAlī, d. 148 A.H./675 C.E., is considered by the Twelver-Shīʿites to be their sixth *imām*. He was a great scholar and a pious man. Famous scholars such as Abū Ḥanīfah and Mālik ibn Anas benefited from his knowledge.

Al-Jaṣṣāṣ, Aḥmad ibn ʿAlī, d. 370 A.H./980 C.E., was an eminent jurist of the Ḥanafī school of law. He is celebrated for his Qur'ān-commentary, *Aḥkām al-Qur'ān*, which is an erudite commentary on the Qur'ān from a legal perspective.

Jesus (ʿĪsā), the son of Mary, was among the most exalted of God's Prophets, who had a miraculous birth from his virgin mother. Jesus' birth has, therefore, been likened in the Qur'ān to God's direct creation of Adam (that is, without the mediation of any father or mother). Notwithstanding Jesus' miraculous birth, he was a human being rather than God, albeit he was God's Messenger. While the Qur'ān lavishes glowing praises on Jesus it categorically debunks the notion that he was invested with Divinity and altogether denies the conception of a Triune God with Jesus as the Second Person.

Khabbāb ibn al-Arat, d. 37 A.H./657 C.E., a Companion and one of the early converts to Islam, was mercilessly persecuted by the opponents of Islam in Makkah.

Khusraw II, r. 590-628, who assumed the title of Parvez ("the Victorious"), was the twenty-second Sasanian king of Persia under whom the empire achieved its greatest expansion. Eventually defeated in a war with the Byzantines, he was deposed in a palace revolution and was put to death.

Korah (Qārūn), who was born among the Israelites but subsequently turned against them, had immense riches which made him vain and arrogant, forgetting that he owed all his wealth to God. Thanks to his iniquity, he became a close collaborator of Pharaoh. At last, God retributed him by causing the earth to swallow him and his mansion.

Labīd ibn Rabīʿah ibn Mālik al-ʿĀmirī, d. 41 A.H./661 C.E., was a famous poet of Arabic as well as a brave fighter. He was born in pre-Islamic times but lived quite a few years after the advent of Islam, embraced the new faith and is considered to be a Companion.

Lot (Lūṭ) was the nephew of the Prophet Abraham (peace be on him) who oversaw his religious and moral upbringing. He was born and spent the earlier part of his life in Iraq but subsequently embarked on a sojourn through several lands and eventually settled in the vicinity of the Dead Sea in the present-day Jordan. Lot's people were steeped in evils, especially sodomy. Eventually God utterly destroyed them by bringing upon them a scourge from heaven.

Makḥūl ibn Abī Muslim, d. 112 A.H./730 C.E., was a scholar of *Ḥadīth* and *Fiqh*. After journeying through different lands, he settled in Damascus and was recognized as one of the greatest jurists of Syria in his time.

Mālik ibn Anas, d. 179 A.H./795 C.E., was a famous traditionist and jurist of Madīnah, and founder of one of the four Sunnī schools of law in Islam. His *al-Mawaṭṭa'*, a collection of traditions as well as legal opinions of the jurists of Madīnah, is one of the earliest extant works of *Ḥadīth* and *Fiqh*.

Maurice was a Byzantine Emperor, r. 582-602 C.E., who helped transform the shattered empire into a new and well-organised medieval Byzantine Empire. Maurice launched a series of wars against Persians, Slavs, Avars and Lombards which drained the imperial treasury and necessitated collection of high taxes. The ensuing discontent led to the outbreak of a revolt under Phocas (q.v.) which led to the overthrow of Maurice and the crowning of Phocas as emperor.

Moses (Mūsā), is one of the greatest messengers of God (*Ulū al-ʿazm min al-Rusul*). Aided by his brother Hārūn (Aaron), he was sent to deliver the Children of Israel from the tyranny and oppression they suffered at the hand of the Pharaoh of Egypt. His story is mentioned in many places in the Qur'ān. According to Jewish sources, he was born on the 7th of Adar 2368 and died on the 7th of Adar 2488 of the hebrew calendar.

Al-Mughīrah ibn Shuʿbah al-Thaqafī, d. 50 A.H./670 C.E., was a Companion. He was highly intelligent and tactful, as well as a good military commander who was also entrusted with the governorship of Baṣrah and then of Kūfah.

Muḥammad ibn Kaʿb al-Quraẓī, d. between 108 A.H. and 120 A.H., was the son of Kaʿb ibn Sulaym al-Quraẓī, a Jew of the Qurayẓah tribe who converted to Islam and was a Companion. Muḥammad ibn Kaʿb became known for his accounts regarding the relations between the Jews and the Prophet (peace be on him) and his knowledge of the history of the Jews as such.

Muḥammad ibn Maslamah, d. 43 A.H./663 C.E., was a Companion who took part in the Battle of Badr and other military campaigns under the Prophet (peace be on him) except the campaign of Tabūk.

Mujāhid ibn Jabr, d. 104 A.H./722 C.E., was a Successor (*Tābiʿī*) and among the foremost Qur'ān-commentators of Makkah in his time. His *Tafsīr*, which has been published recently, is one of the earliest extant works of that genre.

Muqātil ibn Sulaymān, d. 150 A.H./767 C.E., was one of the distinguished scholars of *Tafsīr* (Qur'ān-commentary), who wrote a number of works in the field of Qur'ānic learning.

Muslim ibn al-Ḥajjāj al-Nīsābūrī, d. 261 A.H./875 C.E., was one of the greatest scholars of *Ḥadīth*. His work is one of the six most authentic collections of *Ḥadīth* which ranks second in importance only to that of al-Bukhārī.

Al-Naḍr ibn Ḥārith, d. 2 A.H./624 C.E., was among the staunchest enemies of Islam who personally caused the Prophet (peace be on him) much annoyance. He was the standard-bearer of the Quraysh in the Battle of Badr, during the course of which he was taken captive and put to death.

Nadwī, Sayyid Sulaymān, d. 1953 C.E., was among the foremost South Asian scholars of Islam in the twentieth century. He shared with his teacher, Shiblī Nuʿmānī, the authorship of a 7-volume work titled *Sīrat al-Nabī*. Apart from this encyclopaedic work, Nadwī wrote a number of outstanding books including *Arḍ al-Qur'ān, ʿĀ'ishah, ʿArabon kī Jahāzrānī, ʿArab awr Hind ke Taʿalluqāt, Shiʿr al-ʿAjam* and *Khayyām*. He ably served Dār al-Muṣannifīn, Azamgarh and Nadwat al-ʿUlamā', Lucknow for many years.

Al-Nasā'ī, Aḥmad ibn ʿAlī, d. 303 A.H./915 C.E., was one of the foremost scholars of *Ḥadīth* whose *Kitāb al-Sunan* is considered one of the six most authentic collections of Traditions.

Al-Nīsabūrī, al-Niẓām, d. circa 850 A.H./1446 C.E., was a scholar who richly contributed to Qur'ānic studies, especially by his *tafsīr* called *Gharā'ib al-Qur'ān wa Raghāʿib al-Furqān*.

Noah (Nūḥ) was one of the greatest Prophets. He lived in Iraq and God granted him an inordinately long life. He spent 950 years calling his people to worship none but the One True God and to follow the ways of righteousness. His people contemptibly spurned his calls and remained immersed in their evil ways. In retribution God punished them by the Flood which destroyed all except those who boarded Noah's Ark.

Parwez, Ghulam Ahmad (d. 1985 C.E.), was a civil servant in the Government of India and later in the Government of Pakistan. In 1938 he started a magazine called *Ṭulūʿ-i Islām* ("Rise of Islam"). Parwez had both the ability and the penchant for writing. He authored close to two dozen books on Islam. He became known in the main as one of the leaders of the trend known as *Inkār-i Ḥadīth* ("Denial of the [authority and authenticity] of *Ḥadīth*").

Phocas II, r. 602-610 C.E., ascended the throne from the Byzantine Emperor Maurice (q.v.) and was himself overthrown by Heraclius after losing a civil war.

Pope Sergius I, r. 687-701 C.E., a native of Antioch, was educated in Sicily, ordained by St. Leo II, and elected Pope. Offended by his rejection of the canons of the Trullam Council of 692, Justinian II ordered his arrest and transportation to Constantinople. However, the order could not be carried out owing to strong opposition.

Al-Qalqashandī, Aḥmad ibn ʿAlī ibn Aḥmad al-Fazārī, d. 821 A.H./1418 C.E., was a historian, a litterateur and a researcher. He was born in Egypt in a family of scholars. His most celebrated work is *Ṣubḥ al-Aʿshā* in 14 volumes.

Qatādah ibn Diʿāmah, d. 118 A.H./736 C.E., was an erudite scholar of Baṣrah who was known for his knowledge of Qur'ānic exegesis, *Ḥadīth*, Arabic language and genealogy.

Al-Qurṭubī, Muḥammad ibn Aḥmad, d. 671 A.H./1273 C.E., was one of the most distinguished commentators of the Qur'ān. His *al-Jāmiʿ li-Aḥkām al-Qur'ān* is not only one of the best commentaries on the legal verses of the Qur'ān but also one of the best works of *tafsīr*.

Quss ibn Sāʿidah al-Iyādī was known for both his wisdom and for wide acceptance by the Arabs as an arbitrator of disputes and also for his effective eloquence. It seems certain that he was a *ḥanīf*, believed in monotheism and was opposed to idol-worship. He also relished withdrawal from the humdrum of day-to-day life and lived in the manner of ascetics and monks. While the year of his death appears uncertain, it was reportedly in the fifteenth year after his birth that the Prophet (peace be on him) saw him in the Fair of ʿUkāẓ. The extant specimens of his oration are excellent pieces of Arabic rhymed prose.

Al-Rāzī, Muḥammad ibn ʿUmar Fakhr al-Dīn, d. 606 A.H./1210 C.E., was one of the most famous exegetes of the Qur'ān and the most outstanding scholar of his time who was well-versed in both religious and rational sciences.

Rustam is a legendary figure of Persia known for his valour and chivalry and is credited to be a warrior of extraordinary qualities. He is credited, in Persian legend, with the conquest of many territories in and around Persia and with playing a great role in extricating the Persian monarchs from their difficulties.

Sa'd ibn Abī Waqqāṣ, 50 A.H./670 C.E., was one of the heroes of early Islam who took part in many battles during the life of the Prophet (peace be on him). His fame, however, rests primarily on his command of the Muslim army which led to the conquest of Iraq during the Caliphate of 'Umar.

Sahl ibn Sa'd al-Khazrajī, d. 91 A.H./710 C.E., was a distinguished Companion who died around the ripe age of 100. Some 188 traditions have been reported from him.

Sa'īd ibn al-Musayyib, d. 94 A.H./713 C.E., was a foremost scholar and jurist of the generation of Successors (*Tābi'ūn*). One of the seven recognized jurists of Madīnah, he was known for his knowledge of *Ḥadīth* and *Fiqh* as well as for his piety and devotion.

Ṣāliḥ was an Arabian Prophet of the Thamūd, a people who have been mentioned many a time in the Qur'ān. Ṣāliḥ lived before the Prophets Moses and Shu'ayb. His mission was to direct his people to righteousness, but they refused to respond to his call whereupon they were destroyed.

Ṣarmah ibn Qays ibn Mālik al-Najjārī al-Awsī, d. circa 5 A.H./circa 627 C.E., was a pre-Islamic poet who became disposed to monasticism and abandoned the worship of idols and images. He had a very long life and embraced Islam at a very old age, in the year of the Muslims' immigration to Madīnah.

Al-Shāfi'ī, Muḥammad ibn Idrīs, d. 204 A.H./820 C.E., was the founder of one of the four Sunnī schools of law in Islam. He has had a deep and abiding impact on the intellectual outlook of Muslims.

Al-Shawkānī, Muḥammad ibn 'Alī, d. 1250 A.H./1834 C.E., was a distinguished Islamic scholar of Yemen. He contributed richly to almost all branches of Islamic learning – *Tafsīr*, *Ḥadīth*, *Fiqh*, *Uṣūl al-Fiqh*, History, etc.

Shiroe, r. 628 C.E., a son of Khusraw II, was proclaimed king of Persia as Kavad II after the killing of his father. Khusraw II died the same year he was coronated. As part of an agreement with the Emperor Heraclius, Kavad returned the True Cross to the Romans.

Shuʿayb, an Arabian Prophet of Madyan, was a descendant of the Prophet Abraham (q.v.). He lived before Moses and after the Prophets Hūd and Ṣāliḥ. His tomb is said to be in Ḥiṭṭīn in Palestine.

Al-Suddī, Ismāʿīl ibn ʿAbd al-Raḥmān, d. 128 A.H./745 C.E., was one of the early scholars of *Tafsīr* who has written a significant work in that field.

Ṣuhayb ibn Sinān ibn Mālik, also known as Ṣuhayb al-Rūmī, d. 38 A.H./659 C.E., a distinguished Companion, was famous for his skill in archery and for his familiarity with military tactics which proved of much benefit to the Muslims, especially during the Battle of the Ditch (*Khandaq*).

Al-Suhaylī, ʿAbd al-Raḥmān ibn ʿAbd Allāh ibn Aḥmad, d. 581 A.H./1185 C.E., was a scholar of Arabic language and *Sīrah*. He is especially known for his commentary on Ibn Hishām's *Sīrah* called *al-Rawḍ al-Unuf*.

Suhayl ibn ʿAmr, d. 18 A.H./639 C.E., embraced Islam on the day Makkah was conquered. Before that he was the representative of the Quraysh when they negotiated a peace agreement with the Prophet (peace be on him) in Ḥudaybīyah.

Al-Suyūṭī, Jalāl al-Dīn, d. 911 A.H./1505 C.E., was an eminent historian, *muḥaddith* and linguist besides being an eminent scholar and exegete of the Qur'ān. He was a prolific writer who has about 600 works to his credit.

Al-Ṭabarānī, Sulaymān ibn Aḥmad ibn Ayyūb, d. 360 A.H./971 C.E., specialized in *Ḥadīth*. His works also cover the fields of *Tafsīr* and theology.

Al-Ṭabarī, Muḥammad ibn Jarīr, d. 310 A.H./923 C.E., was a distinguished historian, jurist and Qur'ān-commentator. His extant works include his commentary *Jāmiʿ al-Bayān fī Tafsīr al-Qur'ān* and his *Ta'rīkh al-Rusul wa al-Mulūk*.

Ṭarafah ibn al-ʿAbd ibn Sufyān ibn Saʿd, d. circa 60 B.H./circa 564 C.E., was a first-rate poet of the pre-Islamic times. He is known for his dexterity in *hijā'* (satire). He was presumably put to death in his early youth at the insistance of the potentate ʿAmr ibn Hind who was incensed by his satire.

Thamūd were a people who lived in ancient times in Madā'in Ṣāliḥ (or al-Ḥijr) which lies in Wādī al-Qurā between Ḥijāz and Jordan. The Prophet Ṣāliḥ (peace be on him) was raised among them and invited them to worship and fear God, obey God's Messenger, and not to follow those who commit excesses and spread corruption on earth. Ṣāliḥ (peace be on him) especially urged them not to cause any harm to a she-camel that had been consecrated to God. They, however, wilfully disregarded that directive and hamstrung the she-camel whereupon God's chastisement overtook them and completely annihilated them.

Al-Thawrī, Sufyān ibn Saʿīd ibn Masrūq, d. 161 A.H./778 C.E., was considered an authority in different branches of Islamic learning, especially *Ḥadīth*. His works include *al-Jāmiʿ al-Kabīr* and *al-Jāmiʿ al-Ṣaghīr*, both of which are works of *Ḥadīth*.

Al-Tirmidhī, Muḥammad ibn ʿĪsā, d. 279 A.H./892 C.E., was a famous traditionist whose collection of traditions, *Kitāb al-Sunan*, is considered one of the six most authentic collections of *Ḥadīth*.

Ubayy ibn Khalaf was Umayyah's brother and was extremely hostile to the Prophet (peace be on him). He typifies the attitude of the unbelieving Quraysh who considered resurrection of the dead [to face God's judgement] a fantastic folly. Ubayy picked up a piece of decayed bone and said: "O Muḥammad, do you believe your Lord will revive this bone?" This question occasioned the revelation of the verse: "He strikes for Us a similitude and forgot his own creation. He says: 'Who will quicken the bones when they have decayed?' Say: 'He Who first brought them into being will quicken them ...'" (*Sūrah Yā Sīn*: 36:78-79).

ʿUmar ibn al-Khaṭṭāb, d. 23 A.H./644 C.E., was the second Caliph of Islam under whose Caliphate the Islamic state became increasingly organized and its frontiers vastly expanded.

Umayyah ibn Abī al-Ṣalt, d. 5 A.H./626 C.E., was a poet and savant of Ṭā'if. He went to Damascus before the advent of Islam and was well-versed in the ancient lore. He abstained from intoxicating drinks and idol worship. After the Battle of Badr, Umayyah returned to Ṭā'if from Damascus and lived there till his death.

Umayyah ibn Khalaf ibn Wahb, d. 2 A.H./624 C.E., one of the most influential leaders of the Quraysh and an inveterate enemy of Islam, was put to the sword in the Battle of Badr.

ʿUqbah ibn Abī Muʿayṭ ibn Umayyah, d. 2 A.H./624 C.E., was one of the staunchest enemies of the Prophet (peace be on him) who caused him much hurt. He was put to death after the Battle of Badr.

ʿUqbah ibn ʿĀmir, d. 58 A.H./678 C.E., was a Companion of the Prophet (peace be on him) who was later appointed governor of Egypt.

ʿUtbah ibn Rabīʿah, d. 2 A.H./624 C.E., was among the noteworthy personages of the Quraysh before Islam. He was respected for his maturity, forbearance and benevolence. On the occasion of *Ḥarb al-Fijār* his wisdom and tactfulness bore good results and the contending parties were persuaded to come to an agreement. He was killed in the Battle of Badr.

Al-Wāḥidī, ʿAlī ibn Aḥmad, d. 468 A.H./1076 C.E., contributed to *Tafsīr, Fiqh, Maghāzī* (a branch of *Sīrah*) as well as Grammar and Philology.

Wakīʿ ibn Salamah ibn Zuhayr al-Iyādī was one of the judges of the pre-Islamic times. He was entrusted with the responsibility of the sacred House of Kaʿbah after Jurhum.

Al-Walīd ibn al-Mughīrah, d. 1 A.H./622 C.E., was a chieftain of the Makhzūm clan of the Quraysh who was highly regarded for his ability as an arbitrator. At the time of Islam's advent Walīd, already an old man, responded to it with fierce enmity. He brought together the Quraysh and deliberated with them regarding what should be the main point of their propaganda campaign against the Prophet (peace be on him). Walīd's own view was that they should brand him a magician.

Waraqah ibn Nawfal ibn Asad ibn 'Abd al-'Uzzā was a relative of Khadījah, the first wife of the Prophet (peace be on him). Waraqah had renounced idolatry even before the advent of the Prophet (peace be on him). He was knowledgeable about religions, knew Hebrew, and had embraced Christianity. After the Prophet (peace be on him) received the first revelation at the Cave of Ḥirā', Khadījah took him to Waraqah. After hearing from the Prophet (peace be on him) what had transpired Waraqah assured him that the angel who came to him was the same who had come earlier to Moses.

Zayd ibn 'Amr ibn Nufayl ibn 'Abd al-'Uzzā, d. 17 B.H./606 C.E., is distinguished by the fact that even though he lived in pre-Islamic times he held women in high esteem. He did not live to witness the advent of Islam. He, however, detested the worship of idols and images and considered himself to belong to Abraham's faith. He was among a small group of persons in pre-Islamic Arabia who are called *ḥunafā'* (sing. *ḥanīf*). A Makkan of the Quraysh tribe, Zayd died when the Prophet (peace be on him) was thirty-five years old; in other words, before his designation as a Prophet. Zayd had given up idol-worship but had neither embraced Judaism nor Christianity. He was severely opposed to the pre-Islamic custom of killing daughters in their infancy and abstained from eating the flesh of animals offered to idols.

Zoroaster or Zarathustra, also referred to as Zartosht, was an ancient Iranian religious figure and poet. The hymns attributed to him are the scriptural basis of Zoroastrianism. There is no certainty about the age in which Zoroaster lived, the estimates varying from about 6000 B.C. to the middle of the seventh century B.C., the latter date being more plausible.

Zuhayr ibn Abī Sulmā, d. 13 B.H./609 C.E., was a pre-Islamic poet who is held in the highest esteem for the elegance of his poetry.

Bibliography

Abū Dāwūd, Sulaymān ibn al-Ash'ath al-Sijistānī, *al-Sunan.*

Abū Ḥayyān, *al-Baḥr al-Muḥīṭ.*

Akmal al-Dīn Muḥammad ibn Maḥmūd, *al-'Ināyah Sharḥ al-Hidāyah,* 9 vols., Quetta, al-Maktabah al-Rashīdīyah, 1985 on the margin of Kamāl al-Dīn Muḥammad ibn 'Abd al-Wāḥid, *Fatḥ al-Qadīr,* 9 vols., Quetta, al-Maktabah al- Rashīdīyah, 1985.

Al-Ālūsī, Shihāb al-Dīn Maḥmūd, *Rūḥ al-Ma'ānī,* 30 vols., Cairo, Idārat al-Ṭibā'ah al-Munīrīyah, n.d.

Al-'Asqalānī, Ibn Ḥajar, *Fatḥ al-Bārī,* Beirut, Dār al-Ma'rifah, 1379.

Āzād, Abū al-Kalām, *Tarjumān al-Qur'ān,* New Delhi, 1970.

Al-Azharī, *Tahdhīb al-Lughah,* Cairo, 1967.

Al-Bukhārī, Abū 'Abd Allāh Muḥammad ibn Ismā'īl, *al-Jāmi' al-Ṣaḥīḥ.*

Al-Dāraquṭnī, 'Alī ibn 'Umar, *al-Sunan,* 4 vols., Beirut, 'Ālam al-Kutub, n.d.

Al-Dārimī, Abū Muḥammad 'Abd Allāh ibn 'Abd al-Raḥmān, *al-Sunan,* 2 vols., Cairo, Dār al-Fikr, 1975.

Doughty, Charles Montagu, *Travels in Arabia Deserta*, London, 1888.

Encyclopaedia of the Qur'ān, 5 vols., ed. Jane D. McAuliffe, Leiden and Boston, Brill, 2001-2006.

The Encyclopaedia of Religion and Ethics, 12 vols., ed. James Hastings, Edinburgh, 1959.

Al-Fīrūzābādī, *al-Qāmūs al-Muḥīṭ*, second edition, Cairo, al-Ḥalabī, 1952.

Gibbon, Edward, *Decline and Fall of the Roman Empire*, 5th ed., London, Methuen, 1924.

Goitein, S.D., *Studies in Islamic History and Institutions*, Leiden, E.J. Brill, 1966.

Al-Ḥākim, Abū ʿAbd Allāh Muḥammad ibn ʿAbd Allāh, *Al-Mustadrak ʿalā al-Ṣaḥīḥayn fī al-Ḥadīth*, 4 vols., Riyadh, Maktabat al-Maʿārif, n.d.

Al-Ḥamawī, Yāqūt, *Muʿjam al-Buldān*, 5 vols., Beirut, Dār Ṣādir, 1977.

Hershon, Paul Isaac, *Talmudic Miscellany*, London, 1880.

Al-Hindī, 'Alā' al-Dīn, *Kanz al-ʿUmmāl fī Sunan al-Aqwāl wa al-Afʿāl*, Beirut, Mu'assasat al-Risālah, 1985.

The Holy Bible, Revised Standard Edition, New York, 1952.

Howley, G.C.D., *A Bible Commentary for Today*, London, Pickering & Inglis Ltd., 1979.

Ibn Abī Ḥātim, *Tafsīr*.

Ibn Abī Shaybah, *al-Muṣannaf*, 15 vols., Karachi, Idārat al-Qur'ān wa al-ʿUlūm al-Islāmīyah, 1986.

Ibn al-ʿArabī, Abū Bakr, *Aḥkām al-Qur'ān*.

Ibn Baṭṭūṭah, *Muhadhdhab Riḥlat Ibn Baṭṭūṭah*, ed. Aḥmad al-ʿAwāmir Muḥammad Jād al-Mawlā, Cairo, al-Amīrīyah, 1934.

Ibn Ḥanbal, Aḥmad, *Musnad*, 6 vols., Cairo, al-Maktabah al-Maymanīyah, 1313 A.H.

Ibn Hishām, Abū Muḥammad ʿAbd al-Malik, *Sīrah*, eds. Muṣṭafā al-Saqqā et al., second edition, Cairo, 1955.

Ibn Isḥāq, *The Life of Muḥammad*, tr. and notes by A. Guillaume, Karachi, Oxford University Press, 1955.

Ibn al-Jawzī, *Zād al-Masīr*.

Ibn Kathīr, *Mukhtaṣar Tafsīr Ibn Kathīr*, ed. Muḥammad ʿAlī al-Ṣābūnī, seventh edition, 3 vols., Beirut, 1402/1981.

Ibn Mājah, Abū ʿAbd Allāh Muḥammad ibn Yazīd al-Qazwīnī, *al-Sunan*.

Ibn Manẓūr, *Lisān al-ʿArab*, Beirut, Dār Ṣādir, n.d.

Ibn Rushd, *Bidāyat al-Mujtahid*, 2 vols., Cairo, n.d.

Ibn Saʿd, Abū ʿAbd Allāh Muḥammad, *al-Ṭabaqāt al-Kubrā*, 8 vols., Beirut, 1957-60.

Ibn al-Sinnī, Abū Bakr Aḥmad ibn Muḥammad, *ʿAmal al-Yawm wa al-Laylah*, Hyderabad (Deccan), second edition, Maṭbaʿat Dā'irat al-Maʿārif al-ʿUthmānīyah, 1359 A.H.

Ibn Taymīyah, Taqī al-Dīn, *Majmūʿ Fatāwā Ibn Taymīyah*, ed. Muḥammad ibn ʿAbd al-Raḥmān ibn Qāsim, 37 vols., Riyadh, 1398 A.H.

Al-ʿImādī, Abū Saʿūd, *Irshād al-ʿAql al-Salīm ilā Mazāyā al-Kitāb al-Karīm*, 9 vols., Beirut, Dār Iḥyā' al-Turāth al-ʿArabī, n.d.

Al-ʿIrāqī, Abū al-Ḥasan, *Tanzīh al-Sharīʿah al-Marfūʿah ʿan al-Aḥādīth al-Mawḍūʿah*, 2 vols., first edition, Cairo, Maktabat al-Qāhirah, n.d.

Al-Jaṣṣāṣ, Abū Bakr, *Aḥkām al-Qur'ān*, 3 vols., Cairo, 1347 A.H.

Al-Jazīrī, ʿAbd al-Raḥmān, *al-Fiqh ʿalā al-Madhāhib al-Arbaʿah*, 5 vols., Beirut, Dār Iḥyā' al-Turāth, 1980.

The Jewish Encyclopaedia, 12 vols., ed. Isidore Singer, New York, KTAV Publishing House, n.d.

Kamāl al-Dīn Muḥammad ibn ʿAbd al-Wāḥid, *Fatḥ al-Qadīr*, 9 vols., Quetta, al-Maktabah al-Rashīdīyah, 1985.

Al-Kardarī, Muḥammad ibn Muḥammad ibn al-Bazzāz, *Manāqib al-Imām al-Aʿẓam Abī Ḥanīfah*, Quetta, Maktabah Islāmīyah, 1407 A.H.

Mālik ibn Anas, *al-Muwaṭṭa'*, ed. Muḥammad Fu'ād ʿAbd al-Bāqī, 2 vols., Cairo, 1951.

Mawdūdī, Sayyid Abul Aʿlā, *Rasā'il wa Masā'il* (Urdu), Lahore, 1957.

Muslim ibn al-Ḥajjāj, *al-Ṣaḥīḥ*.

Al-Nasā'ī, Abū ʿAbd al-Raḥmān Aḥmad ibn Shuʿayb, *al-Sunan*.

Al-Nīsābūrī, Niẓām al-Dīn, *Gharā'ib al-Qur'ān wa Raghā'ib al-Furqān*, 30 vols., Beirut, Dār al-Kutub al-ʿIlmīyah, 1996.

Polano, H., *The Talmud Selections*, London, Frederick Warne & Co.

Al-Qurṭubī, *al-Jāmiʿ li Aḥkām al-Qur'ān*, 8 vols., Cairo, Dār al-Shaʿb, n.d.

Al-Rāzī, Fakhr al-Dīn, *Mafātīḥ al-Ghayb*, 8 vols., Cairo, al-Maṭbaʿah al-Khayrīyah, 1308 A.H.

Al-Ṣābūnī, Muḥammad ʿAlī, *Ṣafwat al-Tafāsīr*, 3 vols., fourth edition, Beirut, 1402/1981.

Al-Ṣāliḥ, Ṣubḥī, *Mabāḥith fī ʿUlūm al-Qur'ān*, Beirut, 1977.

Al-Sarakhsī, Shams al-Dīn, *al-Mabsūṭ*, 30 vols., Cairo, Maṭbaʿat al-Saʿādah, 1324 A.H.

Al-Suyūṭī, Jalāl al-Dīn, *al-Durr al-Manthūr fī al-Tafsīr bi al-Ma'thūr*, 6 vols., Tehran, al-Makhtabah al-Islāmīyah wa al-Maktabah al-Jaʿfarīyah, n.d.

———, *Lubāb al-Nuqūl fī Asbāb al-Nuzūl*, II edition, Cairo, Muṣṭafā al-Ḥalabī, n.d.

Sykes, Percy, *A History of Persia*, London, Macmillan, 1958.

Al-Ṭabarānī, Sulaymān ibn Aḥmad, *al-Muʿjam al-Kabīr*, II ed., Mosul: Maktabat al-ʿUlūm wa al-Ḥikam, 1401/1982.

———, *al-Muʿjam al-Wasīṭ*, Cairo: Dār al-Ḥaramayn, 1405.

Al-Ṭabarī, Muḥammad ibn Jarīr, *Tafsīr*.

Thānawī, Muḥammad ibn Aʿlā, *Kashshāf Iṣṭilāḥāt al-Funūn*, Calcutta, 1863.

Al-Tirmidhī, Abū ʿĪsā Muḥammad ibn ʿĪsā, *al-Jāmiʿ al-Ṣaḥīḥ*.

Al-Wāqidī, Muḥammad ibn ʿUmar, *al-Maghāzī*, ed. M. Jones, 3 vols., Cairo, 1966.

Wensinck, A.J., *Concordance et indices de la tradition musulmane*, 7 vols., Leiden, 1939-69.

Winston, William, *The Life and Works of Flavius Josephus*, Philadelphia, John C. Winston Company, n.d.

Subject Index

Abraham (peace be on him):
- His story, 21-30
- Allah delivered him from fire, 26
- Allah bestowed upon him many favours, 30

'Ād:
- Their account, 36
- Their dwellings, 36

Angels:
- Their appearance as handsome young men, 33
- Their assignment, 162, 168
- Angel of death assisted by his staff in seizing souls, 168

Arabs:
- Unfamiliar with monotheism before the Prophet Muḥammad's advent, 159
- Their original faith, 159-160
- Messengers in Arabia before the Prophet Muḥammad (peace be on him), 159
- How they took to polytheism, 159-160
- For centuries no Messenger had come to them, 159

Arrogance:
- Allah does not love it and its condemnation, 136
- Believers do not indulge in it, 170

Associating Others with God in His Divinity (*Shirk*):
- Its variety practised by the Arab polytheists, 59-61, 97-98
- How did it originate? 102-103, 104
- Varieties of the polytheists' idols, 82-84
- It is a lie, 21
- It betrays ingratitude, 62, 103
- Runs counter to the human nature, 102-103
- No sanction for it, 104
- It only causes evil, 109
- The Qur'ānic arguments against it, 21-23, 28, 38-40, 61, 62, 128-129, 132-133, 141-144, 155
- Parents not to exert pressure on their children to indulge in it, 11
- Man should not commit it, no matter who asks him to do so, 11-12, 134
- Its effect on morals and soul, 141-144, 155
- Polytheists will disown their idols on the Day of Judgement, 82
- Their idols will not intercede for polytheists, 82
- It consists in invoking anyone other than Allah, 144
- False idols have not created anything, 128
- Polytheists conceded that Allah is the Creator of the universe, 141
- It is a mighty wrong, 132
- One should not obey even his parents about it, 134

Āyah: pl. *Āyāt* (Sign, Signs):
- As signs of God's power, 40, 88, 89, 91, 92, 93, 95, 96, 98, 105, 111, 145, 174, 177
- For warning, 20, 26, 35
- As miracles, 51, 116
- Standing for the Book and the divine commands, 25, 49, 114, 121, 126, 170, 176
- Those who deny these are unjust, 51
- Those denying these despair of Allah's mercy, 25
- Those denying these are perfidious and ungrateful, 146, 147
- The steadfast and the thankful learn lessons from these, 145
- Allah will exact retribution from those who turn away from these, 174

The Bible: 58-59

Blind Conformity: 139

Call to the Truth:
- What should be done for this cause? 56-59
- Its stages, 46-47
- Traits of those engaged in it, 116-117

Charity in Allah's Way:
- Believers expend out of the sustenance Allah has granted them, 171

Christianity: 67, 70, 73
- Muslims' sympathy for it in the early history of Islam, 73

Christian:
- kingdom, 68
- sects, 67

Church: 67, 70

Companions: 5, 21, 45, 54, 73, 124, 130, 137

Criminals:
- They shall be dumbfounded on the Day of Judgement, 81
- They oppose the Messengers, 111
- Their terrible end, 81, 111, 115

Day of:
- Judgement: 18, 26, 82, 83, 110, 115, 125, 168, 169, 177, 178
- Reckoning, 135, 147
- Resurrection, 17, 18, 28, 115, 148, 177

Death: 168
- Every being shall taste it, 56

Disbelief (*Kufr*):
- Denying Allah's Signs, 51
- Results in Divine punishment, 84
- Allah does not love it, 110
- End of unbelievers, 55, 62, 110, 126, 140-141
- Ungrateful denial, 62, 103, 113, 131
- Manifest error, 128

– Its indications, 146-147
– Blind conformity to forefathers, 139

Divine Decree:
– All power belongs to Allah both before and after, 74
– Allah enlarges and straitens man's sustenance, 59-60, 104
– Allah grants life and death, 108
– Allah grants victory to whomever He pleases, 74
– No one can show the way to him whom Allah lets go astray, 98
– Whose hearts are sealed by Allah? 116
– No one knows in which land he will die, 149
– No one knows what he will earn tomorrow, 149
– Man is tested in this world, 169

Economy:
– The Qur'ānic guidelines about economy, 105-108

Error:
– Who are in error, 128
– Its causes, 103-104, 123-125, 139-140, 148-149

Establishing Faith:
– When can Muslims gain the leadership of the world? 176
– How Allah will help establish Islam, 178

Evil-doers:
– Who are they, 172
– Their terrible end, 172
– They are not like believers, 171-172

Faith (*Īmān*):
– Distinction between a believer and an unbeliever, 3, 14-15
– Its demands, 9, 10, 12-13, 16, 56-59, 140
– Its impact on man's conduct, 105
– Its relationship with good deeds, 10-11, 126
– Why are believers tested? 5-8, 13-16, 27
– Allah aids the believers, 112
– Its consequences, 7-8, 10-11
– Definition of a believer, 172
– Features of a believer, 121-122, 145-146, 172

– A believer and an evil-doer are not equal, 171-172
– Its significance, 175-176
– Belief will not help, if one professes it on the Day of Judgement, 178
– Difference between a believer and an evil-doer, 171-172
– Rewards for believers, 172
– Paradise promised for believers, 172

Good Deeds:
– Reward for these, 10-11
– Its nexus with faith, 126

God:
– All-Wise, 30, 39, 96, 127, 143
– Most Compassionate, 74, 163
– All-Hearing, 9, 58, 143
– All-Powerful, 29, 39, 74, 96, 127, 143, 163
– All-Knowing, 9, 58, 114, 150
– Most Powerful, 114
– All-Seeing, 143
– All-Sufficient, 131
– Immensely Praiseworthy, 131
– Most Subtle, 135
– All-Aware, 135, 150
– Lord of the universe, 156
– He knows all that is beyond as well as what is within a creature's sense-perception, 162
– All-High, 145
– Incomparably Great, 145
– His excellent names in the Qur'ān are closely related to the context in which these occur, 127, 145, 163
– To Him is all praise and thanks, 60, 85
– His is the loftiest attribute in the universe, 96
– He stands in no need of anyone, 10
– He does not go back on His promise, 75
– He alone should be served, 22
– He is exalted above whatever be associated with Him in His divinity, 109
– He has created the heavens and earth in truth, 76

– He brings forth the living from the dead and brings forth the dead from the living, 86
– He has created man, 108
– He created for the first time and will repeat it, 23, 24, 96
– He bestows sustenance upon man, 108
– Sustenance should be sought from Him, 22
– Thanks should be given to Him alone, 22
– He enlarges and straitens the sustenance of His servants, 60, 104
– All creatures are in obedience to Him, 96
– To Him belong all the creatures, 96
– All power belongs to Him both before and after, 73-74
– No one can come to man's aid against Him, 25
– No one can protect man from Allah, 25
– No one can get the better of Him, 8
– He causes man to die and brings him back to life, 108
– He grants victory, 74
– He sends down water from the sky, 60
– He keeps the sun and the moon in subjection, 59
– He revives the earth after its death, 60
– He has power over everything, 24, 113
– He knows whatever is in the heavens and the earth, 55
– He knows what is in the hearts of people, 14
– He has knowledge of everything, 60
– He knows all that man does, 45
– No one can show the way to him whom Allah lets go astray, 98
– He is with those who do good, 62
– Evil-doers cannot get the better of Him, 8
– He does not love the unbelievers, 110
– To Him is the return, 12, 24, 56
– He chastises whom He will and forgives whom He will, 24
– He does not wrong anyone, 38, 79-80
– He is the truth, 144
– He is Immensely Praiseworthy, 131, 142
– He established Himself on the Throne, 161
– He has created everything, 127, 128, 161
– He has excelled in the creation of all that He creates, 163
– He is the owner of all that exists, 142
– The ultimate decision of all matters rests with Him, 140
– He is All-High, 145

- Nothing can deter Him from accomplishing what He wills, 127, 163
- He alone is the truth, and all which the unbelievers call upon beside Him is false, 144
- He has wondrous creative power, 144
- He governs from heavens to the earth, 161
- A thousand years of man's history are no more than a day in His reckoning, 161-162
- He has subjected to man's service all that is in the heavens and on the earth, 138
- He has subjected the sun and the moon to His will, 144
- It is easy for Him to create and resurrect mankind, 143, 166-167
- His promise shall come true, 127
- Man's disbelief makes no difference to Him, 131
- Man does not have any guardian other than Him, 161
- Whoever surrenders himself to Him grasps the most firm handle, 140
- He does not need man's thanks, 131
- He is Compassionate towards His creatures, 163
- He has bestowed bounties upon man, 138
- To Him is everyone's return, 133, 140
- All that He does is fully in accord with the requirements of justice and wisdom, 127
- He will exact retribution from evil-doers, 174
- The ultimate decision of all matters rests with Him, 140
- How to gain His gnosis, 139-140
- Trust in Him ensures firm faith and success in the Hereafter, 140
- He knows even the secrets that are hidden in the breast of people, 141
- His knowledge of the Unseen, 150-151
- Nothing escapes His knowledge, 135
- He will inform man of all that he did, 134
- He embraces everything in His knowledge, 162
- He is well aware of man's deeds, 144
- His Signs and who can benefit from these, 145
- Man does not have any intercessor other than He, 161

Guidance:
- Its means, 139-140, 145-146
- How Allah guides man, 154-155, 173-175
- Who derives guidance from the Qur'ān, 122

Gratefulness:
- Its meaning and implications, 131, 145-146, 165-166
- Its significance in Islam, 145-146
- It is to man's own benefit, 131

Ḥadīth: 41, 52-54, 76-78, 86, 125, 171

Hāmān: 37

Ḥanīf:
- Who were they? 160

Heavens:
- Allah created it without any visible pillars, 127-128
- As a sign of Allah's creative power and as evidence for monotheism and the Hereafter, 127, 138, 141, 161

Hell:
- Who will enter it, 28, 55, 62, 169, 170, 172
- Its nature, 55
- Its punishment, 140
- Allah will fill it with men and *jinn*, 169, 170
- As punishment for man's disobedience and arrogance, 170
- Its inmates trying to escape from it shall be driven back, 172

Hereafter (*al-Ākhirah*):
- Arguments for it, 71-72, 78-79, 166-168
- Its rationale, 24, 81, 88-89, 112, 143, 166-168
- Its need, 75, 76-77
- Consequences of denying it, 78
- Those who deny it have despaired of Allah's mercy, 25-26
- What should this belief prompt one to do? 9
- Why it should be preferred to this world, 60-61
- People would think that they had stayed in the world for a very short time, 115
- All men and devils would appear there before Allah, 84
- How mankind will be split there into groups, 83-84
- All worldly bonds will be cut off there, 28-29
- Its deniers will curse one another there, 28-29
- No one will carry there the burden of others' sins, 16-18

– People will be taken to task there for misleading others, 17
– Wrong-doers will not be able to offer any excuse, 115
– Criminals would be full of despair there, 81
– False gods will not be able to intercede there, 81-82
– It is imminent, 148
– Allah's promise about it is true, 148
– Allah will forget there those who had forgotten it, 170
– Those denying it ask when will be the Hour? 150-151
– Those denying it ask how will they be created afresh after they have become lost in the earth? 166-167
– Reasoning by those who deny it, 166-167
– Why do the unbelievers deny it? 166-167
– Consequences of rejecting it, 170
– It is illogical to deny it, 150-151
– Eventually everyone has to return to Allah, 133, 140
– Allah will judge there all the matters on which people differ, 177
– Allah will gather everyone there, 147
– Rewards for believers there, 171
– Consequences of everyone's deeds will be manifest there, 177
– Everyone will be shown his deeds there, 134
– Culprits would like to be sent back from there to the world, 169
– No one will be granted respite there, 178
– No one will stand for anyone there, 147
– Allah will tell there what everyone did, 134
– No one will bear anyone's burden there, 147
– A true believer and an evil-doer would not be treated alike there, 171
– How will the guilty stand there? 168
– How will the record of deeds be presented there? 135

Hijrah (Migration): 6, 56, 70, 129
– Its importance in Islam, 56
– Its moral basis, 56-59
– Migration to Abyssinia and directives for it, 46-49

Holy:
– Cross: 70
– Sepulchre: 67

Hypocrites:
- Their traits, 13-16
- Distinction between them and believers, 3, 15-16
- In Makkan phase, 3, 6-7, 13-16

Iḥsān (Benevolence):
- Its true nature, 121-122, 140
- Who are the 'doers of good'? 121-122

Intercession:
- Idols will not intercede for polytheists, 82
- No intercessor for those disobedient to Allah, 25, 28
- No one can intercede without Allah's leave, 161

Isaac (peace be on him): 30

Ishmaelite branch: 30

Islam:
- Practised by all the Messengers, 21, 35
- Adherents of every Prophet are reckoned as Muslims until they reject the new Prophet, 73-74
- The natural way, 99-100
- Muslims obliged to believe in all the Scriptures, 49
- Its spirit, 140

Islamic Community:
- Its concept of nationalism, 83-84
- Its concept of love of the country, 56

Islamic Law:
- No one will bear the burden of others, 16-17
- It is unlawful to instruct women in singing and dancing, 124
- Singing and dancing not allowed in Islam, 124
- One's obligations towards his parents, 133-134
- Minimum period of conception, 134
- Gambling is unlawful in Islam, 71
- How to dispense unlawful earnings, 71
- Not to disobey Allah at the behest of one's parents, 12-13

– Marital life, 90-92
– Illegitimate child, 134
– Maximum period of weaning, 134

Israel, The Children of, Israelites (*Banū Isrā'īl*):
– Their brief account, 175
– They held world leadership as long as they believed in Allah's signs, 176
– Corruption afflicting them, 177
– Their differences will be settled on the Day of Judgement, 177

Jacob (peace be on him) (Ya'qūb):
– Reference to him, 30

Jāhilīyah: 43, 130, 159

The Last Hour (*qiyāmah*):
– Arguments for it, 76-79
– All would be raised then, 114-115
– Unbelievers will be called to account, 17-18
– On that Day unbelievers will disown and curse one another, 28
– All the ties among unbelievers will end then, 28
– Allah alone has its knowledge, 149
– Why the unbelievers asked as to when it would occur, 150-151
– On that Day no father will stand for his child, nor any child for his father, 147
– On that Day Allah will settle all the differences, 177

Life-after-Death:
– Its nature, 96
– Arguments for it, 23, 143, 166-168
– Man's spirit survives even after death, 168

Life in this World:
– In what sense it is sport and amusement, 60-61
– Death marks its end, 115
– Why the After-Life should be preferred to it, 60-61
– Its transient nature, 115
– How it deludes man, 72, 75, 148-149
– It is not permanent, 77-78

- As a trial, 169
- Its true nature, 148-149, 161
- Minor chastisement in this life in order to alert man to the greater chastisement in the Hereafter, 173

Loss:
- For whom it is, 55

Lot (peace be on him) (Lūṭ):
- His story, 31-35
- anxiety: 33

Luqmān:
- A familiar figure in Arabia, 120
- Allah bestowed wisdom upon him, 129
- The Prophet Muḥammad's praise for his wise saying, 129

Man:
- The Qur'ānic account of man's creation, 88-89, 114, 163-165
- All human beings have been created with the true innate nature prompting them to believe in Allah, 99-100
- His innate strengths and weaknesses, 103-104
- Basis of man's culture and society, 89-91
- To Allah is man's return, 133, 140
- His own self is a pointer to the Hereafter, 75-76
- Meaning of Allah breathing into man of His Spirit, 164-165
- Allah has subjected everything for man, 138
- Meaning of subjecting everything to man's service, 138-139
- The Qur'ān and the Darwinian theory of evolution, 163-164
- Man's vicegerency, 164-168
- No one will stand for another on the Day of Judgement, 147
- One who gives thanks to Allah does so to his own good, 131
- One who commits polytheism commits a mighty wrong, 132
- His deeds are being recorded, 134
- Allah is well-aware of all that man does, 144
- Allah's favours to him, 138
- Notwithstanding Allah's favours to him, man disputes regarding Allah, 139
- He should give thanks to Allah, 131
- He gives little thanks to Allah, 165

- Limitations of his knowledge, 150-151
- One who surrenders himself to Allah grasps the most firm handle, 140
- He does not instinctively disbelieve in Allah, 141
- The right course of action for him, 174-176
- He should follow those who turn to Allah, 134
- Allah subjects man to minor losses and sufferings in order to alert him, 154, 173
- Man should not follow him regarding whom he has no knowledge, 134
- Allah will tell man all that he did, 134
- Who misleads man, 148, 149
- Who turns lukewarm to Allah, 146
- Death is not man's end, 167-168
- The means granted by Allah to him for obtaining knowledge, 165
- Man's knowledge is too little, 150-151

Makkah:
- Allah has made it a sanctuary, 62

Makkan:
- Muslims: 3, 19
- polytheists, 39, 68, 73, 74, 157, 161
- unbelievers, 2, 3, 16, 35, 38, 52, 59, 69, 73, 74, 153, 175, 176

Midian, People of:
- Reference to them, 35

Miracle:
- It is true, 19-20, 26-27
- How the Prophet Abraham (peace be on him) was rescued from fire miraculously, 26-27
- The Prophet Muḥammad (peace be on him) was granted the Qur'ān as the only miracle, 50-54

Mischief:
- Committing abominations, 31
- Engaging in highway robbery, 31
- Who is responsible for it, 109

Monotheism (*Tawḥīd*):
- This belief is innate in the human nature, 99-100
- Its arguments, 40, 59, 60, 61, 72, 88-96, 102-103, 111, 128-129, 141-146, 161, 162-164, 174, 175.
- Why man should believe in it, 139-140
- Man should hold fast to it, 145

Morals and Moral Teachings: 5-11, 38, 56-59, 104-108, 116-117
- Relations between parents and children, 132
- Obligations towards parents, especially one's mother, 133
- Parents not to force their children into committing polytheism, 132
- Treating well one's parents, though not to obey them if they ask to commit polytheism, 132
- Manifestations of arrogance and their prohibition, 136-137
- Walking at a moderate pace, 136-137

Moses (peace be on him) (Mūsā): 37, 175, 176

Muḥammad (peace be on him):
- A plain warner, 51
- Revelation sent down to him, 41
- Arguments for his being a Prophet, 50-54, 154-155, 156-158
- The Qur'ān as his only miracle, 50-54
- His excellent conduct, 116-117
- He was unlettered, 50-55
- Allah sent down the Qur'ān to him, 157-158
- No Messenger had come before him for centuries to Arabs, 160
- The Quraysh's allegations against him, 154, 162
- The Quraysh themselves realised that their allegations against him were baseless, 124
- The Quraysh's efforts to discredit his mission, 123-125
- Refutation of the false charge that he is the author of the Qur'ān, 156-158

Music:
- *Sharīʿah* command about it, 124-125

Noah (peace be on him) (Nūḥ):
- His story, 18-20
- His long age, 19-20
- His ark preserved as a lesson for all people, 20-21

Noah's:
- Ark, 20
- people, 20
- undaunting resolve, 19

Orientalists:
- Their allegations against the Qur'ān, 129-131

Paradise (*Jannah*):
- Who will enter it, 57, 84
- Those admitted to it will live there forever, 57, 127
- Its bounties, 127
- Man will enjoy eternal life there, 57, 127
- Good deeds will help one enter it, 172

Perseverance (*Ṣabr*):
- Its meaning, 57, 145-146, 176
- Its importance in Islam, 57, 135, 145, 176

Pharaoh: 37

Prayer:
- Its moral and spiritual benefits, 42-46
- Command for establishing it, 135
- Its appointed hours, 86-88
- Refutation of some misperceptions about it, 87-88, 102

Principles of Jurisprudence:
- How Muslim jurists deduce laws from the Qur'ān, 133-134

Prophets:
- Prophets who had come to Arabia, 159
- Their teachings preserved in Arabia, 159, 160

Prophethood, Prophet(s):
- A plain warning, 23
- A Prophet cannot make people embrace Islam, 113-114
- One's kinship with a Prophet cannot save him/her from punishment, 33
- As a blessing likened to rainfall, 112
- It determines the destiny of a community, 176
- Each of them presented Islam, though they had different *Sharīʿah*, 21, 35
- Followers of every Prophet are regarded as Muslim unless they reject the new Messenger, 73-74
- End of those rejecting a Prophet, 19, 34, 36, 37, 112

Prophet Shuʿayb (peace be on him): 34

Prosperity:
- Who will attain it, 106, 122

Punishment:
- Its law, 19-20, 55
- Who will be punished, 25, 84, 125-126, 140, 170, 173
- One's kinship even with a Messenger cannot avert it, 33
- Faith after witnessing it does not help, 178
- Hellfire, 172
- The greater chastisement, 173

Qur'ān, The:
- Its role, 115-116
- Sent down by Allah, 51, 156, 158
- Arguments for this being the 'Word of God', 50-52, 66, 156, 158, 175-176
- Its prophecies came true in full, 66-71, 73-75
- As mercy and good counsel for believers, 52-54
- Reciting it, 41
- Who can take heed from it, 54
- It confirms earlier Divine revelations, 47-48
- Its account differs from the Biblical one, 19
- How to interpret it properly, 105-106
- Instances of its misinterpretation by those who reject *Ḥadīth*, 86-87, 102, 106
- Its unique style, 60, 72, 150-151, 162, 163-164, 165, 177

- Appeals to human reason, 34-35, 39-40, 60, 61, 78-79, 91, 92, 93, 98, 112
- Invites man to observe and reflect on reality, 75-79, 88-96
- On creation and working of the universe, 40, 75-78, 111, 127, 128, 138, 141, 143, 161, 163
- Its philosophy of history, 5-7, 38-39, 78-79, 162, 177
- Its economic guidelines, 105-108
- Purpose of stories, 3, 38, 132
- Purpose of telling the story of the Prophet Noah, 19
- Purpose of telling the story of the Prophet Abraham, 26
- The Prophet's personality testifies to it being the Word of God, 156-157
- Why it is in Arabic, 157
- Who derives guidance from it, 122
- Being a blessing, 159
- Its sending down changed the fate of Arabs, 176
- What challenge it poses to man as the Word of God, 156-157
- Why it is sent down, 155, 157-160
- For guiding man to the right way, 159-160
- It is the truth from God, 158
- Why man should follow it, 155
- It reiterates earlier Scriptures, 153
- The Makkan unbelievers' allegation of its authorship by the Prophet and its refutation, 156-157
- Removing the doubt about its Divine origin, 175
- The Makkan unbelievers' opposition to it, 123-125
- As guidance and mercy, 121
- Its line of argument, 121-122, 127-129
- How to ascertain whether a *Sūrah* is Makkan, 119, 153
- Its moral teachings, 121-122, 136-138, 170-171
- The means it identifies for grasping the reality, 145-154
- Its emphasis on spending in the way of Allah, 121
- Orientalists' prejudice against it, 130-131
- Purpose of its telling the story of Luqmān, 119, 130-131, 135

Qur'ānic Parables:
- Of those who take others than Allah as their protectors, 38

Qur'ānic Stories:
- Story of the Prophet Noah, 18-21
- Story of the Prophet Abraham, 22-30
- Story of the Prophet Lot, 30-35

– Story of the Prophet Shu'ayb, 36
– Story of Luqmān, 129-138

Quraysh:
– They alleged that the Qur'ān is authored by the Prophet Muḥammad, 156-157
– Their opposition to the Qur'ān, 123-126, 154
– They realised that their allegations are not true, 125
– They asked the Prophet to expedite Divine punishment upon them, 162, 178
– Their tricks to dissuade people from Islam, 16-17
– Their objection why the Prophet is a human being, not an angel, 155

Qur'ānic Laws: 132-138, 170-172
– It is permissible to indicate one's disbelief for saving one's life and the conditions governing the utterance of such a statement, 15

Qur'ānic Allegories:
– Words of Allah are inexhaustible, 142-143
– His creating the universe is to Him like creating a single person, 143
– Voice of the arrogant is like the braying of the donkey, 138-139
– Life-after-death likened to the revival of the parched land after rain, 177, 178
– Islam flourishing like abundant vegetation, 178

Religion:
– Islam as the natural way, 99-100
– Originally there was one single religion, 102-103
– Not to be divided into sects, 102
– How to follow it, 98-99, 100-101, 110
– Even the Arab polytheists called upon Allah, 146

Reward:
– Who deserves it, 57

Reward and Punishment:
– Its Divine law, 8-9
– Different recompense for evil and best deeds, 11
– Immense delights as reward for the believers, 171

Roman Empire: 66, 69, 71

Satan:
- Satan embellishes man's misdeeds for him, 36
- He invites man to the chastisement of the Blazing Fire, 140

Sharīʿah Laws:
- Revealed gradually, 107-108

Striving in Allah's Cause:
- Its meaning, 9-10
- Its is to man's own good, 10, 62-63

Successors: 45, 73, 124, 130

Sunnah:
- How it amplifies the Qur'ān, 17-18, 45, 86-87, 99-100

Sustenance:
- Allah enlarges and straitens it, 59-60, 104
- Represents seeking Allah's bounty, 93-94, 111
- Signifies lawful, wholesome earnings, 171
- Spending it in Allah's way, 171

Spirit:
- How Allah breathes His spirit into man, 164-165
- It survives after death, 168

Tasbīḥ:
- Its meaning and explanation, 85, 170
- As a synonym of Prayer, 85
- Allah is exalted above what the polytheists ascribe to Him, 109
- Glory belongs to Allah alone, 85

Test:
- Why are believers tested in the world? 5-7, 13-14, 27

Taqwā (Piety, Fear of God):
- Its requirements, 21, 101

The Torah:
- Allah bestowed it upon the Prophet Moses (peace be on him), 175
- It was a guidance for the Children of Israel, 175
- As long as the Children of Israel believed in it, they enjoyed the leadership of the world, 176

Thamūd:
- Their account, 36
- Their dwellings, 36

Throne (*ʿArsh*):
- Allah establishing Himself on the throne, 161

True Guidance:
- Who is on true guidance, 122

Trust in God:
- Believers put their trust in Allah, 57-58
- Excellent reward for those who are steadfast in their trust in Allah, 57

Universe:
- Allah owns it, 141-142
- The sun and the moon pursuing their course till an appointed time, 144
- Allah has subjected it to man's service, 138
- Its working as a sign for man's reflection, 154
- Allah created it in six days, 161
- Allah governs it, 161
- Its record goes up to Allah, 161

Usury (*Ribā*):
- Its condemnation, 107-108

Verse involving Prostration: 170

Wisdom:
- It demands that man should be thankful to Allah, 129-130

Wisdom in making the Call to Islam:
- How to invite the People of the Book to Islam, 46-47

Wrong-doing:
- It is following one's desires without knowledge, 98
- The wicked commit it, 32
- It consists in highway robbery, 31
- Amounts to giving the lie to the Truth, 62
- A warning to those committing it, 38
- Polytheism is its manifestation, 97
- Wrong-doers deny Allah's signs, 51
- Allah does not wrong anyone, 38, 80
- Its meaning and nature, 132-133
- Why polytheism is a mighty wrong, 132
- Consists in denying the Truth, 128
- Its worst form, 174
- Not taking heed from Allah's signs, 174

Zakāh:
- Its significance in Islam, 121-122
- It is multiplied manifold, 108

Name Index

ʿAbd Allāh ibn ʿAbbās, 45, 73, 74, 85, 107, 124, 127, 130, 134
ʿAbd Allāh ibn Masʿūd, 45, 124
ʿAbd Allāh ibn al-Mubārak, 125
ʿAbd Allāh al-Quḍāʿī, 160
Abraham, 21, 22, 23, 24, 26, 27, 29, 30, 32, 33, 159
Abraham's descendants, 30
Abraham's example, 27
Abrahamic faith, 160
Abraham's people, 23, 26
Abraham's story, 23, 26
Abū Bakr, 69, 70, 71
Abū Bakr ibn al-ʿArabī, 125
Abū Dāwūd, 5
Abū Ḥanīfah, 133
Abū Hurayrah, 130, 171
Abū Jahl, 8, 84
Abū Lahab, 84
Abū Qays Ṣarmah ibn Abī Anas, 160
Abū Saʿīd al-Khudrī, 74, 172
Abū Sufyān, 12, 16
Abū Umāmah al-Bāhilī, 124
Abū Yūsuf, 133
Abyssinia, 1, 2, 46, 65, 68, 74, 130
ʿĀd, 36, 37, 38, 130
Aḥmad ibn Ḥanbal, 12, 99, 100, 133, 171, 172
Aḥqāf, 36
Al-Ālūsī, 45, 107, 137
Al-Aʿmash, 45
Al-Bayhaqī, 45, 124
Al-Ḥākim al-Nīsābūrī, 107, 124
ʿĀ'ishah, 137
ʿAlī, 52, 53, 54
Al-Jazīrah, 21
Al-Kalbī, 124
Al-Khalīl, 32
ʿAllāf ibn Shihāb al-Tamīmī, 160
Al-Lāt, 62
Al-Mutalammis ibn Umayyah al-Kinānī, 160
Al-Naḍr ibn al-Ḥārith, 123
Al-Suddī, 74, 107
Al-Wāḥidī, 124
Aleppo, 66
ʿĀmir ibn al-Ẓarb al-ʿĀdwānī, 160
ʿAmr ibn Jundub al-Juhanī, 160
ʿAmr ibn Luḥayy, 160
Anas ibn Mālik, 125
ʿAqabah, 36, 130
Arabia, 36, 42, 49, 65, 68, 74, 99, 120, 129, 130, 132, 135, 159, 160, 175, 176
Arabian Peninsula, 62, 117, 120, 160
Arabian polytheists, 97
Arabian unbelievers, 176
Arab(s), 36, 43, 49, 72, 120, 129, 130, 155, 159, 160, 177
Armenia, 70
Asfandyār, 124
Aʿshā, 129
Asia Minor, 66, 69
ʿAṣr, 86
ʿAwn ibn ʿAbd Allāh, 54

Aylah, 130
Azerbaijan, 70

Babylon, 30
Badr, 70, 74, 75
Bāqirwā, 21
Barā' ibn 'Āzib, 52, 53
Bible, 19
Biblical passages, 59
Black Sea, 70
Bosphorus, 69
Bu'āth, 130
Bukhārī, 5, 6, 41, 52, 53, 99, 171

Caesar, 73, 75
Carthage, 69
Chalcedon, 69
Children of Israel, 175, 176, 177
Christian(s), 31, 46, 67, 68, 73, 74, 99, 100
Clorumia, 70
Constantinople, 66, 69
Ctesiphon, 67, 70

Ḍaḥḥāk, 107
Damascus, 67
Dastagird, 70
David, 160
Dead Sea, 32, 35
Derenbourg, 130

Edessa, 66
Egypt, 69, 130, 176
Euphrates, 160

Fajr, 86

Gibbon, Edward, 69

Ḥadramawt, 6, 36
Hāmān, 37
Ḥamnah bint Sufyān ibn Umayyah, 12
Ḥarb ibn Umayyah ibn Khalaf, 16
Ḥasan al-Baṣrī, 10, 45, 107
Hebron, 32
Heller, B., 131
Heraclius, 66, 67, 69, 70
Ḥijāz, 36
Hubal, 62
Hūd, 23, 130, 159
Ḥudaybīyah, 52, 70
Ḥunafā', 160

Ibn Abī Ḥātim, 45, 124
Ibn Abī Shaybah, 8, 54, 124
Ibn Ḥajar al-'Asqalānī, 54
Ibn Hishām, 123, 124, 129
Ibn Kathīr, 54
Ibn Zayd, 85
'Imrān ibn Ḥuṣayn, 45
Imra' al-Qays, 129
Isaac, 30, 32
Isaac's descendants, 30
'Ishā', 86
'Iyāḍ ibn Ḥimār al-Mujāshi'ī, 100

Jābir ibn 'Abd Allāh al-Anṣārī, 130
Jacob, 30
Jacobites, 67
Ja'far al-Ṣādiq, 45
Jalāl al-Dīn al-Suyūṭī, 124
Jaṣṣāṣ, 133, 134
Jerusalem, 67, 70, 73
Jews, 6, 31, 67, 74
Jinn, 25, 39, 162, 169, 170, 173
Jordan, 33, 65, 67

Ka'bah, 5, 97
Kadiköy, 69
Khabbāb ibn al-Arat, 5
Khālid al-Ruba'ī, 130
Khālid ibn Sinān ibn Ghayth al-'Absī, 160
Kavad II, 70
Khaybar, 36
Khusraw II, 66, 67, 69, 70
Korah, 37, 38

Labīd, 129
Lot, 29, 31, 32, 33, 34, 35, 38
Lot's wife, 33
Luqmān, 119, 120, 124, 125, 129, 130, 131, 132, 133, 134, 135, 136, 137, 138
Luqmān's scroll, 129

Madīnah, 1, 2, 69, 129
Madyan, 36, 130
Maghrib, 86
Magian, 99
Makḥūl, 124
Makkah, 2, 5, 56, 62, 68, 70, 129
Makkans, 23, 122, 132, 150, 156, 158, 161
Mālik, 41, 125, 133
Mas'ūdī, 130
Maurice, 66
Midian, 35
Moses, 37, 155, 160, 175, 176
Mount Jūdī, 21
Mount Uḥud, 108
Mughīrah ibn Shu'bah, 172
Muḥammad (peace be on him), 3, 4, 7, 12, 18, 30, 48, 49, 50, 51, 52, 53, 66, 67, 68, 74, 84, 86, 120, 122, 123, 126, 129, 132, 155, 156, 157, 159, 160, 166, 175
Muḥammad ibn al-Ḥasan, 133
Muḥammad ibn Isḥāq, 123
Muḥammad ibn Ka'b al-Quraẓī, 107
Muḥammad ibn Maslamah, 54
Mujāhid, 54, 85, 107, 124, 127, 130
Muqātil, 124

Nasā'ī, 5, 6, 12, 99, 100
Negus, 74
Neostrians, 67
Nineveh, 70
Nubia, 130

Orientalists, 130

Palestine, 32, 65, 67
People of the Book, 46, 47, 48, 49
Persia, 66, 67, 68, 70
Persian(s), 65, 66, 67, 68, 69, 70, 71, 72, 73, 74, 75, 109, 110, 124
Pharaoh, 37
Pope Sergius, 70

Qatādah, 21, 45, 85, 107
Qinnaṣrīn, 160
Quraysh, 8, 16, 68, 84, 102, 123
Qurṭubī, 8
Quss ibn Sā'idah al-Iyādī, 160

Rābigh, 36
Rāzī, 13
Roman emperor, 66, 69
Rustam, 124

Sahl ibn Sa'd al-Sa'īd, 172
Sa'īd ibn Jubayr, 124
Sa'īd ibn al-Musayyib, 130
Ṣāliḥ, 23, 159
Ṣan'ā', 6
Sasanid emperor, 66
Satan, 9, 37, 47, 82, 139, 149
Sayyid Sulaymān Nadwī, 130
Sea of Lot, 35
Sha'bī, 107
Shāfi'ī, 133
Shawkānī, 130
Shu'ayb, 30, 35, 36, 38, 159
Sinai Peninsula, 67
Sodom, 35
Solomon, 58, 160
Stillman, N.A., 131
Sudan, 130
Sufyān al-Thawrī, 74
Suhaylī, 130
Sulaymān b. Aḥmad al-Ṭabarānī, 45, 97
Suwayd ibn 'Amr al-Muṣṭaliqī, 160
Suwayd ibn Ṣāmit, 129

Sykes, Percy, 67
Syria, 35, 65, 66

Ṭabarī, 16, 21, 45, 69, 86, 107, 124, 130, 136, 172
Ṭabarānī, 45, 97
Tabūk, 36
Ṭarafah, 129
Taymā', 36
Thamūd, 36, 37, 38
Tirmidhī, 12, 42, 69, 124, 171, 172
Torah, 175, 176
Tunis, 69

Ubayy ibn Khalaf, 69, 70
Uḥud, 6
'Umar, 16, 137
'Umar ibn Shabbah, 54
Umayyah ibn Abī al-Ṣalt, 160
Urfa, 66
'Uthmān ibn al-Ḥuwayrith ibn Jaḥsh, 160

Wakī' ibn Salamah ibn Zuhayr al-Iyādī, 160
Waraqah ibn Nawfal, 160

Yemen, 130

Zabad, 160
Zayd ibn 'Amr ibn Nufayl, 160
Zecharias, 67
Zoroaster, 70
Zoroastrian invaders, 67, 73
Zoroastrianism, 67, 73
Zuhayr ibn Abī Sulmā, 160
Ẓuhr, 86